Distant Reading

MODERN AND CONTEMPORARY POETICS

Distant Reading

Performance, Readership, and Consumption in Contemporary Poetry

PETER MIDDLETON

THE UNIVERSITY OF ALABAMA PRESS
Tuscaloosa

Manufactured in the United States of America

Typeface: Minion

∞

The paper on which this book is printed meets the minimum requirements of American National Standard for Information Science-Permanence of Paper for Printed Library Materials, ANSI Z39.48–1984.

Library of Congress Cataloging-in-Publication Data

Middleton, Peter, 1950–
Distant reading : performance, readership, and consumption in contemporary poetry / Peter Middleton.
p. cm. — (Modern and contemporary poetics)
Includes bibliographical references and index.
ISBN 0-8173-1442-3 (cloth : alk. paper) — ISBN 0-8173-5151-5 (pbk. : alk. paper)
1. American poetry—20th century—History and criticism. 2. Authors and readers—United States—History—20th century. 3. Books and reading—United States—History—20th century. 4. Performing arts—United States—History—20th century. 5. Oral interpretation of poetry—History—20th century. 6. Experimental poetry, American—History and criticism. I. Title. II. Series.
PS325.M53 2004
811′.509—dc22

2004014701

This book is dedicated to
Kate, George, and Harriet

Contents

Acknowledgments

Throughout the writing of these essays I have felt I was part of a growing conversation about a previously neglected area of the history of poetry, one largely taking place within the poetry scene in magazines and internet discussion lists, and even sometimes during the breaks at poetry readings, a conversation whose significance is now increasingly recognized by scholars. The essays in this book could not have been written without the support of editors who commissioned earlier versions of them (their names are listed at the end of the preface), those who invited me to give talks on these themes at several universities and conferences, and the support and conversation of colleagues at the University of Southampton and elsewhere. I would like to thank all those who read and commented on these essays at various stages of development, and I would like particularly to thank Charles Bernstein and Hank Lazer, the editors of this series, for extensive support, comment, conversation, and the inspiration of their own researches in the field of poetry performance and readership. Sabbatical leave from the University of Southampton and a grant for research on poetry performance from the UK Arts and Humanities Research Board (AHRB), were both crucial for completion. Kate, Harriet, and George have been a great source of support and encouragement throughout. This book is dedicated to them.

The author and the University of Alabama Press gratefully acknowledge permission to use the following poems and extended passages:

From *Singularities,* copyright 1990 by Susan Howe and reprinted by permission of Wesleyan University Press.

"Taxonomy" from *Shalers Fish,* Etruscan Books 2001 copyright. Helen Macdonald is quoted in full by permission of Etruscan Books.

From *Mars Disarmed,* copyright 2001 Drew Milne and published by The Figures, Great Barrington Maine 2001.

From *Poems,* published by Bloodaxe Books Ltd and Fremantle Arts Centre Press, copyright 1999 by J. H. Prynne, by permission of the author.

From the poem "Taliban Lamp-Post," copyright 2000 by Rob MacKenzie, in *Foil: Defining Poetry 1985–2000.* Courtesy of Etruscan Books.

Preface

Poems are neither machines nor made of words, although William Carlos Williams understandably felt it necessary to call attention to such affinities by asserting an identity at a time when machines and language were turned into weapons on a worldwide scale. Nor is the poem pure energy or angelic vibrations heard only by the ideal inner senses that transcend historical contingency. The materialist vision of the poem makes it a verbal refrigerator, solid, enclosed, keeping its contents ready for consumption; the idealist turns the poem into an ether that trumps all other physical and metaphysical foundations. Versions of this polarization are endemic to our discourses of poetics, especially our theories of reading and reception. The problem is that poems are not like light, a wave or a particle depending on which way you look at them, they have several aspects. Poems can be manifested as heterogeneous material objects; they can be events in performance; their multiple versions, published copies, and performances cannot be located in any single point of space and time; and they are unusually complex mixtures of all the knowable and unknowable components of consciousness: primary process, reasoning, emotion, memory, and intersubjectivity. The assemblage of dictionary-given words into an optically compressed box of lines on a paper page is simultaneously an unbounded phenomenon extending across time, minds, objects, and meanings.

Reading the poem requires labors whose boundaries are not easily foretold. Poems have to be realized, rendered, performed, or as we ordinarily say, read, for their meaning to be produced (the uncertainty about whether it is more helpful to pluralize "meaning" is part of this problem), just as musical scores require instruments and players for their significance to be fully manifest. Poems exacerbate what most other kinds of text try to minimize: published or unpublished, the nonpoems are circulated with strong controls on pertinent reception that allow minimal opportunities for improvised responses. Popular novels, for instance, follow many strictly conventional story-telling rules so familiar they are largely invisible; letters are addressed to a particular recipient who is figured as standing by the periods of each sentence waiting to hear them; and scientific papers use a style as devoid of ambiguity as possible. Poems by contrast are deliberately made highly vulnerable to the instabilities of transmission by the intensification of the effects of language on ear, eye, thought, and feeling so that they can also explore, celebrate, and critique the intersubjectivity of language practice. Within small communities of readers, the specially controlled environment of the classroom, or a network of devoted scholars, the reading of a poem can nevertheless appear to be very similar to the translation of a text from a foreign language with the help of a dictionary. The poem seems in such situations to be a singular artifice out of which meaning can be distilled by patient exegesis, relying on the elucidation of reference, the analysis of rhetoric, and the investigation of its contingent biography and history. For many purposes this idealized model of reception works fine. It doesn't work so well for the study of contemporary poetry. These poems produce their meanings across networks of readers, performance, intertexts, and visual presentation, meanings that are not usually locatable in a singular, solitary encounter between one printed manifestation of the text and one sensitive reader.

Put simply, there are two reasons for this: the inherent instability of communication and the shaping effects of communicative technologies on the production of meaning. First, linguistic meaning is transactional and negotiable, not fixed in the sign or even in one discursive formation. Actual uses of language are interactive, and the meaning of what one person says to another is meaningful precisely because it is open to interpretation and misunderstanding. Communication is always unfinished, suggestive of further possibilities, and understanding one another is therefore also a form of work, whereby we add to and transform what the other says and draw out its possibilities. Writing, as Plato feared, only takes this condition further. Poems work simultaneously along axes of speech, writing, body, person, sociality, and abstraction (or artifice) that enormously complicate these transformational negotiations because the artificial distinctions between meaning and naming, or meaning and extension, heuristic abstractions sometimes useful to philosophers, don't apply very closely to the actual practice of poetry reading.

Second, poems work at the limits of the technologies of language. Prosody, the use of print layout to create perceptual and cognitive codes, the use of fonts, folded paper bound together, audible voicing, recordings, digitization—this is only a short sample from a long list of the *techne* that poems work with. Almost every feature of language technologies has been put to use by poets as a formal device for the production of meaning, and these formal devices are themselves historically shaped and can sometimes even allude to that construction process as well. The poem on the page is impatiently waiting for its next staging in another technology, a new performance, or some other realization via formally marked interactions, and it is even waiting for the recognition of literary theorists, as the editor of the *New Princeton Encyclopedia of Poetry and Poetics* points out. He allows himself a note of frustration on this very theme in his entry on "Poetry" that carries special emphasis given the comprehensiveness of the reference work itself: "we are still very far from a full and satisfying exegesis of what an intricate complex of formal relations a poem is, and, concomitantly, what precisely is involved in a reader's cognition and interpretation of a poem" (Brogan 941). For once the collective pronoun really carries weight. He recognizes that the problem is partly that the term "reading" refers to several different moments of response—silent reading, reading aloud, and the back-and-forth process of interpretation—but doesn't go a step further and ask whether these formal relations might not be figures of social and historical relations. Without making this connection the significance of these formal relations will probably remain obscured and their visible markers irrelevant.

For many historical reasons, ranging from the legacies of genocide to the growth of universal literacy, social mobility, and many new modes of imaginative pleasure, the patterns of distribution of a poem's meanings across the world of readers have rapidly changed. The ethical urgencies of the visual immediacies created by the news media that have plenty of terrible and pressing material every year, and the vast social institutions dedicated to producing scientific truths of the material world, shrink the public space for the low-budget poet to offer counterbalancing insights. The practice of poetry has changed radically: in the past fifty years the live poetry performance has become integral to the writing and reading of poetry; print layout has, over only a slightly longer period, created many new conventions and prosodic opportunities; and most powerful of all, and the most elusive to describe, social forms of poetry reception, the ways we collectively come to understand poems, have been transformed.

Poets of the past few decades have therefore had to think harder than ever about the means by which they launch their poems into the world of new technologies and cultures of communication. They are all too aware, for example, that most lyric poems written today are cushioned with popular music and published on CD or as internet MP3 files, and their visceral accompaniment easily drowns out textual limitations, and often promises effortless emotional rewards. Should poets take up performance themselves to gain readers? If they do, how much will success depend on voice training, the skills of performance art and theatre, the additional support of social and political passions co-opted for the occasion, and other features of public culture? These pressing questions are matched by the new challenges of publication. Will their readers know how to read their new (and traditional) poetic signs, their line-breaks, shifting margins, special punctuation, allusions, and rhetoric, when the poems are printed in magazines and books? If a reviewer says their poetry "is excruciating to follow, lacking . . . even the slightest pretence to logic and reality" and adds dismissively that "the audience for this kind of poetry is small" (Bartlett 126–27), as one said of Michael Palmer, is the answer to bring back logic and realism, or introduce help menus throughout the poem? Or should they follow Palmer's lead and reply robustly that such poetry is not a "consumer item," it requires "an effort of attention that is as active as that which goes into the writing?" It has become something of a commonplace that the more innovative forms of poetry require readers to be active, almost joint participants in the cultural work of the poem. Such attention requires collective organization, just as the performance does—an entire network of people who edit, publish, review, research, and teach the poetry, or even simply engage it with conversation and correspondence. And the cultural work of producing the meanings of the poem is shared out amongst them.

If all that was at issue here was the delivery of the poem into the hands and minds of readers, this would still be a major element in the making of poetry. But the meaning of a poem is not already there latent in the pattern of words, as a dictionary definition is available as a ready equivalent of any ordinary word in circulation. The production of meaning by a poem is an intersubjective process extended over time, many individuals, and only ever partially available for cognitive reflection. The same network of publication, performance, and reception histories is the field where meaning is constantly in flux. Poets such as Palmer know this and compose with it. Just as a composer of music thinks about the sonic properties of instruments, the skills of performers, and possibly the acoustics of performance spaces, so too do poets anticipate the conditions under which their poems will be realized through the physical, emotional, and cognitive labor of an audience extended across time and space.

I argue in this book that many of the processes whereby poetry is performed, displayed in magazines, imperially controlled by the computer, read by consumers, printed on the page, or carefully labeled with anonymity-defying authorial names become integral to the possibility of meaning in contemporary poetry, and that our relative neglect of the significance of these activities is one cause of the continuing resistance to reading that Palmer mentions. All readership represents some effort, however much it can apparently be mitigated by the easy reading techniques developed by the poetry of entertainment and autobiography today (much of this poetry is actually a lot harder to read than it appears—if its complexities and confusions were better acknowledged its ascendancy would be more questioned), and this labor of reading can be considerable for the poetry of inquiry or extended imagination. Poetry communities instinctively know this: many poems are offered within networks that help organize their reception. Readerships do not spring into life as a new poem rains down upon them. They need training, they need to be brought into being as economies of affect, memory, and interpretation. Poets are extremely aware of this, as they are also aware that their writing has to try hard to be heard in public cultures where other forms of discourse and knowledge have far more legitimacy.

The first essay introduces these issues in terms of a metaphorics of distance and biography, arguing that the temporal and other distances between reading and composition are active contributors to the work of the poem. Poems by John Ashbery and Frank O'Hara are traced across differing communities of reception represented by the magazines and anthologies where they have been published in addition to their appearance in collections by the poets themselves. These poems owe their popularity to the way they anticipate cultural conflict and shifting constructions of poetic tradition. The following two essays stand at the center of the arguments within the book. They offer a theoretical and historical account of the modern poetry reading that reaches back into elided histories of elocution and rhetoric and questions the neglect of linguistic sound in literary theory. This research leads into arguments about the staging of authorship, the sounding and intersubjectivity of oral performance and then into the history of poetry, and into its future on computer and the internet. A talk on the first person in poetry was rewritten to become the essay "Anonymous Poetry," making the original talk the object of several layers of reflexive commentary that enfold it like a triptych that becomes its own version of the long biography of the text.

The final four essays track different modes of reading and the formalisms that they engage with. "The Line-Break in Everyday Life" stages an experiment to see how much the activity of the active reader of poetry is reliant on emotional and symbolic investments in the material form of a text. "The New Memoryism" starts with the observation that computers have changed the way most Westerners with access to at least a modest degree of financial support communicate with one another, as well as becoming the standard tools for writing. Have they also affected the way we read poetry or made more visible what were somewhat hidden parts of the processes of readership? The essay takes up these questions in the context of the recent surge of interest in memory as a base for individual and national identity. "Dirigibles" is a series of fragments or writing balloons that steer through the ins and outs of textual exegesis in modernist poetics and use the recent controversy about the leading British poet J. H. Prynne as a test case for study of the tensions between poetic difficulty and the institutions of explication. The final essay addresses that target of Michael Palmer's dislike, the reader as consumer. Stephen Vincent dismisses poetry that is written just to make an immediate impact as performance in front of a large audience, saying that "the work tended to become a commodity that the audience devoured and forgot" (51). What do such metaphors of consumption tell us about our uses of poetry? This concluding essay starts with an autobiographical dilemma manifested as a problem with the literal act of consuming and then investigates the many strands of metaphor from literary theory, poetics, and history that are woven into it. Its inquiry into the consumption of meaning generates a split into parallel sequences of poetic autobiography and cultural theory that are as unreconciled as their larger counterparts, poetry and criticism.

This explicit division between discursive scholarly writing and autobiographical and poetic writing is also questioned by the form of several other essays, which variously fold back on themselves so that the form questions the materials in play. This is not just an implicit claim that essays on radical poetry need themselves to be complicit with convention-breaking struggle, although I do believe that the ordinary expository essay has certain blind spots and cognitive limitations that we need to understand better if we are going to be able to sustain pertinent discussion of the more innovative recent poetries. Nor is it advocacy of autobiographical frameworks for critical writing. I hope rather that the form of the essays can be enjoyed as an integral accompaniment to the specific reasoning within the essays themselves.

The historical period under review here is largely the postwar era of American and British poetry, although the historical discussions go further back. The poems I discuss are almost all either American or British, although the arguments here could be extended to other poetic traditions. Even to bring these two sometimes divergent histories into dialogue is much less common that it should be, given the intricate patterns of influence and development that often tie them closely together in practice, and the lack of mutual knowledge of each other's traditions and achievements beyond the high-profile poetic immigrants to each country.

These essays had their beginnings in magazines and book-length collections that enabled me to work out the ideas in receptive contexts, where I benefited greatly from editorial advice, revision, and above all encouragement. I would like to thank in particular Charles Bernstein, Ivan Gaskell, the late Salim Kemal, David Kennedy, Roger Luckhurst, Anthony Mellors, Ty Miller, Peter Nicholls, Miriam Nichols, Bob Perelman, Keston Sutherland, and Keith Tuma. All the essays have been extensively revised for this collection. I have wanted to avoid homogenizing them too much in the spirit of hindsight, personal or historical, and so I have mostly not tried to update their relation to the latest scholarship, unless it seemed absolutely necessary. Many fine and interesting studies, such as Susan Stewart's *Poetry and the Fate of the Senses,* or Brandon LaBelle and Christof Migone's *Writing Aloud,* are already taking these issues in new and sometimes unexpected directions. My hope is that this discussion of the many stages, oral and otherwise, through which poetry is realized will contribute to this growth of understanding of contemporary poetry and its ambitions, achieved and still embryonic, in an age where much poetry is often poorly understood and looks irrelevant alongside the issues of the time.

Distant Reading

Chapter 1
The Long Biography of the Poem

A scene of reading

Start with a scene of reading. Will it be office, library, classroom, or study armchair? A clear mind charged with rigor and wholly committed to the text? Or one drowsily switching between the page and my friend Tony, who looks odd in new reading glasses that trouble me because they remind me of advancing middle age, as he works his way through a pile of children's novels he is judging for the Smarties Prize. Our wicker chairs are some distance from the rented holiday house, under the shade of a large cedar, and we are enjoying the quiet time after breakfast while our four children sleep off their late night, and our partners go for a walk. Both of us are a little resentful, a little tense about working on holiday even for a couple of hours, and I am worrying about how to explain the idea of distant reading I want to summarize for this collection of essays on poetry performance, readership, and consumption. This chapter needs a couple of examples of modern lyric poetry, and the books by Allen Fisher, Susan Gevirtz, and Lissa Wolsak I have brought haven't yielded anything that would be familiar enough for readers to enable me to make general observations, so I am now leafing through an anthology I threw into my bag at the last moment, J. D. McClatchy's *The Vintage Book of Contemporary American Poetry* (1990), looking for material. This "mainstream survey" that "draws on and addresses the MFA/Creative Writing program circuit for its contents and audience," in the words of Alan Golding (35), is the best I can do; there are no libraries or bookshops likely to supply modernist English language poetry within a hundred kilometers in this part of France. Eventually I decide on Frank O'Hara's poem "Ave Maria" and John Ashbery's "Syringa," and begin scribbling in the margins of the soft paper, and then speaking to a dictaphone. My thoughts are a disjointed overlay of memories of other readings of the two poets; of friends' comments, articles, and student essays about them; images of Ashbery himself looking frail alongside Denise Levertov at a reading in Cambridge, and then looking distinguished on the platform at Senate House in London; a recollection of buying an intriguing yet baffling copy of *The Tennis Court Oath* in the early nineteen-seventies from Better Books in the Charing Cross Road; and the horror of a description of O'Hara's protracted deathbed scene, a memory now stuck to another of a friend reading aloud the lines, "And up the swollen sands/ Staggers the darkness fiend, with the storm fiend close behind him," in an attempt to introduce me to "The Skaters." A child interrupts these reveries to ask if we are going to the lake, and a clattering from the kitchen doorway reminds me that lunch has to be prepared. The scene ends. It is hard to imagine a more perfect location to read these poems (nor one as calculated to create stereotypes of the bourgeois holiday in the minds of my readers), yet it still falls short of a familiar ideal of what reading a poem ought to be like, the moment of complete cognitive and emotional transformation of self by the text.

Reading is always like this, embedded in an everyday world, one more usually of even greater distractions, of buses and taxis, computers and phones, deadlines, hunger and anxiety, always partial, tendentious, and tainted with both recollection and anticipation. If we think about this at all, we are likely to assume that ideally reading should not be like this, that it should be a moment of intense absorption excluding the contingencies of leisure, work, or supervening passions. Most attempts to represent interpretation of poems discursively as "readings" still elide the implications of the contingent history of actual sessions of reading in favor of a supposedly more comprehensive understanding that rises above the messiness and temporal incompletion of individual run-ins with the text, on the premise that their singularity plays no part in the significant meanings generated by the poem. A "reading" resembles a composite image in which all the oddities of particular angles of vision have been rounded off, and the poem can be treated as a material object for which a complete description is at least potentially possible, even if what amounts to this totality may change as culture, knowledge, and ideologies alter.

These poems by Ashbery and O'Hara had traveled a long distance from their composition and first publication to the house in France, a distance measured in space, time, and culture. Such distances, I shall argue, are not extrinsic to the meaning and significance of poems. The text is altered by the wear and tear, repairs and remodeling it undergoes as it is read over time by many different readers, and as Michael Palmer says, in some texts "the very fact of decay is what is generative of new meanings" (276). This history of responses, uses, memories, expectations, and other actions (much more heterogeneous than literary criticism usually acknowledges) constitutes the only unity the poem has. Since writing is a technology of varying degrees of success and failure for the management of spatial and temporal distances, and poetry an art that intensifies selected aspects of language and writing to create the patterns that generate meaning, distance is a potential poetic material as much as rhythm is for a metrics. This distance is created by the scale of our culture, however, much more than by geographical measures. The diversity of venues for poetry has enormously increased along with the sheer numbers of readers, readings, publications, and critical responses, and the timescale for these responses has undergone that same acceleration that is widely reported in other areas of contemporary life, with the consequence that what used to be a period of time in which relatively little would happen to the poem is now a crowded and complex history, each new decade packing in more than the last. Distance as a density of reception is also produced by public culture, and within it by the institutions of education and the economies of cultural capital, by the legitimating institutions of knowledge such as institutional science, and the political maneuverings of public spheres and their counterpublic spheres. The density of social spaces within a specific geography has also increased enormously, producing social distances that contemporary literary texts have to weather somehow, treating them either as local differences of climate against which the text must be proof, a background noise to be ignored, or a field of difference to be celebrated and incorporated into textual production. In these circumstances, features of the poetic condition that have always existed become suddenly much more salient than before, have much greater influence on the reception of poetry, and are, at least potentially, more visible to both writers and historians.

I shall call this condition "the long biography of the poem" following the introduction of the idea of a long biography of the commodity in recent research by Arjun Appadurai and others. They argue that only by adding this diachronic analysis of the commodity can we understand the full implications of the changing status of an object that may at times become a different sort of commodity or cease to be one altogether, for theories of the commodity, consumption, markets, and gift economies. The textual condition of poetry also manifests itself in long biographies of the poem, although the argument has to be wary of making direct analogies between commodity and text. Poetry makes more visible than any other form of text the implications of the simultaneous existence of many copies within the culture, so the many different histories of reading are twined together in complexities and simultaneities largely beyond our ability to record them. The different realizations of the text of the poem, orally, visually, and memorially, are parts of a wider semantic field that is generated by readers of the text, and in the modern condition those readers are increasingly volatile and demanding, not only, as is often suggested, because they want easy consumer gratification, but also because they increasingly possess new and often advanced modes of reading competence. These readerly talents present opportunities and challenges to poets. Readers finely attuned to sexist, misogynist, and racist language; readers able to isolate a proposition and consider its logic in relation to ordinary language use; readers accustomed to quickly assimilating long, managerial documents presented as hierarchies of information through bullet-point summaries; readers trained in the intricacies of literary interpretation; or the users of specialist scientific and technological languages—these and many more forms of specialist competency are now so widespread that poets can factor in an expectation of such reader abilities as they compose a poem, and perhaps put those skills on their mettle.

Poems cannot be passive in the face of such rapid change without losing their power to affect readers, making it increasingly necessary for the poem to work more deliberately with the anticipated career of the text than before. Poems become more futural (notably in the dominant form of the memory poem that is now the default literary mode of the lyric). Whitman's poignant tease to the reader when he says, "I consider'd long and seriously of you before you were born," and then proposes a mutuality of recognition by using the same verb—"Consider, you who peruse me, whether I may not in unknown ways be looking upon you"—is a relatively rare pre-twentieth-century explicit acknowledgement of the importance of this impending long biography for the poem. To conceive this dimension of the poem requires poetics to make a temporal turn in order to acknowledge that texts can project their reading forward in time, attempting to anticipate and thereby negotiate their possible reception. The resultant long biography of the poem is not only a record of former interpretations; it is also prospective and still unfolding as the language reaches toward further possibilities and transformations. This is especially true of the lyric poem, whose exceptional linguistic sensitivity to the wide orchestral instrumentation of language (its sound, rhythmic organization of time, etymological depths and physical production, and many other possible features) exposes it more fully to effects of distance than almost any other type of text.

DISTANT READING

"Practical," "new," "close." These three adjectives span most of the traditional academic scholarship and pedagogy devoted to the intricacies of actual literary language, and by a *via negativa* they also point to the subsequent ideologies that challenged and, to a considerable degree, replaced them. Literary *theory* claims to expose concealed ideologies at work in *practical* criticism, and argues that the foundational aspirations of practical criticism to provide an unmediated descriptive judgment of texts upon which wider contextualization—linguistic, philosophical, historical, and biographical—could then be based with confidence, presupposes concepts of language, self, and time that should be analyzed. *New* historicism counters the belief that a *new* criticism is possible in the modernist sense in which it was proposed: no criticism can simply detach a literary text from the past of its making and circulation because texts are precipitations of historically situated discursive activities. To read with care such a text is to track backward along many lines of filiation into the past of both reader and text. *Close* reading, our preferred contemporary term for a heterogeneous and largely unorganized set of practices and assumptions, may seem to have met its replacement in the growing importance of the distances of diasporic and postcolonial studies, which take away the likelihood that most reading situations could be proximal approaches to a shared (cultural) capital, since there is no longer any center where a text could be located. If the usefulness of the metaphoric name for the practice has not yet been entirely supplanted in our affections it is because other connotations still rouse expectations of insight and achieved argument. Attentiveness to the phoneme-by-phoneme structure, the images, the line's syntactic architecture, the cross-weave of etymological, semantic, and homonymic associations, metaphor, metonymy, and other highly localized features remain important. So does the sense that authorial circumstance, even if no longer conceivable as intention of bumper-sticker salience, is often highly pertinent. Close reading's additional suggestion of intimacy and its fields of desire also helps sustain the currency of the term for justifying scholarly method, although the tacit abandonment of conceptual or modernist terminology underlines the loss of importance attached to textual analysis by this latest phase of literary theory. The practice of close reading persists, pretty well unmodified, as a lowly chore prefatory to the sophisticated use of theory.

One critic who has done much to resist the subordination of close reading to theory in poetry studies, without simply reaffirming literary value uncritically, is Marjorie Perloff, whose essays persistently demonstrate great hermeneutic sensitivity to the material text. In a review of Chaviva Hosek and Patricia Parker's collection of essays, *Lyric Poetry,* Perloff argues that even these would-be reformers of criticism of the lyric have not sufficiently recognized the historicity of form: "theoretical and rhetorical terms—'apostrophe,' 'allegory,' the word 'lyric' itself—are assumed to have transhistorical, typological validity" (17). Taking her lead from an essay by Annabel Patterson, Perloff argues that it is a mistake to define the genre of the lyric "normatively," with its corollary that "there is no reason why the poetic structures of the 1980s should differ perceptibly from those of earlier centuries" (2). By contrast, Perloff's many essays on modernist poetry treat such forms as architectures constructed within cultural moments from the available technologies, politics, histories, and memory. She reads closely with the care of a historically attuned ethnographer for the significance of distinctive features of sound, use of line-break, and patterns of meaning, as culture indicators local to a specific history and place.

This investigative curiosity toward the possibility of new ways of creating meaning through innovative textual practices makes her close reading a process of discovery and alerts her to the shifting conditions of reading, including those manifest as distance. Writing about D. H. Lawrence's later poetry, she dismisses the orthodox views that they display a late Romantic pantheism, or empathic communings with the world beyond the human (as one might say about Ted Hughes or James Koller), and turns to the intended effect on the reader, because the poems "have a marked theatrical edge," which suggests that Lawrence might almost have been "a performance poet":

> the addressee here, as almost everywhere in the sequence, must be construed as a devoted—which is not to say a like-minded—listener, a close companion, say, or worthy antagonist. . . . [W]e can posit the audience to be a group of friends in a café or country house, and beyond this circle, the readership of certain books and journals that 'everybody' reads. (102)

The adjective "close" does subtle work in the argument here, intimating that her own close reading simulates that of a reader who would actually have been in proximity, or "close," to the author, and in turn, then describes a series of increasingly distant social circles radiating in time from the inception of this text. In the process, the term "close" has to work hard while Perloff's account of the Lawrence poems traces in compelling detail their shifts and turns of mood and address. The question that remains, however, is where such a reading can itself be located in relation to those widening circles of anticipated readers, and whether the "performance" alters as the distance increases (and what does this scaling up signify as interpretative effect, both quantitatively and qualitatively?). How can close reading fully factor in the distances of the textual condition?

The inclusion of all contingent readings of a poem or body of poetry into one vast encyclopedic record is not an attractive option, and yet without some such strategy it would appear as if we would simply revert to the misleading ideal of the reading that pushes as close as it can to the text by setting aside all incidentals of actual reading. Perloff's account of Lawrence's readership points to another way of conceptualizing our dilemma, by following through the question of the temporal location of our belated interpretation. In an unusual essay on the ethnography of reading, Susan Noakes offers a speculative model of how this might be done. It is commonly assumed, she argues, that: "in what might be called 'ordinary' reading, as it is still conventionally taught in high schools and colleges, it is supposed that the reader looks backward in time to try to establish contact with the authoritative character of the text" (47). Or, one might add, the reading of literary texts is usually hermeneutic. What doesn't generally happen is what Perloff achieves in the discussion of Lawrence: "the text" says Noakes, "does not look forward to, and await, the reader" (47). By this she means that the text does not anticipate its fulfillment in a singular culminating future reading. I shall argue that texts can be said to anticipate contexts of reading and reading strategies, however, moments when potential melodies in the text will be taken up and sung loudly, quite possibly at the expense of other latent soundings. This is what Whitman teases us about in his forward-looking address. What needs to be questioned is the supposedly objective viewpoint of the interpretive critic who implicitly claims to have closed the loop that the text began. The seemingly neutral practice of looking backward can arrogate a quasi-divine authority to the occasion of one's own scholarly interpretative reading, and she shows why, in a clever analysis of the famous scene in Luke's gospel where Jesus first announces his vocation. He goes to the synagogue at Nazareth, and like others who participate in the informal theological debates there, reads from the prophetic verse of Isaiah before offering his own interpretation. Unlike the others, however, Jesus makes a startling claim: "Today this scripture has been fulfilled in your hearing" (39). He alone can know what Isaiah's poetry really means because he speaks with God's direct authority, and as Noakes comments, it is this that "makes possible his claim about the temporal relationship between what he reads and his reading of it, the claim that his reading is the last correct one, the definitive interpretation" (47). Unfortunately, most critical writing on literature attempts to emulate what could only be a unique "erasure of temporal distance," and therefore loses sight of what is involved in being a contemporary reader. Luke's Jesus "affirms in the present that he is the future to which the (past) text looked forward," whereas the other, everyday reader of the religious books at the synagogue, "looks to the (past) text in hopes of understanding it at some moment in the future" (48). The contrast between these two types of reading illuminates the limitations of most contemporary interpretations of literary modes, because the standard model of literary interpretation similarly assumes that it can transcend the distance between itself and the inception of the text in a fulfillment of the meaning of the text. The other type of reading represented in Luke's narrative (by the ordinary disputants) corresponds to what I shall call "distant reading," an interpretation that acknowledges that it is only one moment of the text's future, and only one of many "interpretants" (Noakes borrows the term from Charles Sanders Pierce). Criticism needs to rethink "the temporal dimension of the non-identity" (50) of its close reading of the texts with which it begins, and this will necessitate, however authoritative its scholarship, the admission of the effects of temporal distance, attention to the shaping densities of intervening history between composition and this act of reception, and to textual performances of the temporalities of both the horizons and the moment.

Common-sense understanding of close reading therefore conceals a paradox: a specific close reading of a poem is almost always perceived as an approximation to an ideal reading of a poem, although at the same time such an ideal is tacitly admitted to be unattainable. The implications of this paradox are ignored for the most part, because for ordinary purposes, especially the reading of poems from earlier epochs or the discussion of populist contemporary texts whose possibilities of poetic interaction are deliberately limited, the assumption that a singular reading in one time and place, as well as the transmission of this reading in writing (or by other means), can be treated as such an approximation works well enough. Intrusive problems arise, however, when dealing with the texts that innovate with form, publication, performance, reception, and other conditions of textuality, because even scholarly practices of interpretive care and attentive judgment cannot overcome the distance. Then an interpretive deficit becomes glaringly apparent.

An avant-garde poet might incorporate distance by using, for example, specialist scientific discourses likely to exceed the expertise of poetry readers, who then have to track down their sources and work out their rhetorical implications, as well as to deal with the emotional disturbance of such interruption to understanding and the unsettling reflections on readerly competence this internal distance creates. Or she might create a text as the poet Harryette Mullen does, out of registers from great distances apart, and then invite the reader to listen to the resulting harmony and dissonance in compacted lyrics, like those of *Muse & Drudge*. In an interview for *Contemporary Literature* she responds to a question about the categorization of poets by saying that there are different literary worlds coexisting in Los Angeles, and she likes to move between them: "I know that in Los Angeles, for instance, I can go to some poetry readings and see basically the same people, and I can go to other venues and there will be a whole different cast of characters who don't participate in this other literary world. And I like traveling. I enjoy the different perspectives—I have always done that, out of necessity, since my childhood" (402). She is what we might call a "long-distance specialist" even though the distances are cultural not geographical, because she works her knowledge of these distances into the aesthetic forms of her poetry, which incorporates elements of several different (and distant) contemporary worlds of poetry.

"Long-distance specialist" is the term used by the anthropological theorist and historian, Mary Helms, to describe those in premodern societies who used their knowledge (real or alleged) of faraway places to augment their social authority (3). We moderns may assume that distance holds no aura for us; the indications are that it still does, that our arts and politics still write their scripts in the language of distance. Helms argues that in earlier and preindustrial cultures, distance measured in spatial terms takes on a recognized cultural value that can then invest those who associate themselves with it. The belief that distant places enjoy greater proximity to the sacred or supernatural can be found in many past cultures. Expeditions or foreigners would be valued not only for the trade goods they brought but also for the cultural intangibles of distance, the stories, inventions, customs, that could be interpreted as signs of other metaphysical worlds. The ability to manipulate the effects of distance in everyday and special human affairs was often an important part of the power of leaderships, and therefore Helms believes that "anthropological understanding of the locus of esoteric materials, the 'other worlds' of political-religious exotic experience, should be expanded to include the realm of geographical distance and the peoples, places, and things found therein; second, that knowledge of these domains has long formed an important part of the corpus of esoteric materials controlled by learned political-religious elites" (261). Her summary of what these esoteric materials include covers practices that are the counterpart of what some contemporary poets expect of poetry:

> comprehension of the dynamics of the sacred powers that fuel the operation of the universe and all things and beings therein, and recognition of the diverse expressions of these powers in the sounds and odors, colors and consistencies, shapes and sizes of phenomena of the natural world [. . . and] the means to contact and control such powers for the benefit (or harm) of individuals

> or of society at large, and mastery of often awesomely large corpuses of lore as expressed in song, myth, ceremony, and secret or ritually distinctive formulas or languages. (261)

Secret languages, sacred powers, initiation rituals, lost traditions: these are frequent topoi in contemporary poetry, and one indication that distance is widely performed in contemporary poetry's reading and interpretation. The persistence of the concept of the avant-garde is partly due to the explicit emphasis of the concept on the metaphorics of distance, because what makes these arts resistant to assimilation and even understanding is their skill at prolepsis, their ability to appear to be ahead of social time, and even when this furtherance of possibility is largely illusion, it is a picture painted boldly in the colors of distance from a palette of estrangement.

The concept of distance focuses attention on the transformational pressures at work on the salient linguistic forms in a poem because the concept of distance requires us to acknowledge the effects of aggregative readings within these different locales as mediated at once by both these textual fittings and the political necessities of emphasis. Distance is also a sign of a text's intersubjective embeddedness in mutually negotiated histories of cultural and social exchange. New Historicism and Editorial or Textual Criticism both recognize the longitudinal historical dimension of texts, how different authorially instigated states of the text may coexist, how different publishers' editions may influence reception, and how prominent critical judgments can add to this constellation with no single center. Although histories of reception have been composed for many canonical authors by now, these almost always tacitly pass over the distance I am most concerned with here. Once a new composition is performed and published it passes out into many distinct but intersecting personal histories of reception simultaneously, which may then develop their own relatively autonomous lines of development through assimilation, interpretation, emotion, cognitive response, and actions of literary and nonliterary kinds. These multiple concurrences soon add up to very large numbers of "reading-years," to express the idea in a provisional and quantitative mode in order to emphasize how much it extends beyond any individual's capacity to chart every moment of such a history. This concept of reading-years is not meant to imply that the book has been continuously interacted with, but that the text's potential as an accompanying elicitor of thought and feeling extends over such times. If all the readers live in much the same condition, a single town or city with a small number of literary scenes, or a common class, then these reading-years would be so little distinct as to be collapsible into a few paradigmatic responses. The distances within contemporary culture across which texts move greatly increase the temporal depth that helps constitute the textual condition, especially of poetry. Accelerated reception often means that a text can now have an active reading life within many different parallel microhistories, which sometimes precipitate as reviews, essays, other poems, or just conversation directed specifically at an articulated response to the text. Much of the response to the text will of course dissipate entirely and be directed outward away from it into new projects or most likely into memories that are casually integrated with quite other experiences.

FRANK O'HARA, "AVE MARIA"

The audience for a poetic text can be small compared to those for novels or cinema, and yet be comprised of readers distributed across the world, able to share a reading experience from their distant locations. Although communities of readers may thereby seem to have been lifted from their local space and time into transglobal networks, this disembedding is never complete, and any text which, like poetry, already pulls away from a well-rehearsed set of referential anchors is put under an unprecedented strain by this process, since the readership will almost certainly encompass a much more centrifugal diversity of response than a geographically localized collective readership of the past would have done. The poetic text has to work harder to sustain its situationally transcendent forces in the futures it encounters. Moments like that in Whitman, or John Donne's "The Canonization," when the poem explicitly figures this futural relation between composition and reading, are rare, although a poetics of distance has been a distinguishing achievement of contemporary avant-garde poetry. It was the search for familiar poems that would provide telling examples of the use of distance as poetic material that led me to choose the poems by Frank O'Hara and John Ashbery, both poets in whose body of work this projection remains entirely implicit.

One of the best known formulations of a distance inhering in literary texts is Adorno's account of the negation of existent conditions in modernist art whose utopian distances or abstraction from the reality of its time offers a perspective of expectation and cultural labor that would be needed to instantiate its projectivity. One form of this is the poem that assumes an ethics that does not yet exist. Some radical modernist texts do this through sexualized images by which readers are made conscious of a tardiness, a shortfall in their own culture and perhaps in their own outlook too, but without more reflexivity the text's own distances can still be collapsed and the hopes or disappointments fall back into a reified confirmation of the reader's rightness in despair or marginality. Frank O'Hara's brilliance as a poet lies partly in his ability to project a world that negates the existent because it assumes an ethics of sexual and imaginative trust that is manifested as improvised playfulness, and in doing so calls into doubt the possibility that such futures can be imagined in this way. A flagrant instance of this is one of his most anthologized poems, "Ave Maria."

"Ave Maria" was first published in May 1961 in a men's magazine, *Swank*, that mixed female nudes with literary pretensions, and was then reprinted in the year before O'Hara's death first in *C* magazine, and then in *Lunch Poems*, before appearing in the *Collected Poems*, as well as several anthologies, including Paul Hoover's Norton anthology *Postmodern American Poetry*. The teacher's guide to this school textbook (also written by Hoover) proposes this question about "Ave Maria" for students: "What is the *moral* of this poem? Are the 'darker joys' in fact important?" (39). This is a poem that seems to invite such old-fashioned questions. It cleverly invites condemnatory moral judgments in a context that makes readers uneasy about their own historical relativism, for its reading will depend very much on historical distances. The rhetorical appeal to the mothers of America, the arbiters of the law in the private world, to allow their children out to the cinema in order to encourage the children's aesthetic imagination, and let them enjoy both the erotics of cinema and possibly even their own eroticism too, is as indirect as a rhetorical question. The idea that children may be lucky enough to be seduced by a stranger is offered as if there were nothing shocking about the proposal, and this paradoxially therefore makes the appeal impossible. At the time the poem was composed, even homosexuality was illegal, not to mention underage sex. Today, homosexuality may be legal, but it still elicits reactionary political opposition and as for pedophilia, it is now, if anything, even more fiercely hounded than when the poem was written. O'Hara's poem cannot afford to trigger unbending attitudes therefore and the poem seems to know this; it charms the reader with its sentimental patriotism and nostalgia for childhood awe at cinematic wonders.

Distance can interfere with scholarship. I have been unable to locate this issue of *Swank,* either in libraries or for sale (and hate to admit it). The poem was part of a section of texts by new writers edited by Seymour Krim. My impressions are based on looking at another issue from the same year, the issue for January 1961 that has poems by Ginsberg and LeRoi Jones ("Hymn for Lanie Poo" where he brilliantly satirizes the idea that black people have the jungle in their make-up), as well as articles with titles like "Plush Pad for Mobile Playboys," "Big Business Takes a Sex Break," and an article on London night life, "The Pleasures of Percy." In this type of company, "Ave Maria" would read as a literal incitement to (hetero)sexual pleasure and a celebration of cinema sexuality. The poem would also gleam like the expensive commodities in those bachelor digs, where new writing would be part of the lifestyle.

The poem's form and structure screen future distances in several ways. There is no audience for the rhetorical address of this poem. Written at a time when mothers were still regarded as the sole shapers of personality through their influence on the first five years of life (one form of the poem's ethical negativity is the question of why the fathers are absent), the poem assumes that the audience its opening apostrophe harangues so explicitly can never be the audience that reads it. Publication in *Swank,* a magazine that is about the least likely to be read by women with children, adds further emphasis to the absurdity of the gesture. It acknowledges this in its broken vertical column of caesurae, as the strongly voiced free-verse line is repeatedly interrupted by a drop down to the next level as the line continues on across the page. These dropped lines articulate a more knowing attitude, a glancing aside to a different audience than the explicit addressees, the mothers. The poem enacts a continuing failure of reception, which might eventually, it is implied, succeed in the future, and in this way ensures a continuing interest in trying to be there when it does.

Such odes to the impossibility of being the intended reader stir thoughts on the difficulties of finding an audience and can arouse complicity with what the distant reader is likely to mistrust as a flattery that we are not so narrow-minded and do recognize the importance of pleasure. Just as the love of cinema miraculously presents itself as avatar, the fantasy lover of cinema who seems to step right out of the screen to take the viewer home to consummate the seduction of fantasy, so the poem's persona steps away from the political rhetoric of the appeal to the mother nation to take the reader home to consummate a seduction into the aesthetic.

Although the poem might seem to be rooted in the culture of *Swank,* it cleverly anticipates a long future of shifting responses that will constitute its biography. Ted Berrigan provided a very different context in his mimeo magazine, *C: A Journal of Poetry. C* was born out of resistance to censorship, and flourished transgressive sexual material as a sign of its radical poetics and politics. The idea for the magazine arose, as Daniel Kane recounts, when Ron Padgett and his fellow editors were prevented from publishing allegedly obscene poems, including one by Ted Berrigan, in an issue of the *Columbia Review,* which they were editing at the time. After a special issue called the *Censored Review,* which reinstated the poems, Berrigan decided to produce his own mimeograph magazine called *C,* and by the time he printed O'Hara, his front page announced that both *C* and Ed Sanders's even more sexually provocative *Fuck You,* had been nominated for a magazine award, thereby linking the two magazines in the mind of the reader. From the very first poem, this issue plays on the possibilities of sexuality as transgression. The opening line of the first poem, a translation by the poem machine of Francis Picabia, "Poop" begins: "1. / If it's inspiration you want, drop your panties," and a poem translated from Giuseppe Ungaretti, "December," alludes to the incestuous desires of siblings: "Brother and sister departed / With apologies to the mother for intercourse / In their hearts." Dick Gallup's "The Return of Philista" celebrates "Kid love! Billy love!" in a faux naïve style.

"*C* will print anything the Editor likes, and will appear weekly." Berrigan liked a lot that week: forty-seven poets including O'Hara appeared in the issue for February 14, 1965. Here the "darker joys" made possible by the social space of the cinema are also the joys of poetic imagination, and already the poem's use of distance as part of its metric is beginning to emerge. Some poets have several poems in the issue (O'Hara also has "Button Birthday") but they are scattered through the magazine, as if poems not authors are the most important feature of the work. "Ave Maria" forms the midsection of a tall page, the first part of which contains the final section of Tony Towle's poem "Supplements," which ends metapoetically with "a final wave at the ships." After "Ave Maria" is a prose poem by John Dent, "Fits of Affection," which continues the theme of sexual liberation and must have been juxtaposed to O'Hara's because of its similar, if somewhat blurred, preoccupations with sexual fantasy. These are the first three sentences of Dent's short five sentence poem:

> It is only the tiny pill that brings forth life. The young girl will only produce the whistling void. Go forth, then, into the fitted missile that you occupy, the bone, the juice, the meat of social intercourse. Go forth into the high oven of the Giantess or into the lowly furnace of the fiery Dwarf. Mix with the roaring blood, or mingle amid the sweat and tears of quiet desperation, carrying into whatever hand you fill a wildness, and you will radiate around you cheers and high stakes, and leave behind you snatches of fearful memory.

Then on the next page is "The Ecclesiast" from John Ashbery.

In this company, O'Hara's poem becomes almost modest, restrained, and authorial intent is submerged in what Kane describes as "a kind of progressive autobiography charting the growth of a circle of friends" (121). Its appearance in *Lunch Poems,* a selection in which the first person is heard strongly and the lasting image of O'Hara the lunchtime flaneur was created, had given the poem the appearance of a deeply felt personal request to middle America. Now in *C,* the "sheer gravy" of the cinema's door to sexuality appears necessary dressing for Dent's "meat of social intercourse." The poem's masculine emphasis on the dangers of oppressive mother-love that was uppermost in the *Swank* version, is subdued by a strong push toward the phallic "fitted missile" and pervasive insistence that all sex is good. Even Ashbery's poem, in which sexuality is only ghosted in, manages to fit the same pattern, so that "the new dimension of truth" gives way to the assertion that "there is no time like the present for giving way to temptation."

By the time the poem reaches McClatchy's anthology, the need for interpretative control has become evident, and this time the poem is relocated to the zone of nostalgia for the unweeded sexual fantasies of adolescence. Anthological parataxis is the device that achieves this. Immediately after O'Hara's poem there's an introduction to the poet David Wagoner, followed by a narrative poem, "The Best Slow Dancer," an endearing recollection of the sweaty fumbling of a high school dance that shares an interest in emergent sexuality with O'Hara but entirely lacks his subtle handling of textual distance. Whereas O'Hara's poem is subjunctive in mood, Wagoner's poem insists on the authenticity of the events recounted. It stakes the poet's reputation upon his own honesty, leaving no space for readers to reflect on the seductions of this gesture and its elisions of time. It has no textual strategy for creating the potential history of different reactions to teenage heterosexual masculinity's desire. Placing this poem alongside O'Hara's subtly intimates that it might be hiding a transgressive sexual advocacy, while also muting O'Hara's ethical dissonance with a nostalgic haze that makes it look more innocent and purely personal than most of its earlier appearances did. McClatchy's editorial manipulations are just what we might say the poem expected, a distancing (whose precise social make-up could be ethnographically investigated) produced by shifts in the locale and scale of the social spaces of reception. This particular showing of the poem elicits admiration for the poem's willingness to play to adult nostalgia for adolescence, as well as its flexibility and resilience in changed circumstances.

"Ave Maria" has been a heavily anthologized poem because of its expert handling of the poetics of distance. Throughout the period of more than forty years in which the poem has been read, ideas about motherhood, sexuality, the power relations of seduction, and the nature of child development have been volatile, highly political issues. This is a poem for which there is no neutral ground other than a complete withdrawal into the tenets of aesthetic autonomy. Otherwise, whatever the reader's views on these issues are—liberal, right wing, queer, feminist—they are going to bring in their own distances from the supposed starting point when this liberated sexuality was espoused. The positional instability of the ethical ambiguities at the heart of this poem enables the poem to continue to raise awkward questions about the autonomy of aesthetic judgement. It is self-consciously proleptic of future readings as attempts to find its moral line and allows for large variations in where that line will be placed. To read the poem is to read the morality of one's own time and place too, and so to articulate the poem's meaning as a reading of distance.

JOHN ASHBERY, "SYRINGA"

O'Hara's poem can never have a reader who fulfills its meaning, and this gives it enduring (but not everlasting) force, although over time this is less a matter of shock and more a matter of an accumulated history of sexual and identity politics. What the poem can't do is reflect explicitly on its treatment of distance. This remarkable feat is what Ashbery sometimes manages, notably in "Syringa." By contrast with O'Hara's poem Ashbery's is quite uncontroversial and was published in the most respectable of all poetry journals, the April 1977 issue of *Poetry,* then edited by Daryl Hine. McClatchy himself had a poem in the same issue, so perhaps that proximity (don't poets read issues that have published their own work a little more closely than usual?) was the start of his anthologist's interest in Ashbery's poem. *Poetry* magazine was eclectic up to a point and would publish formalist and New American Poetry alongside one another. A considerable number of Frank O'Hara's posthumous poems appeared in the magazine that year, as well as poems by Philip Levine, Gary Soto, David Wagoner, Diane Wakoski, and many others less well known. The magazine always had a policy of publishing young writers and not allowing a coterie of poets to make it their house magazine, and Ashbery himself was now as close to a regular as the magazine permitted. He had been the lead-in with "Self Portrait in a Convex Mirror" for an issue a few years earlier.

"Syringa," a poem based on the Orpheus story in Ovid, is not the opening poem this time. This honor goes to David McCann's poem "David," a prose poem about a beautiful Renaissance "rent-boy" who inspired several Italian artists to sculpt versions of the biblical figure. The following poem, "All Present," by Randy Blasing, tells us that the "secret / of being" is "becoming," a poetic tribute to the influence of Sartrean existentialism in American university education, and in the next poem, Blasing asserts that "Change / raises time / to the power / of *now,*" completing the poetic preface to "Syringa." I mention these forgettable poems (and teasingly call them a preface) because like so much else in the magazine that month, they appear to talk either directly or indirectly to Ashbery's poem. The editor even placed another poem about Orpheus immediately after Ashbery's contribution, and reading on, several other poems are also remarkably consonant with Ashbery: classical references abound; light philosophical speculation is rife; the effects of time and memory are mentioned repeatedly; and there's an explicit interest in male sexuality, even to the extent that McClatchy's poem "Suffering the Cut" meditates on the connection between castration and art. A line from his other poem in the magazine, "Scenes from Another Life," might even have come from Ashbery himself: "The merest regret seemed another stage / in some grand scheme." Particularly striking is Chris Wallace-Crabbe's coded image of a message shot by an arrow and written in blood, which is found on a Roman tent on the border with Parthia, a message ultimately aimed at Caesar: "We come on you in time. / We will fall everywhere like flakes of snow. / You do not know us. We are history" (11). One of the main cities of the ancient empire of Parthia was Ecbatana, the image of the "perfect" city in Ezra Pound's *Cantos,* and so it is possible to read this warning as the hope of poets who wish to threaten the Caesars of today. Alongside Ovid, Rainer Maria Rilke is also in evidence in many poems, in the "stars" and brave meditations on loss, and even in the "radiant / angles" where Rilkean angels still hover in the transposed letters.

This is partly clever editing, but the material was there for the editor to use, and Ashbery was just one player. Finding parallels to Ashbery is slightly misleading, in fact, because it is not necessarily the case that other poets are simply emulating Ashbery. Perhaps all the poets are anticipating scenes of reading organized by this and similar magazines in which such modes, tones, and styles will be highly pertinent. Certainly the two reviews in this issue support this view. Robert K. Martin, now best known for his book on homosexuality in American poetry, reviews a book of poems by Richard Howard. "In memory," he writes, "all the arts have their source," and then goes on to argue that "if we construct ourselves out of our memories, we also construct ourselves out of our past reading." J. D. McClatchy's review (he was a particularly active contributor that month) also celebrates memory, although not so emphatically, using asides deftly to outline appropriate expectations of poetry for the reader of the magazine: New York's literary scene "resembles an Our Gang comedy" (42); we should remember that it is speech "in its clearest utterance we call poetry" (43); and poets are desperately needed in our world of "incomplete significance." Like Martin, he also thinks the mind's muse is memory and believes "the poem of consciousness" (his example is from John Hollander but he is generalizing) "finally masks the soul." Ashbery's poem matches this pattern of thought, and then helps it undergo a new meiosis.

Readership was very much on the mind of the poets who contributed to this issue of *Poetry.* Loren Eiseley's poem asks, "Why do I write / to myself?" Richard Stull is quite explicit about the difficulty of thinking about audiences. What happens to the poet? "People leaf / through his books / and die," he says cynically, and drily adds, "they do not / sell well" (26). Stull even cites an anonymous voice saying what many contemporary poets must have been asked: "Doesn't it bother you / that no one can read / your poems?" A second poem by Stull takes the dilemma into a cruder version of Ashbery's meditation on writing's failure to resist transformation. Ashbery writes: "And no matter how all this disappeared, / Or got where it was going, it is no longer / Material for a poem." In Stull's attempt at a surreal fable, "the words began / erasing themselves."

"Syringa" works very effectively within the field set up by the magazine as a quasi-philosophical meditation on the nature of change. The classical form of the allegory offers aesthetic comfort to the phenomenology of loss as a condition of time only partially mitigated by memory. It is this very effectiveness that is a sign of its brilliant handling of distance.

It is a moment of literary history that could be framed by a historicist question that asks how poetic narratives derived from Ovid and Rilke circulated amongst different discourses within that historical moment. The poem has tricks up its sleeve, however, to resist such dissolution. Reading forward, as it were, the poem might be transformed into a lyric more about the effort to represent transformation than about phenomenological or epistemological issues themselves, and with this transformation, an insistent metapoetic strain becomes more evident: "You must / Wait til it's over" says the poem, and it might be talking about itself here (and elsewhere), as if the poem were also on the outside of itself, reading the poem in its own distorting mirror. Textual memory could be faulty: " 'But what about / So-and-so?' is still asked on occasion. But they lie / Frozen and out of touch until an arbitrary chorus / Speaks of a totally different incident with a similar name." In passages like this the poem playfully reflects on its future readers' attempts to read history back into it, and its many periphrases for the materializations of rhetoric use metaphor so strikingly that metaphor becomes an intersection of the corporealization of thought and the decorporealization of action. This metapoetic self-commentary repeatedly and endearingly flirts with failure (ambition would seem arrogant), as if the poem could not succeed, and yet in not succeeding, the poem implies, lies its success at enacting a lived experience of the metalingual dilemmas of language.

Reading this Ashbery poem (as so many others), is more like reading an anthology of poems of the kind to be found in that distant issue of *Poetry* than reading just one of those poems that tries to achieve poetic transcendence from within its single location of thought and feeling. In Ashbery's poem there is no such transcendence, just the endlessness of metamorphosis itself. "Syringa" flourishes when placed in a context like *Poetry* because it so evidently shares the preoccupations with classicism and change, while it starts to "erase" the other texts with its insistence on the poem reading itself. Soon they are largely forgotten, broken reeds. How then has this poem managed to gaze into the future eyes of readers? "You must / Wait til it's over," says the poem, but when is it over? Although it concludes with an alleged memory cue, which might be very like that in the Wagoner poem—"hidden syllables / Of what happened so long before that / In some small town, one indifferent summer"—the poem's indifference to any epiphany or passion that memory might contain, coupled with its absorbent boundaries, makes it hard to say when the poem *is* over. Its poetic interminability enables it to go on traversing the distances of reading and gives the illusion that there is no end to the metalingual turns that can be made. What does fade, however, is the context provided for by *Poetry*, so that the "hidden syllables" could be identified as literary scenes now almost entirely forgotten, and this adds to the force of the loss and consequent nostalgia explored by the poem. Euridyce becomes a figure for the receding contexts of readership in the long biography of the poem.

What Noakes calls an "authoritative reading" would play straight into the poem's hands, and this is what happens when the critic John Shoptaw tries to provide a backward look at the text. The title, he says, "sends us in several directions" (211), and then he proceeds to offer detailed glosses: the flower, the direct Ovidian reference, the possible allusion to Ovid's Syrinx, and a debt to Whitman. The "us" who are "sent in several directions" are presumably scholar-readers who go in several directions into their reference books. Are we meant to assume that readers keep reenacting this educational project, that this is what the poem does to a reader—everyone goes hurrying off to find out what the words mean even when Shoptaw has already done it for us? Asking this question shows that the collective noun is a convenient fiction. Shoptaw has done this, and then presents his reading activity as the paradigmatic reading of this poem. He also traces everything backward in time to the outset of meaning, especially to Ashbery, who is repeatedly referred to as directly speaking the poem, and even assigned a diagnosis by the critic-psychologist: "Like Proust and Wordsworth before him, Ashbery has learned that one must turn away from the frontal happiness of those prophetic moments in order to keep them" (211). This assumes an author who, one day, learns something new, and then records it for readers who are able to retrieve this discovery intact despite the distances of history and culure. But isn't it Shoptaw who has learned this? Saying so would risk, from the critic's standpoint, trivializing the insight by localizing it to just one later stage of distant reading. "Syringa" is surprisingly agile then, for it can encourage readers to attribute other poems to Ashbery as well, it can play the sound of classical myth, and its pipe can lead readers off in not one but several directions. Like "Ave Maria" the poem has a full biography.

CONCLUSION

The discussions here of poems by Frank O'Hara and John Ashbery have been deliberately presented so that the distances of reading catch the eye. The various disadvantages of the starting point of the reading (the absence of libraries, computers, and reference materials and the pleasant distractions of a holiday) in my opening caricature of a scene of reading also stand for all the other stages of this project—the years of revisions, talks, and research trips to archives in London and the United States, as well as my forgetting, my reading of the poems on trains and in other editions, my questioning of the interpretations I made earlier, and my dialogues with others. The editions, the time, the space, and the numerous other readers are the conditions of this distance from which I have been reading and cannot be avoided. Contemporary lyric poetry can either treat distance as constituted by the density and variety of social space through which all texts must pass, as an obstacle to be overcome and a background noise to be ignored, or as a field to be celebrated and incorporated into textual production. Much contemporary avant-garde poetry, like that of O'Hara and Ashbery, does this with great brilliance through its skillful management of reading futures shaped by its handling of form, publication, performance, internal relations with readers, and other conditions of textuality. Distance is only one of a changing repertoire of poetic practices that can generate meaning and with which poets like O'Hara and Ashbery innovate. For literary critics of poetry, distance is overdue for recognition. To some degree what I am advocating here as distant reading is a development from a somewhat sidelined feature of Hans-Georg Gadamer's model of hermeneutics. Most accounts of his hermeneutics concentrate on his emphasis on the fusion of horizons between present and past, and the need for a conceptual, methodological, and imaginative dialogue that this entails. His model of reading also includes a future however. He insists that the present-day reader is put at risk in a truly hermeneutic reading by the encounter with the text from the past. To be "open" to the past, as Gadamer puts it, is like a two-way relationship, because it "includes the acknowledgement that I must accept some things that are against myself, even though there is no one else who asks this of me" (324). Therefore, he adds, "I must allow the validity of the claim made by tradition, not in the sense of simply acknowledging the past in its otherness, but in such a way that it has something to say to me." This putting at risk could be redescribed as a willingness to take the projects of the text, as they realize themselves in the reader's present, forward into some future, not passively but as an active reader who both challenges them and experiences their force. To do this is to read forward, to recognize the imperatives of distance in distant reading. Another way of expressing this is offered by J. M. Bernstein, this time in the terms offered by Theodor Adorno: "Like a promise, a work of art is a fully (materially) substantial present object; like a promise, a work of art 'intends' a future that is not legible from the present other than through its very being, only providing a sign that a certain nonpredictable future will come to pass; and finally, like a promise, a work of art is impotent in the face of future reality" (420). Maintaining this modal relation and not trying to end it by claiming that the future is now, ought, according to the account of literary interpretation I have offered here, to be the ethical task for criticism.

Distant reading of a poem would entail mining what is available of the aggregative textual archive that composes the textual memory of the poem, its showing in magazines, performance, anthologies, its construal in reviews and commentaries and other treatments. Distant reading would do this to investigate how the poem's reception enables it to participate in these situations and what realignments are being made. The more detail we know about these engagements, especially their diversity or similarity, the more we can work out the possibilities of the poem as a temporal entity that produces imaginative thought and feeling. The economy at work with these merged resources results in: (1) extension of formal analysis, (2) analysis of the potentials of this form revealed by its long biography, and (3) a reading that would then not represent itself as the fulfillment of the poem but as a partner in the poem's continuance, its projective orientations that may require engagement with its commitments, as much as attention to the speed of its forms. It considers the poem as probably unfinished, and even possibly interminable, business, and in that will be its value and pleasure, a continuing struggle, a renewing music.

Chapter 2
Poetry's Oral Stage

A person stands alone in front of an audience, holding a text and speaking in an odd voice, too regular to be conversation, too intimate and too lacking in orotundity to be a speech or a lecture, too rough and personal to be theatre. The speaker is making no attempt to conceal the text. Signs of auditory effort in the audience are momentarily lost in occasional laughter, tense silences, sighs, and even cries of encouragement. Sometimes the reader uses a different, more public voice and refers to what is being read, or to some other information of apparent interest. No one talks to the reader. No one proposes a second take. No one reflexively discusses the ritual itself. It is, to borrow the words Catherine Bell uses to describe ritual, "a particularly 'mute' form of activity . . . designed to do what it does without bringing what it is doing across the threshold of discourse or systematic thinking" (Bell 93). This ritual is an ordinary poetry reading of the kind that has become widespread in the past forty years, and therefore so familiar to most readers of contemporary poetry that its strangeness requires an alienating description in order to be visible at all. Listeners and poets have had almost nothing to say (until very recently) about this phenomenon despite its importance for financing and fostering their careers, assisting the distribution of their poetry, and even shaping its very forms. Public readings seem to belong to those "background expectancies" of poetry, which are "recognizable and intelligible as the appearances-of-familiar-events," and about which a participant "is at a loss to tell us specifically of what the expectancies consist" (Garfinkel 37).[1] What could be more natural than people interested in poetry gathering together and singling out someone to present a low-budget demonstration of the full emotional and sonic effects of their poetry so that dedicated readers can comprehend the author's intentions to the full? The apparent indifference to explanation may also be simply the result of a commonplace assumption that nothing remarkable happens to the poetry itself at these events, that meaning stays fundamentally unchanged.

This elective mutism should be questioned. It could be that poets and audiences just put up with readings that don't in themselves mean much, and that there isn't much to say about an obviously successful way of publicizing poetry. Audiences seem to enjoy seeing the poets live, seeing their faces, shapes, clothes, and mannerisms. Surely this would be too cynical. Many poetry readings since the Beat poets read at the Six Gallery have radiated a belief in poetry's revolutionary cultural power. Perhaps on the other hand too much self-analysis might destroy this confident radicalism by revealing that what appears to be an entirely new venture at the limits of representation has a long embarrassing ancestry. Calling attention to the manipulation of powerful collective affects might also make the poetry seem parasitic on other political struggles, and at best a vehicle for social bonding. When a feminist poet claims that "poetry readings are an integral part of the contemporary feminist movement, and these acts of art . . . not only reflect, but forward, women's political struggle" (Machan 120), and cites Judy Grahn saying that "we used poetry to help energize women and speak to women's needs" (123), the risk with such openness would seem to be that such an assessment might lead to the conclusion that the poetry could be jettisoned altogether, and "communitas" built more directly in other ways, despite the author's claim that poetry is a necessary art that projects possible social change. Maybe poets and audiences share a desire to believe in some collective magic and don't want to look too closely at the hidden compartments and trick wires by which the illusions are created. The persistent interest amongst those who do discuss oral poetics, in shamanism, bardic lineages, mysterious energies, and transformations, might make one think so. Maybe Victor Turner's conviction that "performance is often a critique, direct or veiled, of the social life it grows out of, an evaluation (with lively possibilities of rejection) of the way society handles history" (Turner 2), applies to poetry readings, and their critique works best when veiled with a silence about aims.

Poets certainly become uneasy when they do occasionally reflect on poetry readings. Michel Deguy is bothered by the "technical conditions involved, the possible staging of an 'act,'" and prefers to separate out the poem from the "festival moment, the regulated, preconceived moment of a vociferal act, itself operating within the field of a whole complex of technological apparatus . . . the microphone, the recording session, the sound conditions for the audience on a given evening" (Deguy 71). Donald Justice calls poetry readings "a kind of vaudeville," and as another poet points out, "writers have become well known not because of the value of their work, but because they're good performers" using "methods of delivery and gimmickry that owe more to show-biz than to literature" (Wojahn 268). Maybe the whole thing is a con. John Glassco recalls a large poetry reading organized by the League in Toronto in 1968, where the "showmen" and the "mindless diatribe" were "the sensation of the evening" (Glassco 57). He complains about the "naive listener's belief that he is getting 'closer' to a poem by hearing it from the poet himself," and the way that "not only is one listening to *him* more than to what he is saying but, as part of a crowd, one is not so much having an aesthetic experience as participating in a communal one." Performance degrades cognitive apprehension of poems because "the educated *inward* ear can do more with the rhythms, vowels, syncopations and stresses of any poem than the amateur human voice can hope to do." As a result the performance movement may have irreparably weakened poetry. Donald Hall reports an unnamed poet complaining that "the poetry reading has ruined a generation once promising, because in pursuit of platform success poets wrote simplistic poems; no poem that is decently or humanly complex, he said, can reach an audience of twenty year olds at one sitting" (Hall 74). These are important criticisms, and few poets and critics have tried to answer them. Even Frederick Stern, in a careful, introspective analysis of his own experience of poetry readings, feels compelled to conclude that "the act of 'speaking,' while it may affect our apperception of the poem, does not change its meaning in any fundamental way" (Stern 77). He doesn't share Glassco's dislike of readings because he values the celebration of the poet and community that can take place, although he is careful to distinguish between the "formal" reading and "festivals." He has a place for poetry readings as celebrations of embodied humanity: "the presence of the living voice and body of the creator of the text—the poet as public reader—affirms the significance of the text, helps to overcome the abysmal fear that the poem—

even poetry, is *no more* than sign" (78). Revealingly he admits that when listening to William Everson read despite an advanced case of Parkinson's disease, he eventually ignores the poetry altogether and simply watches the man. Everson's bodily courage is the real performance (as was John Wieners's struggle with mental confusion when I saw him read not long before his death).

This essay takes issue with the view represented by Stern and argues that meaning is extended, complicated, and sometimes transformed by performance. For many poets, however, the question of meaning is subsumed into that of performance itself, which they consider a primary value both because it draws on the performativity of identity and makes an open display of the processual dimension of art. If a poem is "energy transferred from where the poet got it . . . by way of the poem itself to, all the way over to, the reader" (Olson, *Selected Writings*, 16), this dynamic would seem likely to be most fully realized in the interactive performance of poetry. If as Creeley says of Zukofsky, "all that is, as whatever has spoken it, may occur as it is, each time it is spoken" and "there is nothing which anything so existent is 'about'" (Creeley, *Essays*, 55), then all such poetry is performance irrespective of whether or not it is being voiced aloud by an author to an audience. Robert Kelly says that the sections of *The Loom* emerged from the energy of a first line that produced the ensuing "Recital" (using a word for performance that had entirely different connotations before the Second World War).[2] Douglas Oliver deliberately uses the word "performance" instead of the word "reading," saying "when I talk about poetry as a poet, as an artist and not as a critic, I always focus upon performance of poems: artistically that's where the action is, where the possibilities begin." He disarmingly admits that when he reads a poem like Dryden's "Absalom and Achitophel" to himself, he is performing it so intensely that he becomes aware of the degree to which he is being truthful and honest as he does so, and is made aware that some of its scorn for the Earl of Shaftesbury could be directed at his own dissenting politics. Such reading is an event because performance is necessarily an embodiment of the poem in time and space. Current performance writers stress the importance of the unique location in history, space, and interaction for the significance of the poem, a condition which is paramount in performance. Steve Benson summarises this very thoroughly:

> Within the generic context of "poetry readings" and "talks," I hope that my performances, involving improvisatory oral generation of texts, intermedia real-time relations, site-specific engagements of circumstances proper to the social and physical properties of the event setting, dramatic inflections of the presentation, and interpersonal collaborations with other writers, have called attention to a performance as a constructive, constitutive act, over and above its representation of previously determined plans.[3]

Such general use of the term "performance" to describe the actions of poetry has powerful but unexamined support from the use of the word in current theories of sexuality and identity, as well as theories of deconstruction.[4] When Judith Butler uses the term "performance," she, like Douglas Oliver, is using certain features of performance as the ground for what is effectively a form of analogy:

> The forming, crafting, bearing, circulation, signification of that sexed body will not be a set of actions performed in compliance with the law; on the contrary, they will be a set of actions mobilized by the law, the citational accumulation and dissimulation of the law that produces material effects, the lived necessity of those effects as well as the lived contestation of that necessity. (Butler 12)

Such a formulation could be reapplied to the performance of the identity of a poem, as a dialectic of interpretation and reinvention, since according to Butler, identity is constructed through a process of active reiteration and citation of discursive elements. Her theory uses the mobility of this rhetoric to claim that drag performances are also allegorical performances of "*the sign* of gender" (237). Cultural theory is part of an even wider appropriation of this rhetoric of performance in philosophy, where its use ranges from Lyotard's pejorative description of the functionalism of expertise, to deconstructionist interpretations of Austin's theory of performatives in speech acts. Actual poetry performance can therefore assume a much wider significance for the participants than the actual texts might indicate, and in particular, as Butler's hypothesis shows, can be read as if it were a performance of the affirmation or transgression of foundational social structures.

What *is* that person doing reading aloud from a text (or iconoclastically improvising without) to a patient audience? Do readings change the meaning of poems in fundamental ways? I shall try to answer these questions by discussing the significance of the improvised venues and presence of the author before going into detail about the reasons why poets read their own poems and the significance of sound symbolism for poetry readings. This discussion will demonstrate that there is much more semantic activity in a poetry reading than the dogmas of literary theory have hitherto allowed.

POETRY'S DREAM

Most poetry readings are ragged affairs taking place in venues temporarily liberated from other activities—pubs, bars, lecture rooms, art galleries, halls, and theaters where the readers stumble over stage sets, talk above the noise of drinkers returning from the bar, or try to figure out how best to use a PA system installed for other purposes. Readers are rarely as proficient as actors at articulating the words, and are often surprised by their tongue and larynx into false starts, repetitions, and sinusoidal amplitude. Listening to poetry requires effort, and the audience's attentiveness is vulnerable to distractions of every kind (beer, traffic, hard chairs, comings and goings, even the distracting appearance of the poet). The space is precariously and only partially transformed from its mundane use as gallery, pub, or lecture hall, whose signs remain prominently in evidence throughout the scene of textual performance, and this transformation of the backdrop tells the participants that the everyday world, despite the way it is crowded with other activities and purposes, can still provide a space for poetry. Unplanned sound, material objects that insist upon other social purposes, obtrusive failures of attention, and an insistent temporariness are common features of readings. Poetry is only in the ascendant for a moment during which it is still in competition with many reminders of the everyday world waiting to rush back into its borrowed space and expel it. The messy, incomplete, heterogeneous poetry reading is quite unlike the well-regulated art of opera, for example, where everyone sits in specially designed seats in a specially designed auditorium, reading a program telling them the biographies of the stars and the significance of the plot; the event starts at the advertised time, and the performers are separated physically from the audience. Poetry becomes sonic performance in the face of considerable odds, a conquest of the resistant contingency of everyday life, which provides a ground bass or insistent inescapable rhythm. Meaning arises out of the noise of the life-world, both as sign and other materially intelligible forms of order and significance.

The temptation is to set these imperfections against an ideal, which is imagined to be the aim of the event, even if it can only be adumbrated by the flawed actuality, a deficit that it would appear might be made up through better funding, the use of dedicated spaces, proper voice training, and management of the audience. The persistence of these momentary ascendancies of poetry in an everyday world that threatens at every instant to flood back in and reclaim the space for its everyday function suggests another possibility. Aren't these supposed flaws all part of the act, important constitutive elements of the performance event? The myriad distractions that mitigate against the ideal are stage villains representing the resistant conditions of the contemporary culture in the drama of poetry's tentative appearance and overcoming of inertia and opposition, when space, time, and poetry collude to produce a temporary dream of triumph for the power of poetry over the noise, routine, and institutions of everyday life each time a poetry reading is held.

These grating, nonsemiotic aural intrusions, and other seemingly irrelevant signs of unwanted occupancies, are antagonists in the dramatic appearance of poetry's temporary rule over the everyday world in which it is usually marginal. The hissing background is a constant reminder that readers and audience have taken hold of a space defined by the dominant culture and, as Michel de Certeau explains, have "diverted it without leaving it" (de Certeau 32). These visual and sonic incursions may also have another more liminal effect. The insistence of these fricative imperfections can help create an awareness of the space in which the performance is occurring, in an experience of what John Cage calls "an utter emptiness" in which "each sound is unique . . . and is not informed / about European history and theory," and "one can see anything can be in it, is, as / a matter of fact, in it" (Cage 176). Many contemporary poets consciously strive to extend the semantic repertoire of their performances, and this wide troublesome frame around the actual performance helps cue the audience's attention constantly to possible extensions of the field of significant action. Avant-garde poets are aware, like Carolee Schneeman, that the space of the event itself induces recognition. She recalls the traditional dancer's tense withholding of spatial response in terms that also describe the situation of the reading:

> Space was anchored in their bodies, space was where they felt their spines. They didn't realize a radiator behind them equaled their mass, asserted verticals against their legs. I want a dance where a body moves as part of its environment; where the dancer says Yes to environment incorporating or says No transforming it . . . where that choice is visual as a dancer is Visual Element moving in actual real specific dimensions. (Schneeman 18)

Poetry readings add an aural choice, although it has to be admitted that space is still an uneasy participant in the poetry reading, because most readings only faintly acknowledge the location as any more than a vehicle for the generation of spoken language. The extempore poet of the unanswerable talk, David Antin, can ask "what am i doing here?" in his performance at the San Francisco poetry center and have it be a question specific to a time and location.[5] Most poetry is read from an existing text, or at least emerges from the kind of preplan that Steve Benson refers to in his notes on performance, and its relation with the audience produces what Schneeman calls a "projective space" generated from within the person, an abstract space similar to that used in the theater, but much more raggedly, so that the actual site constantly shows through rips in the fabric of the reading. Virtual space and material space jostle uneasily as the poems are read, and this unstable coexistence forms part of an allegorical counterpart to the dramatization of a fundamental instability between writing and speech center stage of the reading.

The staging of these aspirational dramas of poetry's potential relies on the largely unconscious desires of the poets and audiences working within the material, economic constraints of an art that generates little income and only moderate levels of cultural capital. But the staging is not mere empty wish fulfillment. Just as dreams help manage the psychic economy by drawing attention to what the ego wishes to forget, so poetry readings can also be moments when the discursive network of poets and poetries is encouraged to reflect upon the conditions under which its communications, writings, and publications necessarily occur.

THE PERFORMANCE OF AUTHORSHIP

A specter is haunting poetry readings. The "dead author," risen from the text again and trailing the rags of the intentional fallacy, claims to be the originating subject from which poetry is issuing right in front of your eyes. At most poetry readings the author reads the poetry and firmly occupies the first person. When Allen Ginsberg read "Howl" his magnificent assertion of prophetic judgment filled the first person with his substantial presence from the very first word, the pronoun "I," closing the gap between author and text, saying in effect, "I, this Allen Ginsberg you see before you, witnessed these things and am telling you about them now." This is all part of the drama of the poetry reading, an acknowledged illusion in which everyone participates. The poet *performs* authorship, becoming in the process a divided subject by reproducing language constructed into a poem at some time prior to the reading, while reading aloud as if it were a spontaneous speech act arising in the present. This is why the reader is almost invariably the author, although there would seem to be no good reason why accomplished readers and actors couldn't take their places. Only the dead are represented in this way as if death for a poet meant that others had to represent you.

It ought to be surprising that an author is still the cynosure of every contemporary poetry reading, usually uttering the words of a written text as if every single one bore the indelible mark of their composer. This fixed element might appear to depend upon beliefs about authorship well past their sell-by date. It's not surprising that some critics blame it for the limitations of much contemporary poetry. Hank Lazer links the familiar format's excessive spotlighting of the author to the overwhelming hegemony of the autobiographical lyric today:

> The format for most poetry readings—a brief introduction (usually a mixture of vita and praise), a 45- to 60-minute reading where brief poems are the going thing, with explanations of personal references, some literary references, some circumstances of composition and/or intention—reinforces a narrow conception of poetic accomplishment. . . . That is, the poetry reading, with a few notable exceptions, exists in complicity with the dominance of the carefully crafted voice-lyric. (52)

Although I agree that there is a connection, I think that other socioeconomic factors have also contributed to the inexorable rise of the personal poem, and that the reading does more than just provide a bare stage for the poetic ego. Could the poetry reading, for instance, be a ritual to reestablish the authority of authorship in the face of its downsizing by the academic industry, and the performance of authorship an attempt to resist this delayering while tacitly working for different collective ends? The socialist specter hints that authorship may be a radical force in this shifty, untheorized practice.

Modern print cultures allow a surprising number of opportunities for explicit reversion from text to speech, some by authors, some by readers. Many institutional and intimate situations require texts to be read to an audience, whether of conference delegates, churchgoers, or children at occasions where the contingent relations of place, people, and history can mold the actual performance of reading aloud. The reader in turn uses these elements to produce a multidimensional commentary on what is read, through tones of voice, asides, and physical gestures. Such a medium is a highly flexible signifying vehicle for the affective and cognitive information presented alongside the reading itself, adding further semantic tracks to the performance. It is almost always informative to hear a lecture read aloud although no substitute for reading it silently at another time. Listeners can be made aware of the illocutionary force of the utterances in ways that cannot always be signaled by written linguistic markers. This is because the ordinary act of speaking in conversation is assumed in our culture to be a reliable index of the individuality of the speaker. Reading aloud relies heavily upon this axiom. However ironic or skeptical the tone of delivery, the words uttered are momentarily given a life-context, as if the reader were showing what it means for a life to say these words because the physical presence of the speaker acts as their warrant for their relevance to a specific body, point of view, and history. Such effects are obviously greatly amplified when the speaker is the author, when the moment of reading acts as a figure of an imaginary moment of composition. This radiant core then illuminates the attendant interactive commentary and gives energy to the implicit acts of asseveration.

In both the formal events and the informal occasions the person of the reader embodies an answer to a potential question: what does it mean to say these things to you now? Writing's iterability is put into tension with the contingency of the moment of production represented by the person of the reader, whose presence and delivery produces a reflexivity received as a penumbral commentary upon it. This process is perhaps most accessible in the ritual familiar to academics, the conference paper, which might also seem one of the most redundant. A complex conference paper could surely be read far more effectively by the audience beforehand in private, and the time which would have been devoted to the seemingly mechanical, oral act of delivering the paper, given instead to the all-important discussion of its contents.

The generally accepted criteria for measuring a good delivery of a good paper suggests why oral presentations may continue. The good lecturer addresses the audience directly rather than, as we say, simply "reading" the paper (an apparently paradoxical statement since reading is precisely what the lecturer is often doing). This address, which is contingent upon the actual relation between speaker, audience, and site at a particular time, can produce a continuous commentary on what is read aloud through changes of tone and emphasis in the voice, through additional verbal annotation, through asides that elaborate on the material, and through body language: a commentary similar to the second voice of the footnote beloved of academics. Such a multilayered commentary on the written text can indicate hierarchies of importance, affective investments, and relations to existing norms (using shifting tones of voice to indicate approval, irony, a sneer). In this way it is not dissimilar to the possibilities of reading a story aloud to children and bringing it to life. If the speaker is also the author, a person well placed to produce such an interactive commentary, this performance also produces an exaggerated, dramatized picture of authorship. These words arise out of the speaker, whose bodily presence and identity is their *warrant,* and whose delivery shows what it means to think and say these words and ideas, indeed, shows what it means to live them for at least the moment of their delivery. The presence of a speaker is a reminder that the words are temporarily invoked from an individual with a particular point of view, a particular body, a particular experience and history. A parallel with the reading of the children's story makes this plainer. For young children, authorship is not a clear concept, and the parent or teacher who reads the story to them will become the author or originator of the narrative, permeating it with their own identity and effectively acting as its source. Authorial reading suffuses a text with the person and their relation to the listeners.

Authorship and liminal commentary coalesce in a repertoire of asseverational gestures common to all performances of writing as speech, allowing a wide range of nuances of intensity, direction, and quality of assertion to be indicated. Most ordinary spoken utterances carry an implicit aura of assertion with them, which depends on the presence of the speaker to the auditors, because this presence metonymically represents the individual origin of the utterance. The speaker endorses what is said by saying it, whatever the positivity or negativity of the utterance itself, in a process of embodied asseveration.

The poet who reads her or his own poetry aloud in public is performing authorship, a practice that fascinates poets and audiences because the author is the subjective crossroads for the enormously complex transactions of institutional legitimation in the contemporary world. Unremitting efforts go into maintaining the authority of specialized knowledges and the rights of individuals to be its authors, critics, and revisionists. Poets cannot claim that the authority, truth, and pertinence of their work is directly dependent upon such existing institutional networks, and instead they have to generate this platform from within the work and its distribution, adding any authority they can from their standing as a poet.

This difficulty is also a source of radical power just because it puts authorship into the contested field of the poem. Gillian Rose's brilliant investigation of the damaged modern understanding of ethics in *The Broken Middle* leads her into a discussion of authorship and its paradoxes of authority and pseudonymity, which she argues are the only means for avoiding the arrogation of the authority that ethical philosophers are questioning. In her discussion of three Jewish women philosophers, Varnhagen, Luxemburg, and Arendt, she suggests that their greatness emerges from just this commitment to a performative authorship.

> They neither opt to abandon political universality, even though it is demonstrably spurious; nor to resolve its inconsistency and antinomy in any ethical immediacy of love: "community," "nation," "race," "religion" or "gender." Remaining within the agon of authorship they cultivate aporetic universalism, restless affirmation

> and undermining of political form and political action, which never loses sight of the continuing mutual corruption of the state and civil society.

One sign of their commitment is that they recognize that "the politics of this 'middle', conceived now as 'social' and as 'civil' in the sense of sociability or civility, and of *gesellschaftlich,* contractual, civil society or civil law, involves indirect communication, not 'ideal speech situation' or ideal communication" (Rose 155). This subtle and complex argument offers a clue to the politics of the poetry reading. The ambitions of the poetry reading to place its art within a community of listeners should not be collapsed into either a moment when a work independent of the collective process is handed over in speech, nor into a moment of collective shared understanding that "reads" the work within its own encompassing discursivity. Rose points us to the need to consider the poem outside any ideal beginning or end, and to recognize its large ethical ambitions in performance, a figure for the middle ground between objectified poem and its interpretation, which is a field of flawed ethical and semantic ambitions where the agon of authorship waits.

To say this is to say something very different from Denise Levertov, who argues that a poet can't really spoil the reading of a poem by adding personality to it, because the poet's personality and the personality emulsified in the poem are the same, so that "his voice will clarify, not distort" (Levertov, "An Approach," 53). For her, authoriality is already inherent in the poem and the poet, just as ideology would have it that there is a gender already inside us (according to Judith Butler). Levertov's misleading assumption may derive in part from her misapprehension of the contemporary fascination with metapoetic displays of authorship, from Robert Duncan's "sometimes I am permitted to return to a meadow," to Ron Silliman's iterative references to the pen in *Tjanting,* which both effectively question any simple egoistic derivation of intent.

This begins to explain why poetry readings usually feature authors reading their own poems, but still leaves questions about the remarkable degree of emphasis on authorship in the ordinary poetry reading. A signal only needs to be amplified when it isn't strong enough to resist the circumambient noise on its own, and the amplifying gestures of asseveration can be read as a further symptom of the agon of authorship, when the poem's actual and potential disturbances of authority are registered by more encompassing modes of power. Indeed asseveration may be closely connected to problems of authority, especially moral authority, as Alasdair MacIntyre shows in his critique of modern moral philosophy, *After Virtue.*

He stigmatizes most modern ethical theories as emotivist, because they can offer no foundations for moral claims other than their advocate's own individual convictions, the personal assertions of value ultimately grounded only in desires and affects, which has reduced moral argument to no more than a competition for the upper hand between the self-proclaimed authentic feelings of different people or groups. The passionate sincerity of my views is the ultimate basis for deciding the value of my moral position in any specific case. His answer to this evacuation of all objective criteria from ethical terms is not to argue for some new system of constructing moral laws, perhaps in the manner of Kant's categorical imperative, but for the somewhat utopian possibility that the reestablishment of valid moral debate might re-create a new form of the type of language communities built on a densely shared common experience found in highly traditional societies. In such conditions the language is tied almost completely to

> a particular community living at a particular time and place with particular shared beliefs, institutions, and practices. These beliefs, institutions, and practices will be furnished expression and embodiment in a variety of linguistic expressions and idioms; the language will provide standard uses for a necessary range of expressions and idioms, the use of which will presuppose commitment to those same beliefs, institutions, and practices. (MacIntyre, *Whose Justice,* 373)

It is a community where a moral language would have foundations in actual common practice and understanding, where "by saying something a speaker or writer communicates more and other than he or she has actually said" (373).

When Barrett Watten read from his collection of poems, *Conduit,* at the University of Southampton in 1993, his performance was carefully poised to withhold assertoric support. *Conduit* is composed of emphatic utterances, and the poet delivered them in a neutralizing style that collaborated with their lack of coherent sequence to unsettle expectations that these are existentially backed propositions. *Conduit* takes its title from an essay by George Lakoff on what he calls the "conduit" fallacy, the belief that language transports something tangible, a meaning, between a speaker and a listener. In the preface to *Conduit,* Watten explains the new conditions for the writer as a reconfiguration of the distance between writer, text, and reader:

> The forms of contemporary writing are entering into an acknowledgement of this stricture—that the work is only completed, apart from the writer's intentions, in a response. . . . The writer is faced with adjusting himself to what accurately is the medium, a missing person that is a space for projections, the ground for what wants to be perceived. This new medium is the resistance between writer and reader, speaker and hearer. . . . Nothing can be compelled from the site of the speaker except the outlines of his form. This new resistance of the medium, then, demands from the speaker an intuitive mastery of blanks and negations. The speaker no longer hears only himself; he must also hear what the absence of himself would mean to another. (Watten 9–10)

The field of interaction, of intersubjectivity, in which the performance occurs, is the work, not some meaning or assertion the uttered text might contain. Watten's opening line to section four, "to whom am I speaking," a distinctively English idiom, sounding odd to American ears, is placed in quotation marks to exhibit it and suspend its force. Yet spoken by Watten, it sounds as if he were asking the question of his auditors, since the quotation marks are heard only as a tonal hesitancy, a slight shrinking from this unfamiliar way of asking the question. Watten's sentences start to raise a hazing disturbance of response that gradually coheres around questions of the possibility of something to replace the vanishing text.

Sometimes authorship is performed in a manner that appears excessive or under-inhabited, and at both extremes the tacit frameworks of expectation are more than usually apprehensible. The poet David Bromige, born in the UK but a part of the West Coast poetry network, provides a rare instance of a detailed report on all aspects of a poet's performance in his critical account of the British poet Allen Fisher's 80 Langton Street (an arts center in San Francisco) artist-in-residency in 1982.

Allen Fisher's work is distinctive because of its conversance with a wide range of contemporary scientific discourses. Few poets use up-to-date knowledge from the natural sciences as part of their compositional strategy, not only because of its intrinsic difficulty, but also because of problems of authority, their own and more troubling still, the authority of the knowledge itself, which has such a short half-life in most cases. In his recent poetry, Fisher has been working in this challenging area with results that led Bromige to complain that Fisher attempted to present too much material in the four days of his residency, an excess symptomatic of a problem with the poetry itself: "the mimesis of information overload destroying any and all attempts at the discrete and limitable cannot take place on the scale of life without rendering itself defunct as art" (Bromige 42). These problems the audience had with Fisher's work were, Bromige suspected, displacements of a more general problem with audience in England: "Fisher has to use his poetry to tell a possible readership how it is to be read" (41). Fisher's difficulty, one might say, is how to perform authorship for his audience in a persuasive manner, and so Bromige takes up a role as representative naïve American listener to Fisher in terms which overstate the audience's fascination with the hitherto unfamiliar poet. The report on the actual reading begins with the kind of attention the press gives to celebrities: "Wearing gray shirt with red buttons, electric-blue baggies, shiny white shoes with red trim and laces, bright red socks, wristwatch with red strap, and browny-gray belt, and revealing himself to be a youthful 38, a little over six feet and lean, with dark hair and attractively limber wrists etc. . . . His voice—Denise Levertov as a light baritone—disguises the Olsonic address of his poetry" (22). This ironic imitation of the language of the journalist feature writer works because we do indulge such inquisitiveness at readings. Emphasizing the audience's immediate reaction to the poet is a means of reminding everyone of the importance of that relation. The hitherto unwitnessed writer reveals himself to be lean and limber, a sharp dresser, who reads in a tone of voice that reveals the anxiety of influence by merging the tones of two poet predecessors.

Bromige's witty account makes critical points about both the timbre of relations between performer and audience and the poetry itself. He quotes some lines from the reading ("that poetry can medically do you good / through evoking deliberate shadow / of unmentioned imago / defeating expectations and stock responses") and comments that they posed a problem for this particular audience: "as so often, Fisher did not indicate where he stood with regard to this definition" (28). The unmentioned imago becomes the well-dressed person of the author, which may defeat expectations and do the audience good, but does so without the poetry. By telling us what Fisher looked and sounded like, Bromige tells us too literally where Fisher stood, but of course this information fails to tell us where Fisher stood metaphorically with regard to such statements in the poetry. Fisher withheld the asseverations that Bromige wanted, so that the author he performed, the Fisher who stood in a known place, was (unusually) not immediately translatable into the Fisher in the discourse of the poetry, in the manner that Ginsberg triumphantly achieved in his famous reading of *Howl.* Bromige's almost ethnographic report doesn't however consider whether Fisher might deliberately be attempting just such a diremption. I would argue (making my own attempt at asseveration and an appeal to common values) that this uncertainty is a necessary element in the wider project of Fisher's poetry, which attempts to develop an ethics of contemporary urban life by deliberately juxtaposing in the field of the poem some of the many different knowledges used by the authorities as the basis of their decision making, and then confronting them with ethical and aesthetic challenges created by his own implicit, and sometimes explicit, commentary in an attempt to transform them into new, radical projects for the future.

Authorship can be very difficult to perform even on the page. When poets like Fisher do plug into the standard networks of scientific knowledge, they sometimes produce texts whose use of the conventions for negotiating authority and authorship's indebtedness appears as poetic idiosyncrasy. J. H. Prynne, for instance, tried printing a list of scholarly endnotes referring to his sources in learned journals and books on the page following his poem "Aristeas, in Seven Years" without any heading, so that they read as a further stage in the poem, their status unclear. The notes tell the reader where to look for more information but they don't validate the poem nor allow it to emerge as a corrective, extending critique of this existing body of historical knowledge. Instead the poem unsettles the authorizations it negotiates. *Brixton Fractals,* Allen Fisher's narrative series set in the South London of Blake and the Greater London Council, finishes with a "bibliography" of one-hundred-and-twenty-three items that runs to several pages. These listings extend the range of the poems and certainly repay investigation but they cannot lend the kind of authority to the poems that even the citations to a humanities essay like this one will provide, as the preface admits:

> A bibliography has been added under the title "Resources" in the back of the book, and has been kept as simple as possible to emphasise some of the indirect perception involved in making *Brixton Fractals.* This is not intended as an itinerary for suggested further reading, or a listing to give authority to the text. It is to thank those who have taken part in the perception and memory that has made the text, and to keep open the opportunity to hear them. (Fisher 4)

In both cases the status of information, whether the dates for the invasion of the Scythians or the possibility of "phases between nematic and smectic parallelisms" (Fisher 69) of an ice sheet, does not have a direct dependence upon the accepted value of these facts, which may change with scholarly and scientific developments. It is not enough to shrug and say like the Wife of Bath, "Experience, though noon auctoritee / Were in this world, is right ynogh for me" (Chaucer 158). Poets like Prynne and Fisher recognize that they have to find some way of staking a claim to be heard, and the more their work moves in the wider public and scientific sphere, the more there is a problem. Poetry readings stage this difficulty recognized by Lisa Robertson's amusing strategy for outlining her sources in *XEclogue.* She defines the relation between poem and authority in a manner that echoes Fisher's gesture of gratitude and avoids any implicit claim to borrow scientific codes, by saying that "XEclogue has had many houseguests" and then naming various writers and performers as people who "taught me the necessity of women's tactical intervention in the official genres" (Robertson, no page nos.).

Bromige's account shows how integral the staging of authorship can be for the reception of the poem's meaning and demonstrates that this need not be a simple matter of wholehearted approval, since the fissuring of authorship that he witnessed can also be interpreted as a wider condition of authorship as well as an intentional effect. Sometimes poets go so far as to turn such splitting into a metapoetic narrative of reception alongside its other narratives within and outside the poem, by incorporating reference to the anticipated relations with a live audience. Denise Levertov's poem, "The day the audience walked out on me, and why. (May 8th, 1970, Goucher College, Maryland)" (Levertov, *Footprints,* 26), is available as part of a reading done as a studio recording specially for issue on tape, so is not quite the same as a public reading, but nevertheless demonstrates one aspect of what would be likely to be its effect when performed at a reading. The poem is an account of how she read two poems against the Vietnam War in the college chapel at a ceremony to mark the killing of the students at Kent State by the national guard, and then followed the poems with a reminder of all the other students, especially African-American students, murdered in the civil rights struggle. The audience gradually walked out on her as she spoke, and one man told her that "my words / desecrated a holy place," a denunciation which implicitly acknowledged the power of her speaking, and her poetry, although he strongly disapproved of these results.

Levertov's delivery deliberately blurs the boundaries between speech and writing, making her writing sound extempore, and making explicit reference to itself ("while I spoke"), particularly by referring to the speech that provoked the walkout as her "rap," associating it with oral African-American culture. As she reads the poem, Levertov keeps closely to the line-breaks, yet manages to make them sound inevitable, as if she were just telling an anecdote. Her voice, which sounds unclear, thick, laden with some uncomfortable affect, suddenly clears and softens when she recalls the signs of May outside the door. Her lighter tone stands in the same relation to her earlier heaviness as the spring outside does to the dark cultural interior of this time and prefigures the voice that would be possible if the audience for the new poem were able to meet her in her wish for them to form a group capable of both mourning the murders in this intersubjective ritual, and vowing to make reparation. This poem is about an audience, an audience that refuses to listen, because to their ears her "rap" illegitimately extends the occasion to a ritual observance for all the murdered students, black and white. Her talk had tried to conscript its white listeners into a ritual they cannot accept, and so they left, refusing to be an audience at all. The poem recounting this walkout is therefore itself a ritual made self-aware, a ritual of remembrance for another reading, as well as the murdered students, and anyone hearing her read the poem aloud would be constantly aware of the contrast (and possible similarity) of their own behavior and that of the complacently white churchgoers of Goucher. The poem seems to be about one past incident, but when performed as a reading, even on tape, becomes through the authority of the poet's voice, a challenge to the white listener to acknowledge the significance of African-American campaigns for justice. Levertov's poem is explicit about the way performance stages the presence of the author as a challenge to listen and confront what it means to assert these words, or depart, literally or figuratively withdrawing from the negotiations enforced by the presence of the author alongside, and not only within, the text.

Levertov's strategy also creates a history of herself as performer, and is a reminder that the power of live performances to establish a readership for even poets working on the margins of the public sphere should not be underestimated. Public readings can help establish authority even in a world where the bureaucracies of knowledge are more powerful than ever before. One cause of the divisions between the antimodernist and modernist poets in the UK is that detractors of modernist work have often never attended a live performance by these practitioners. When readers have only read a text on the page that is also written with performance in mind as part of its promulgation, they can fail to understand what they are reading.

A unique instance of a survey of readers' responses to poetry that is highly performative shows just how important it can be for the readership to have witnessed performances in order to grasp the significance of the printed page. In the Maggie O'Sullivan issue of the magazine *Responses* (each issue presented one poem followed by a series of short paragraphs of immediate, unrevised responses from anonymous readers) edited by Steven Pereira and Anthony Rollinson, O'Sullivan's poem "Giant Yellow" was published alongside a series of revealing attempts to discuss or reject it.[6] The extremes in these eleven responses are striking. Comments by readers of this poem who had not encountered her work before suggest that without witnessing her performance, the work's imagined readership can be hard to discern. Some of the readers were defeated by its neologisms, insistent sound patterns, and lack of integrating syntax, and they were "made to feel uncomfortable" because the poem "creates ignorance" (the respondent doesn't entertain the possibility that this might be valuable) and it is like listening to a foreign language or just white noise. Some are even more abusive, calling it verbal butchery, vomit, or that most awful term of abuse, an "academic exercise."

Other respondents seem to have read a different poem and are full of praise for the work. It is noticeable that these poets, who identify themselves as having been part of the London scene for years, immediately summon up a picture of the poet herself performing the poetry aloud. For them, the author's vocal performance is a memory now inscribed within the text. One poet summons up "striking if not conventionally beautiful dark Irish features" which are "transformed, transfused with beauty as she reads unhurriedly." Another poet contrasts the "permanent disruption" on the page with the "elusive meanings" heard in the air by the "mental ear." Lawrence Upton has strongly internalized an image of the poet reading: "Maggie O'Sullivan has a remarkable reading voice—and manner, her manner is quite compelling though friendly and supportive, drawing in audience (they who hear)—which is warm, resonant and *not* colloquial, *not* casual but *causal*." One way of contrasting these positive readings with the other hostile ones is to say that the others have not heard O'Sullivan, so that instead of hearing her voice inscribed within the poem, they can only experience disorientation and nausea. A dissenter says perceptively, "I have no knowledge to sustain me," and shows how unpleasant this feels by spewing forth images of an abattoir, of eating offal, excrement, blood. To a reader who knows what the writer actually looks like, this respondent's comment that "through this carnage runs a blonde" shows how easily readers project their own mistaken images of the writer into the act of the poem. The seventh respondent allows primary process to take over and figures the poem as vomit and masturbation before saying that the poem "shits all over the reader." This litany of abjection, of images of the expulsion of taboo bodily substances, is evoked by the belief that the poem is a deliberate act of contempt for "dull bastards." The reader feels that the poem denies the patrimony of its readers, making them illegitimate as well as illiterate, because it fails to involve the reader and instead "forces the reader into the position of spectator," which only a "sick" poem would do. Exclusion from a relation to the poem's performance produces these extreme reactions, in which by imagining the poem as having been taken into the body, the critic abjects it her/himself, throwing it violently away from attention. This reader is actually reading attentively, noting the performative style and the importance of sound, but is then unable to process the information and explodes, rather like the early Dada audiences, in a violent rejection. Although one of the readers unfamiliar with O'Sullivan's poetry does guess hesitantly that it "could be a poem for voices," even this is not enough to enable the new reader to feel part of the implicate readership.

The poetry reading dramatizes authorship because the authority of the poet and poetry is so questionable in an age where the production of any kind of public discourse, especially ones which make any kind of statement about the way the world is or how we ought to act, depends for its legitimacy on institutional validation if it is to be any more than personal opinion, which itself depends for its significance on the status of the person. Academic conference-goers know all about the struggle for legitimation and have many rituals besides the reading of conference papers to establish the credentials of what is to be scientific, properly theorized, empirically established, and so forth. Unless poets are content to dramatize only their own inner struggles according to recognizable criteria of what counts as psychologically possible, they will be perceived as eccentric one-person research outfits, and will need to meet the question of authority head on. Lacking many of the other forms of legitimation available to academics in academic settings, poetry readings become another means of negotiating the authorization of the claim to a public voice and the right to state facts and make judgments. Asseveration is central to this. The poetic utterances carry an assertoric force that depends on the presence of the performative author, and the result is a local, momentary attempt to draw listeners closer into such communities, however fragile and temporary, to provide partial foundations for ethical and aesthetic assertions, and at the same time, is a reminder of their partial absence, because its degree of emphasis is commonly in inverse relation to the degree of consensus.

SOUND SYMBOLISM

Denise Levertov believes that "the sounds—the vowels and consonants, the tone patterns, the currents of rhythm . . . are the chief carriers of content" (Levertov, *Light*, 49). Steve McCaffery goes even further, claiming that "it is energy, not semantically shaped meaning, that constitutes the essence of communicated data. . . . [I]t is the scripted signifier, the phonematic unit that marks the crypt of a vast repression, where energy is frozen in the articulated and subordinated elements of repression" (McCaffery, "Sound Poetry," no page nos.). Unfreezing these sound symbols is difficult even when reading enables us to glimpse them. Should for example a reader encountering the phonestheme "gl" in the word "glad" in a poem try to hear traces of light symbolism in the word? The answer probably depends upon the context, yet in actual examples the relevance can be hard to gauge. Consider the following passage taken from Maggie O'Sullivan's "Hill Figures" from the recent anthology *Out of Everywhere: Linguistically Innovative Poetry by Women in North America and the U.K.*:

> Skull—
> alarge, Oth
>   Twisted
>   merry-go
>   superates,
>   congregates,
>   rolled-a-run
>   lettering
> (O'Sullivan, *Out of Everywhere,* 70)

"Oth" could be an obsolete form of "oath" or "otter," it could be a segment of "Goth," "other," "troth," or it could echo the sound of words like "loathe." It can therefore be pronounced in several different ways and be linked to several associational networks, allowing an imprecision of pronunciation that performance cannot replicate. The phonestheme "gr" in the word "congregates" is a particularly strong one, with associations of unpleasantness, complaint, and unwanted rubbing (Waugh 77), yet the pertinence of this iconicity is deliberately unclear, although the tone of this poem about the poisoning of outdoor freedoms does seem to encourage a reader to hear such a semantic trace. Performance could linger with a growl or quickly open out into the following vowel, without resolving the question, unless one grants the author's pronunciation an absolute authority. Take another instance from the same anthology. When Deanna Ferguson writes "Had I seen square when / eyeball suture teethed with / cankorous proclivity" (O'Sullivan 131) in the poem "It's Bad for You," should we hear an active phonestheme in the "sq" with echoes of the crushing in squash, squelch, squeeze? We can say with more confidence that the replacement of "seethed" by "teethed" brings the teeth more actively into use to make the "th" sound and gives the awkward adjective (with verbal overtones) more bite.

"Words change in spoken language," as Ted Greenwald puts it (Greenwald, "Spoken," no page nos.). Since most poets agree with the general sentiment of Louis Zukofksy's claim that "the sound of the words is sometimes 95% of poetic presentation" (Zukofsky, *Test*, 58), if not always about the exact percentage, it is not surprising that poets, and those who go to readings to hear them, generally agree that the opportunity to hear the poem vocalized is the best justification for contemporary poetry readings. They say that hearing a poet read work aloud helps them comprehend it better because the author's oral interpretation of tone, gesture, and emphasis can clarify what was not always immediately perceptible on the page, providing a training session in the effective reception of the poems, especially in how to hear the actual sonic qualities of the poem. Are they right? Couldn't this apprenticeship be equally well, if less readily, done on one's own? Does a public reading reach its apogee when the poet enables listeners to appreciate the full frequency range and dynamics of the performed sonorities? Or can some value be attached to the sound of poetry as also a cognitive element of the poetry and would this be similar to the nonsignifying arts of music?

Literary theory has lacked a conceptual framework for analyzing and justifying these phenomena and therefore sidelined attention to the actual qualities of sound in language. Saussure's concept of the arbitrariness of the signifier has been taken to mean that the actual sound of a word is nothing more than a nonsemantic girder on which the sign can be built. As is now a commonplace, it is the differences between the phonemes which count, not the audible qualities of the actual sounds themselves, and this dogma led to the closure of enquiry into the semantic potential of sound apart from the differential structure, despite wide agreement amongst writers about its deep significance to their craft.

The poet J. H. Prynne, whose own poetry relies heavily on encoded associations linked by sound, questions the dogmas of aural indifference in two lectures that demonstrate the range of ordinary interpretative strategies for reading poems that rely on the assumption that sound effects are "motivated" rather than arbitrary. Literary theorists claim to believe that: "If language is a system of meanings and meaning-relations, then any kind of efficient carrier which could encode and deliver its discriminations would be adequate to efficient performance; there is no need for an idea to be matched by a word-form at an individual level: the sign is *arbitrary*" (Prynne, "Stars," 1). In practice almost everyone ignores the rigidity of this claim about arbitrariness. Poets have always cared for the sound effects of their vocabulary, for its roughness and smoothness, its harmonies and tones, its rhymes, alliterations, and onomatopoeias, and therefore the sound quality of signifiers in poetry can be said to be at least partially motivated or thickened with intention. Prynne argues that all language in use actually encompasses a dense texture of diachronic "secondary relations, allowing functional connection from sense to sound (violating one system-generated rule) and from sound to sense (violating another); such connections may in intensely witty or language-conscious performance be recognized to run alternatingly back and forth, or even in both directions at once" (32). These secondary relations are historically local associations between sound values and both ideas and emotions, associations that are pragmatic rather than systematic and do not undermine the system itself. He makes this latter point because linguists have insisted on the arbitrariness hypothesis partly to retain the seemingly necessary concept of language as system. Prynne proposes that such poetic play with sound as sense can be a

> complement to essentialist analysis of structure, not so much because it operates more in one dimension than another (e.g., historical space rather than conceptual space), but because it is an aggregating and proliferative instigation, recursively back-folding and cross-linking, and this kind of incorporative opportunism is idiomatic for a whole pattern of cultural practice in which language is a centrally-mediating agency. (34)

Although Prynne wishes to retain the concept of system, he also recognizes that language is inherently performative—spoken, dialogic, contingent. He indirectly acknowledges the potential of performance by emphasizing the way signifying media extend beyond basic phonetic units: "If language is a social code of interactions, in which performance is an expressive procedure within a context of sense-bearing acts, then anything that *can* count toward meaning *may* do so: intonation, style-level, choice of words and of their sounds and echoes" (1). Prynne's insistence that the set of potential sense-bearing material practices is open-ended is particularly important—it encourages us to look for others and to expect some new writing to generate new designs for such "sense-bearing acts." This leads him to be ambivalent about the status of the arbitrariness hypothesis, at once calling it into question and then backing off into qualifications that reduce the significance of sound pattern to contingent, occasional, and local collaborations of interpretation. His discussion does recognize the difficulty of applying a theoretical method, designed to isolate the phenomenon of language for analytic study, to a performative event in which the boundaries between different structurings of significance, both linguistic and nonlinguistic, become permeable and at times indistinguishable. His conclusions help explain his own unwillingness to read his poetry in public, since if a poem is already an expressive interaction generating the tonal and decisionist range he mentions, then it might have no need for any additional resources, making performance redundant; indeed performance might only obfuscate the intended field of readerly engagement. The continuing prevalence of poetry readings suggests that few poets and readers believe that poems are capable of achieving this ideal without further performative resources.

Poets' interest in the "de-emphasis of the written medium" (Beach 124), their insistent call to recognize a nonsemiotic, and sometimes nonlinguistic, dimension, has often embarrassed modern critics trying to establish the intellectual gravity of poetry, especially after what have been widely perceived to be symbolist and Keatsian excesses of some late-nineteenth-century poets. Lacking theoretical resources to analyze its positivity, they have mostly sidelined it, treating it as an unwelcome distraction from the proper rigor of fully developed rationality and the richness of distinctive voice. Even the high theorists follow this line. The oral stage of psychic development is the earliest, according to psychoanalysis, and this sense of the primitive character of orality has been carried over into literary and cultural theory. Julia Kristeva's association of sound in poetry with the unconscious chora is characteristic.[7] Her concept of the *chora*, the presemiotic space of rhythmically organized psychic drives characteristic of the oral stage, presupposes that the psychic experience of sound occurs on the far side of conscious rationality and representation. She describes the foregrounding of sound in poetry as a disruption of the political laws and orders of the symbolic, but in doing so sees only the destruction of sense and not the innovative constructions that the poetic virtuosity of phonic display can create according to poets. The oral stage is imagined as incapable of development without relinquishing orality itself. Literary theory has not provided an adequate account of sound in poetry, and hence a way of considering poetry readings, largely because of its somewhat unexamined reliance on Saussure's assumptions about sound.

Saussure's *Course in General Linguistics,* the primary source for a model of language in recent literary theory, is as much an account of how to study language as an account of what language is. In the following key passage where he underlines the importance of assuming that the linguistic sign is arbitrary, his reference to the collective action of the analysis is a reminder that this is a deliberate process of isolating and defining a phenomenon for a particular kind of study:

> The link between signal and signification is arbitrary. Since we are treating a sign as the combination in which a signal is associated with a signification, we can express this more simply as: *the linguistic sign is arbitrary.* There is no internal connection, for example, between the idea "sister" and the French sequence of sounds *s-ö-r* which acts as its signal. The same idea might as well be represented by any other sequence of sounds. (Saussure 67)[8]

This formulation is notoriously hard to interpret rigorously. What, for example, is meant by an internal connection? Many commentators have written as if the connection would be between a referent and the signifier, citing another of Saussure's examples, the word "arbre" and his accompanying diagrams, yet he surely means that the ideas of tree or sister exist independently of any particular signifier and are only linked up to them by some arbitrary, unconscious, and consensual process. A further uncertainty of great relevance to poets is that Saussure is not quite accurate to say that idea and sequence of sounds have no connection. Patterns of ideas often have corresponding patterns of phonemes. The words for family members—sister, brother, father, and mother—all end in *er,* and the latter three share the ending *ther.* In French a similar asymmetric pattern of endings links the last three and distinguishes them from the first. As the linguist Linda Waugh, who worked closely with Roman Jakobson, points out, such patterns mean that just any sound would not do as a representation of the idea of sister. Saussure's remark that any sound would do as well to represent the idea of sister conceals a tacit assumption of great importance, that given a different cultural history in which sounds and meanings had come to be associated in different ways, then the idea of sister could have been marked by a different sound, but he makes it appear as if some kind of arbitrary decision, made independently of the rest of language and history, is the abstract paradigm for there to be a signifying connection between sound and sense. Affinities between the sound of words are, however, likely to be indications of other historically determined cultural associations. The psychoanalyst Paul Kugler, for example, notes that such sonic isomorphisms occur even in different languages and are based on different root sounds. The sound pattern manifest by the words *violet, violate, violent,* seems to have counterparts with the German *Blut* (blood), *Bluten* (blossom), *bluten* (to bleed), the Hungarian *ver* (blood), *veres* (bloody), and *verag* (flower), and the English trio *carnation, carnage,* and *incarnation* (Kugler 23). He attributes these patterns to Jungian archetypes but they could be explained as resulting from culturally established associations of ideas reinforced by aural similitudes that have been common to European countries with convergent histories. Such examples suggest that Saussure is wrong to claim that the whole sequence of sounds bears no relation to the idea. Can the principle of abitrariness be rescued by moving the claim one step further down the chain and saying that the individual sound is arbitrary? According to the linguist Linda Waugh, even this is not enough to account for the patterning or "iconicity" of language. Saussure himself seems to recognize this later in the *Course* in a passage less often cited: "A linguistic system is a series of phonetic differences matched with a series of conceptual differences." (Saussure 118 [167]) This description doesn't assume that the matching or correlation only takes place at the level of a word, although some kind of mapping must occur between the two systems.

Jacques Derrida's deconstruction of Saussure takes up this point in the *Course* and argues that it exemplifies the metaphysical idea of the sign, which has had a hold over the modern period. Derrida thinks that Saussure fails to sustain his arbitrariness hypothesis, which Derrida endorses, because of a competing claim that there is a natural bond between sound and sense. Although the link between a specific signifier and a specific signified is arbitrary, this is still governed by the natural relation between "phonic signifiers and their signifieds in general." This interpretation of Saussure depends on a tendentious reading of a passage that Derrida repeatedly cites. In a discussion of the proper object of linguistic study, Saussure argues that the prestige of writing has misled many linguists into making false generalizations about language chronology. Thinking of linguists, Saussure argues:

> The written form of a word strikes us as a permanent, solid object and hence more fitting than its sound to act as a linguistic unit persisting through time. Although the connection between word and written form is superficial and establishes a purely artificial unit, it is none the less much easier to grasp than the natural and only authentic connection, which links word and sound. (Saussure 26 [46])

Derrida picks up that last claim, "the natural and only authentic connection, which links word and sound," and makes much of it: "This natural bond of the signified (concept or sense) to the phonic signifier would condition the natural relationship subordinating writing (visible image) to speech" (Derrida, *Grammatology*, 35). A critic of his commentaries on Husserl and Saussure, J. Claude Evans, argues that he is making an unwarranted leap from Saussure's point that linguists studying the structure of language should concentrate on the system of utterances, to the claim that Saussure, in common with modern philosophy, imagines that speech gives direct access to thought. Saussure would seem to be saying something very similar to Derrida, that there is no such thing as phonetic writing, that the link between written word and spoken word is superficial, and that the proper or natural subject matter of linguistics is the sign, which at this point in the course of lectures he has not yet clearly defined as a combination of concept and sound-image, or signifier and signified. Derrida's point, however, is a broader one than Evans recognizes. Saussure does conceive of a language taken as a whole as a system of sound-images linked to thoughts, as if sound were the inevitable first stage whereby thought develops into language. Much work evidently remains to be done in this area of poetics because existing theory does not offer all the discriminations necessary for the task.

Outside literary theory, however, two developments in linguistics do offer some ideas as to how theory might begin to rethink its resistance to sound. Prynne's argument has affinities with the work of Roman Jakobson and Linda Waugh, and McCaffery's image of the crypt, presumably an echo of Abram and Torok's theory of "cryptamnesia," has more distant resonances with the work of the cognitive linguist, Reuven

Tsur. Linda Waugh argues that the concept of arbitrariness has led to confusion because it has been muddled-up with the concept of conventionality. Words can have a phonetic form that is a matter of convention without at the same time being arbitrary, a feature of language most evident in the way the sound forms of words exhibit relations amongst themselves, which function rather like visual diagrams, and so can be called iconic. Saussure himself recognized that many words displayed what he called "relative arbitrariness," or "degrees of arbitrariness," because some signs are "motivated to a certain extent." The word "dix-neuf" is composed of two words whose meaning literally adds up to the meaning of the entire word. Waugh shows that this is only one of many kinds of iconicity and estimates that about 80 percent of all words are motivated in some fashion. Her range of examples and reports of linguistic research back up what poets have always said, that the sound of words within a specific language is highly significant, and their composition requires great artistry to create effective patterns of meaning, which means that: "speakers of a language differ widely in how salient the associations are for them. There seems to be a continuum all the way from those who find such associations quite strong and important, to those for whom they are negligible, with many subtle differences in between" (Waugh 75). Linguists have described a link between high-pitched front vowels and the idea of smallness and light, and low-pitched back vowels and largeness and darkness (a *chip* involves a small cut and a *chop* a large one). The words *glitter, glisten, glow,* and *glimmer,* for example, all use the phonestheme *gl* associated with an indistinct light (Hinton 5). A poet might therefore manage to convey these ideas simply by some pattern of vowels that will convey this suggestion subliminally or use words that do not use this kind of iconicity (the antonyms *big* and *small* are familiar examples) in contexts where the lack is also significant.

The concept of sound symbolism has not had much influence on literary theory, and so the linguistics does not help us resolve several key issues concerning the poetry reading. One possibility is that poetry readings are spaces in which readers can improve their attentiveness to this area of the semantic repertoire. Waugh herself notes that: "some language users are poets, while others are deaf to the music of language" (Waugh 75), and this analogic use of poetry to describe a high level of competence suggests that the poetry reading might plausibly be considered in this manner.

A quite different approach to the same problem is offered by cognitive linguist Reuven Tsur. Sound symbolism is resolutely linguistic, yet sound itself is a bodily experience, and most sound in the world is extralinguistic, a continual vibration of the air by all the movements in the plenum. Dennis Lee describes an experience of sound that so permeates him it is not strictly heard at all: "Most of my life as a writer is spent listening in to a cadence which is a kind of taut cascade, a luminous tumble. If I withdraw from immediate contact with things around me I can sense it churning, flickering, dancing, locating things in more shapely relation to one another without robbing them of themselves . . . I speak of 'hearing' cadence, but in fact I am baffled by how to describe it. There is no auditory sensation" (Lee 397). Poetry readings position the sound of the poem on this sound stage quite deliberately, if somewhat unconsciously. One way of interpreting this is to say that all the sounds audible at a reading are part of a world of sound, which the minds of the audience then scan in search of meaning. According to the Tsur, our minds process language-bearing sound in an automatic manner. When we hear a sound our minds make a decision whether to treat it as speech or pure sound, and once it has been processed as speech, we find it hard to recall the sounds out of which the linguistic units were made. We direct our attention away from the sound to the muscular movements that create the sound and from there to the phoneme itself. "We seem to be tuned, normally, to the nonspeech mode; but as soon as the incoming stream of sounds gives the slightest indication that it may be carrying linguistic information, we automatically switch to the speech mode." (Tsur 11) These processing modes are not hermetically sealed, so some crosstalk can occur and at times "some tone colour from the processing in the nonspeech mode faintly enters consciousness" (Tsur 18), but this will vary according to many factors, especially the tone structure of the phoneme and the way the speaker delivers it. A slow, punctuated delivery will be much richer in this acoustic information than one delivered at ordinary speed (although a very rapid delivery will start to produce a breakdown of the reception ability and also create semantic effects that link with the larger semantic units). The acoustic structure of the particular verbal sounds will determine how readily the neural system can exit speech mode. A front vowel with its formants widely spaced across the frequency spectrum is more likely to enable such switching than a back vowel which has a tighter less distinguishable structure (Tsur 23). Writing that uses neologisms, nonsense words, partial segments of words, and syntactic disjuncture is likely to encourage an uneasy oscillation in a listener's mind between the "auditory and the phonetic modes of listening" (Tsur 73) during a performance. Tsur claims that when some of the "rich precategorical sensory information" is noticed by listeners of poetry they interpret this nonlinguistic acoustical awareness as part of the mystery of sound (Tsur 47).

The problem with Tsur's theory is that it still isolates sound too much from the wider social practice in which the making of sound as language is taking place. Roland Barthes's homage to old-fashioned singers shows what is missing in Tsur's account, and perhaps this is because the singer he singles out for especial praise learned voice techniques with some affinities to those promulgated by the elocution movement. In his essay "The Grain of the Voice," Barthes praised old-fashioned singers like Panzera, whose body itself seemed audible in the performance. According to Barthes, Panzera advocated something quite different to an emphasis on clear enunciation, especially of consonants, because he thought the consonants should be "patinated" or made to seem worn in the way consonants are in actual use, showing "the wear of a language that had been living, functioning, and working for ages past" (Barthes 184). In a romantic description of Russian singers, he says that one can hear in their performance something of their entire cultural matrix, "something which is the cantor's body, brought to your ears in one and the same movement from deep down in the cavities, the muscles, the membranes, the cartilages, and from deep down in the Slavonic language, as though a single skin lined the inner flesh of the performer and the music he sings" (181). The acoustic dance of language in performance stems from the roots of culture, the deeper, least articulated fields, tradition at its most unconscious. One can interpret this claim using the insights of sound symbolism and cognitivist poetics to mean that in a performance in which the corporeality of the voice glints through the semantic delivery, this apprehensible sound carries with it a culturally informed patterning derived partly from culturally determined habits of body, which when merged with the culturally formed iconicities of sound at the linguistic level, carries a significance beyond the individual. It can do so also because of the intersubjectivity of the event of performance itself.

Communication is not limited to mental acts mediated by language; it has many other material routes through matter and movement, and poetry readings are powerful reminders that sign systems are also dynamic material structures because sound is a material phenomenon experienced as vibration in the body as well as a mental perception. The audible sound of a voice performing a poem literally amplifies the words, and in doing so can make salient features that are muffled by the near silence of private reading. When a word is vocalized, much more than the larynx and a small part of the mouth are involved, the entire body resonates with it, as it does with all audible sound waves (this must be one reason why the deaf percussionist Evelyn Glennie has been able to develop such a sophisticated art). The amplification is a bodily process common to all the live performance arts in which the performer uses the body directly and the audience "delegates its corporeality to the stage."[9]

The implications of this are easier to grasp in the case of other kinds of performance, such as dance. At a dance performance the audience does undoubtedly interpret specific movements as identifiable units, such as pliés, arabesques, and grand jetés for example, and then attributes symbolic significance to them, saying to itself perhaps that the dancer is sad, or greeting the dawn (in traditional ballet at least—the symbolism of contemporary dance is more localized). Alongside this conscious activity of semiotic interpretation is another kinesthetic response, equally cognitive, but not linguistic, in which the audience senses the movements of the dancers in terms of their own bodies, not as a possible action upon them, so much as an action they might be making. The watcher dances with the dancer in an imaginative empathy that is not allowed to call the musculature to action, and there is no necessary intervening stage of conscious interpretation between seeing the dancer and this inward imaginative movement, although many watchers will consciously consider what they see and reflect upon what they sense kinesthetically. Similarly, a sound heard as the voice of another also produces virtual responses throughout the bodies of the audience. When the speaker utters the poem, the listeners also speak it in virtuality.

The American poet, Louis Zukofsky, author of the long poem *A*, was fond of comparing poetic composition to Bach's art of the fugue, even citing Bach's suggestion that "the parts of a fugue . . . should behave like reasonable men in an ordinary discussion" (Zukofsky, *A-12*, 127). For Zukofsky this was a literal possibility. Music's sound patterns could convey argument. This emphasis on argument is significant because it counters the usual tendency amongst nonmusicians to equate the sound of poetry with its emotional, nonrational dimension. Music theorists themselves have also had to resist this assumption that music is only patterned emotion, and the prejudices and suppositions that brings in its wake. Suzanne Langer understood this danger and argued that music is a symbolic form different from language and not translatable into it, a symbolism that "makes things conceivable" (Langer 244). Music is not simply a language of emotions even if it is capable of emotional significance.

Sound, like the drama of authorship, and the tension between speech and writing, provides a resource for poets to extend the semantic range of their poems. It can add another level of conceptual complexity by creating complex networks of association via sound and iconicity, a layering of ever fainter echoes and distant meanings. It can also open into the senses through the material experience of sound waves themselves and the bodily knowledge of their production. David Michael Levin calls this aspect of sound, echoing Heidegger, the "dimensionality of Being" (Levin 7). For Levin, one important dimension of being in the world is sound itself, and it calls for an attention that is too often neglected in a culture that overemphasizes vision. He cites Merleau-Ponty saying that "in a sense, to understand a phrase is to welcome it in its sonorous being" (Merleau-Ponty 155), a sentiment echoed by the voice coach Patsy Rodenberg, who writes from the experience of training actors to speak writing in more effective ways: "When we need a word—really connect with it and release it in a brave, physical sense—the experience is not just an act of intellect but a feeling act felt throughout our entire being" (Rodenberg 3). Poetry readings strive to offer such a welcome to the sound of words in all their fullness, and to reflect on the consequences and responsibilities of the encounter.

For many artists and philosophers, music has symbolized an art that evades the limits of representation. Albrecht Wellmer cites Adorno's belief that music was the lost counterpart to philosophy in a form that many poets would endorse in preference to cognitive analysis, even if they might hesitate about some of the implicit claims about music's direct line to the absolute. Wellmer argues that for Adorno, "the language of music and discursive language appear as the separated halves of 'true language'" (Wellmer 7). Such claims derive in part from Dada. Hugo Ball justified the Dada experiments with sound poetry in very different terms to Tzara's antibourgeois polemics, arguing that the Dada performers "should withdraw into the innermost alchemy of the word, and even surrender the word, in this way conserving for poetry its most sacred domain" (Motherwell xxvi). Richard Huelsenbeck reports that Kandinsky wanted to stop "darkening" the purity of the human voice with meaning. A contemporary philosopher, David Appelbaum, in a wonderful account of the voice, echoes such sentiments today: "With the great gift of speech, an unknown something is stolen from voice" (Appelbaum 85). The activity of speech, language, is a phenomenon about which we theorize and develop linguistics, philosophy, and technologies of analysis, but which, like all phenomena, is not thereby exhausted or fully explained by our current practice of knowledge. Much is still unknown, perhaps unknowable, not because it is transcendent, but because actuality necessarily exceeds understanding.[10] Language opens onto the unknown, and performance is one direction into it.

CONCLUSION

Poetry's oral stage is not, therefore, a childish regression to a mere babble of sound; oral performance actually makes possible an extended semantic repertoire in which poetry fulfils more of its potentialities. Staging, authorship, sound, and intersubjectivity are constitutive elements of a poetry reading that are revealed as elements of reading itself and reveal how much all reading, silent as well as public, depends on the network of hermeneutic communicative interactions within which we live. The different senses of the word "reading" turn out to be more than superficially related. Poems by contemporary poets use these resources projectively just as composers anticipate performances in their scores, because these are the conditions of contemporary reception. Readings are only the most salient form of oral circulation for their texts, however, and even poets who never read their work in public still produce work for a culture that is not simply engaged in the direct interpretation of written texts as if they were mute objects waiting for a fairy tale reader to awaken them to life. Texts are already active projects, already on their way through an endlessly reconstitutive pattern of linguistic transactions that momentarily sustain meaning. The answer to my opening questions about poetry readings is then neither yes nor no. Poetry readings do not do anything very different to silent reading if we recognize how active a place that silence has in a wider dialogue of language and action. Such a recognition depends on acknowledging that subjectivity is neither singular nor reducible to the act of self-reflection or linguistic cognition. Language shades away at the edges of the sign into significances that are not yet theorized. Poetry readings can operate in this territory, extending the meanings of written poems by providing a many-dimensioned experience of significance occasioned by the poem and inextricable from it, a semantic performance that could not be recreated even in the most perfectly eidetic and imaginative mental theater.

Poetry readings are also far from perfect. By trying to show how poems are enriched by public reading I may have overstressed the success of this, and its value, as if all readers managed as well as those I discuss here, and as if all poems were blueprints for a better society. Poetry readings, whatever their possibilities, can also be demonstrations of failure, acrasia, and disintegration. Like other public performances they can seduce, terrorize, and indulge their audiences, provoking outrage, dread, sentimentality, and fantasies of every kind. The oral life of poetry is not simply regression, any more than it is exempt from the vicissitudes of social relationships in the lives of performers and listeners. Yet each poetry reading represents a collective effort to create something out of written texts that is still unarticulated. There is no typical poetry reading.

Chapter 3
A History of the Poetry Reading

One of the most famous of modern poetry readings took place at the Six Gallery in San Francisco on October 13, 1955.[1] To help launch the new gallery, an artists' co-op newly converted from a commercial garage, the poet Michael McClure, a friend of the organizers, arranged for six poets to read, and one of them, Kenneth Rexroth, then opted to act as master of ceremonies. The other five, Philip Lamantia, Philip Whalen, Michael McClure, Gary Snyder, and Allen Ginsberg, already formed a distinct group soon to be widely known as the Beat poets. About a hundred people turned up, and as the readings began, another writer, Jack Kerouac, who had been invited to read but was apparently too shy to do so, collected money for jugs of wine and then passed them around, becoming drunk and excitable himself and encouraging the audience to throw themselves noisily into the spirit of things. By the time Allen Ginsberg began reading his new, unpublished poem *Howl*, the audience was already very receptive. Ginsberg describes what happened then:

> I gave a very wild, funny, tearful reading of the first part of "Howl." Like I really felt shame and power reading it, and every time I'd finish a long line Kerouac would shout "Yeah!" or "So there!" or "Correct!" or some little phrase, which added a kind of extra bop humor to the whole thing. It was like a jam session, and I was very astounded because "Howl" was a big, long poem and yet everybody seemed to understand and at the same time to sympathize with it. (Kramer 48)

Ginsberg's biographer, Michael Schumacher, pictures him beginning timidly, but "before long he gained confidence and began to sway rhythmically with the music of his poetry, responding to the enthusiasm of the audience" (Schumacher 215). Another biography describes him "chanting like a Jewish cantor, sustaining his long breath length, savoring the outrageous language" (Miles 196). Afterward Lawrence Ferlinghetti offered to publish the poem, and the success of the event sparked off a wave of poetry readings across the bay area.

The most notable feature of the entire reading was undoubtedly Allen Ginsberg's sheer presence as he performed his testimony, beginning with the emphatic first-person assertion "I saw the best minds of my generation," etc. (Ginsberg 126). His magnificent assertion of prophetic judgment filled the first person with his substantial presence, closing the gap between author and text, saying in effect, "I, Allen Ginsberg, saw these things and am telling you now." Much of what happened as he read must remain speculation. We can guess that as the anaphoric link word "who" was repeated again and again its polysemy was brought fully into play, and it shifted almost imperceptibly back and forth between relative and interrogative pronoun, making its audience question just who these unknown soldiers of the underground were. The listeners probably felt encouraged to admire and perhaps emulate the "best minds" even as they mourned them. Some members of the audience, like Kerouac, who knew what Ginsberg meant when he said that his generation had "bared their brains to Heaven," were already busy drinking assiduously enough to reexperience that mental disrobing as the reading proceeded. Audience participation must have had something of the force of a mass chorus brought into being by the poem in performance, as they created a litany in response to Ginsberg's delivery.

Performances like this are rare. What is the point of ordinary poetry readings in contemporary culture? What accounts for their popularity even when poets read material of such verbal complexity that only the cumulative intensities of silent reading would seem likely to do the texts justice? People commonly say they go to readings to see the poet and to hear the sound of the poem, but curiosity and a love of phonetic harmonies don't seem enough to justify all this activity. Is there something more? Is the meaning of a poem affected by performance in ways that make performance seem indispensable even for complex written texts? These questions address a heterogeneous scene ranging from academic gatherings where a poet sits and reads from a book or manuscript, to club performances accompanied by music, a diversity that might seem to resist analysis. What unites them is that a written text is turned into a verbal performance in public by the author of the poetry. This transformation becomes more puzzling if we consider the outlines of a history of poetry readings.

The *Howl* reading seems to have unintentionally played an inaugural role in the proliferation of contemporary poetry readings, but to make this claim would require research that is yet to be done. To the best of my knowledge no general history of poetry reading exists, although the diversity and complexity of oral poetics has been widely studied in the past thirty years.[2] In societies where there is partial or widespread literacy, and poetry is commonly written down, poems have still been read aloud to public audiences, circles of friends, and simply as part of ordinary social life, as well as fulfilling more specialized roles in education, public rituals, and other cultural practices. Literacy itself has even sometimes been measured in schools by the ability to read poetry aloud effectively. Until quite recently, this widespread, and largely unremarked reading of poetry aloud by all sorts of people, was a common practice in English speaking cultures. Today, such occasions as Maya Angelou's reading at President Clinton's inauguration are reminders of how unusual this now seems. The oral reading of poetry is no longer a common feature of everyday life and in its stead is the largely postwar phenomenon of the more formal poetry reading. Famous poets of the premodernist era, like other well-known writers, did in a few cases go on speaking tours in the past (Dickens and Whitman are familiar examples), but these have been relatively exceptional, and even the major English language poets of the early part of the twentieth century did not spend their time on reading tours. The contemporary poetry reading, firmly structured around the presence of the author, is a new variant on the old practice, made possible by social changes such as greater social wealth, leisure, mobility, and education and more necessary in the face of the technological anonymity of mass culture.

The *Howl* reading also demonstrates another feature of these readings, their radicalism. Poetry readings since the latter part of the fifties have been popular with dissident intellectuals who believe these events can make visible the power of hitherto alienated individual imaginations, passions, visions, and creativity. Yet such political aims on their own would hardly have generated the fervor of such readings as those at the Albert Hall in London in the late sixties and in similar large, popular venues in America, which became iconic of the new poetries, nor would radicalism have sparked the continuing interest in hearing even the most textually elaborate poetries. Something else was going on at these readings besides the generation of collective euphoria at the possibility of mass action or the practice of a new cultural politics, something that depended on the poetry itself, and what happened when written poems were transformed by being read aloud in public performances. Of the many kinds of contemporary poetry reading, the avant-garde[3] readings of the past forty years are the most striking, because these poets have used all sorts of unfamiliar stratgies to resist easy assimilation and to articulate new ranges of thought and experience, devices such as innovative page layouts, diminished reference, and newly invented verse forms (many of which are very long, non-lyric structures), all of which would seem to make impossible demands upon performers and listeners. It is to these poetries that this essay is largely devoted (although many of its conclusions apply to other more traditional, politically activist, or entertainment-based poetries[4]) because in these readings the intransigent presence of the written text is most prominent and in need of explanation.

Exceptional in degree rather than substance, the Six Gallery reading in the newly converted garage shares many features with typical, less epochal poetry readings. It is therefore a good place to begin considering the common elements of poetry readings and their significance. *Howl* was premiered at the reading. How, if at all, was it transformed by Ginsberg's reading? To begin with, the semantic repertoire of the written text was extended by its performance in several notable ways: by the location of the poem in a particular place within a defined ritual, by the force of the poet's presence as he read, by the addition of sound to the act of reception, and by the enfolding intersubjective drama generated as the lines were spoken. The author read aloud work conceived and written elsewhere, giving special salience to the sound of the language, in surroundings temporarily borrowed as a performance space for poetry, to an audience who experienced some common purposes partially articulated through the poetry itself. Attempts to describe the event by the poet and his biographers reveal further aspects of it, not least by the differences in their accounts. Ginsberg, like many people who take part in poetry readings, emphasizes the importance of hearing the sound values of the text by comparing the event to a jazz session, in which voice plays a secondary or nonexistent role compared to the nonlinguistic communications of instrumental music. His biographer Miles recognizes that the event extends beyond the poem and implies a parallel with sacred ritual in which poetry is a means of making God present. Both interpretations step away from the literary text as if that alone were not sufficient to sustain an explanation of what happened. The contradictions between these and other accounts (Ginsberg gives slightly different ones in different interviews reminding us that performance depends crucially on memory, whatever the technical means of recording) typify the problem of recreating and analyzing any performance, however much documentation is available. Analysis is always archeology. Performance events vanish as they occur, like the "best minds of my generation" who "vanished into nowhere Zen New Jersey" (Ginsberg 127), leaving behind such traces as polysemic texts, photographs, memoirs, and interviews, which are as slippery to interpret as the trail of mystifying postcards of Atlantic City Hall left behind by one of the Beat heroes of the poem. Any answer to the question of what happened to *Howl* when it moved from writing into speech must factor in its own reconstructive uncertainties, ambiguities already figured by the poem itself, as if it knew that collective memory would try to transplant the "absolute heart of the poem" (131) from performance into text as it died into silence at the end of the reading, as all performances must.

Literary theory on the other hand would say that its real life was only just beginning. Not until the City Lights edition appeared could the poem fully claim to be a text ready for reading and analysis. Theorists apparently see little of significance in the oral performances of poetry reading because they assume that meaning arises solely at the interface between subject and the linguistic structure represented by the written text, whether power is assumed to reside with the active, decoding subject or with the discourse of the text that produces the subjectivity of the reader. Poetry readings where a written text is read aloud seem no more than entertaining ornaments to the solid edifice of reading. As a result, poems like *Howl* lead a secret life. Walter Ong believes that "intertextual analysis has commonly paid relatively little attention to the interaction between texts and their circumambient orality. The orality of a milieu can deeply affect both the composition of texts and their interpretation."[5] This comment on the period when the Gospels were written might equally apply today. Literary theorists tend to ignore the effects of oral interaction on literary texts, perhaps because orality seems no more than an anachronistic survival from an earlier stage of social development, made even more redundant by the Internet and hypertext, although the official reason is linguistic. Saussurean linguistics, which has provided the skeleton for structuralist and poststructuralist theory, downgrades speech in favor of the system of linguistic codes that supposedly govern it, and which most theorists regard as the proper subject of inquiry.

The term "poetry reading" contains an ambiguity that helps explain this neglect. In writing this essay I have to make clear by context when "poetry reading" refers to a public performance rather than a private, silent act of interpreting writing without audible sound, because this latter is the dominant meaning. Moreover, literary theory has widely used the term "reading" to mean "interpretation," and critics describe their practice as readings of specific texts. For most literary critics, poetry readings are simply particular versions of reading, because they are committed to interpretative relativism. A public poetry reading is different only in the trivial sense that every reading is different because readers and communities of readers ultimately determine the meaning of what is read, and their differences produce different interpretations. These differences may be all too slight within communities of readers organized by ideology or other largely unconscious structures. The problem here is what is meant by different. As Reed Way Dasenbrock points out, if this is taken to mean that different interpretations emerge from the incommensurable worlds of different interpretative communities, it would entail the absurd conclusion that one reader could not understand another's reading at all, even to establish incommensurability: "we cannot know whether we are seeing something different unless we can understand each other's perspective, translate each other's language; and if we can understand and translate another's perspective, it cannot have the radical otherness supposed [by some theorists]" (Dasenbrock 25). Why does it seem so important to claim interpretative relativism in contemporary theory? The answer must surely be that it is part of the important commitment to recognizing diversity, difference, and marginalization, expressed in different interpretations, which can be suppressed by hegemonic institutions that claim that there is only one proper meaning, their own. Interpretative relativism is made to do too much work, however, because other practices of difference have been elided from theoretical recognizance. Feminist linguists have pointed out a similar problem with theories that language is male, and women therefore need a female language, arguing against this theory that it mistakes the character of language entirely and becomes a substitute for considering other social divisions in which power produces silence and distortion.

The seemingly important emphasis on different readings conceals an unwarranted homogenization of the heterogeneous concept of reading. Readings are assumed to be fundamentally one kind of process so that an ethnographic stance, for example, which places a text in a much wider network of systems of representation or active subjectivities, appears irrelevant to interpretation and reading. Such analysis of literary productions is rarely admitted within the charmed circle of the high art of first-world cultures, whose significant texts are imagined to transcend the contingencies of local cultural practices.[6] These limitations are the result of assuming that reading is a homogenous, singular activity, whatever indeterminacies of language and subjectivity it produces. The implicit model of reading at work in most contemporary literary theory owes its outlines to the epistemological project of Kantian philosophy as it has been mediated through its encounters with science, positivism, and linguistics. A singular, autonomous subject is imagined to encounter a bounded instance of language in an ideal realm transcending ordinary material limitations. Ordinary acts of reading are approximations to this, limited by the everyday interruptions of concentration and textual presentation. Poststructuralist theory empties out the humanist interiority of the subject, which is the stage for the encounter, only to reinscribe its contours via the putative actions of the signifying process and the positionalities of discourse. Writing and silent reading have helped create assumptions about reading that would not seem so obvious in an oral society, and theorists forget that reading depends on similar conditions to discourse, and like discourse, is always an uncompleted stage in heterogeneous transactions that exceed the moment of encounter, which is itself always taking place in a material space and time. The case of the poetry reading will show why recognizing the inescapably intersubjective, plural condition of reading is necessary for an understanding of the meanings that contemporary poetries are allowed to produce.

SPEECH AND WRITING

The topos of the poetry reading places a highly charged inversion of the history of language center stage. Writing becomes speech as the poet reads, ontogeny recapitulates phylogeny, and nostalgia for lost oral cultures is in the air. But this may not be the pure logocentrism it seems, for the passage from orality to literacy, and from conversation to print, is a transformation that can never be complete: "orality insinuates itself, like one of the threads of which it is composed, into the network—an endless tapestry—of a scriptural economy" (de Certeau, 132). Poetry readings could be imagined as attempts to perform a temporary reversal of this long revolution. Such oral backsliding could even be interpreted as a collective yearning for an earlier era when the poet was a bard, a figure endowed with the powers of a shaman and leader, an era when, according to Eric Havelock in *Preface to Plato,* poetry was the repository of history and knowledge for a community where written records did not exist. The contemporary oral poetry movement has sometimes talked aspirationally as if this was so, invoking "older tribal cultures" (Rothenberg 20) and valorizing the primitive, as if there were a direct continuity from the reading in the gallery to this early human past. The vatic enthusiasm of some poetry readings in the sixties and early seventies (events at the Albert Hall, some of the readings associated with the antiwar movement in America, for example) might suggest that poets and audience hungered for such a return to vanished poetic glories.

Contemporary poets have certainly been very much aware of the anomalies of the standard poetry reading, so much so that some have tried to resolve them by abandoning one or other side of the process (anthropologists have been through similar upheavals). A few like J. H. Prynne even refuse to give readings, implying that oral performance in public is irrelevant to their project, whilst others like David Antin have abandoned print for improvisation.

One way to begin to grasp the significance of the translation from writing to speech is to consider what would happen if it were not an opposition of mouth and paper, if some quite different bodily action were substituted for the spoken words. Stephen Rodefer ends his poem "Pretext" with the sentence: "To my left is Philippa, who will be signing for me" (Rodefer 11). What *would* happen if poets actually "signed" their poetry themselves instead of speaking it aloud? Rodefer's clever pun hints that even the idea that another quite different form of bodily action might encode the poem is enough to call into question ordinary assumptions of authorship, of who signs their name to the poem. What relation do speech, sign language, and writing have to one another? Oliver Sacks, in his popular account of the sign languages of the deaf, says that today: "Sign is seen as fully comparable to speech (in terms of its phonology, its temporal aspects, its streams and sequences), but with unique, additional powers of a spatial and cinematic sort—at once a most complex and yet transparent expression and transformation of thought" (Sacks 90). What does it mean to say that sign language is both "fully comparable" to speech and at the same time has "unique, additional powers"? The addition of capabilities not shared by speech surely means that the signed reading would be different from the spoken one. According to a researcher into sign language, it "produces a structurally different approach" to an ordinary task like explaining the plot of a movie, because it is more "image-based," although it is just as capable of abstraction and complexity as spoken language (Kyle 193). Sign language is a reminder that phonetic language is not the only possible performative rendition of a written text, and that this is not the same as translation from one spoken language into another, say from English into German. Speech is no more fully represented in writing than it is in sign, as any phonetician or conversation analyst knows. The oral performance of a poetry reading is not therefore a mechanically determined outcome of a written text, but involves a choice of medium and some form of transmutation.

Poetry readings make fleetingly perceptible the unstable transitions between different signifying media, as if the poem's significations could be best understood at the margins of signification where such radical transformation occurs, and poetic meaning is produced on the border of transition between sound and visual marks, oscillating unstably back and forth, making evident by this interruption of the ordinary, imperceptible, smooth functioning of signification, the *responsibilities* of meaning-production to the audience and poet.

From the standpoint of deconstruction, a poetry reading would seem to be shirking these responsibilities and endorsing a belief in the power of speech that is no longer tenable. Textuality is the real area of activity for deconstruction. Actual speech is only an uninteresting secondary phenomenon, an assumption already prefigured by Saussure's linguistic redirection of attention from actual utterances ("parole") to the codes ("langue") that make them possible. In his study of the relations between speech and writing, *Of Grammatology,* Derrida locates many of his arguments at just the margin between speech and writing that is activated in poetry readings, because he believes that this border has given rise to many misapprehensions. One of his central arguments isolates the moment when a speaker becomes her own listener and thereby closes the circuit of language production, in a simpler version of the poet hearing herself read aloud poems she wrote on another occasion. This familiar self-conscious experience of simultaneously speaking and listening to oneself speak has, according to Derrida, provided a misleading image of the relations between language and subjectivity for the Western philosophical tradition. Aristotle, for example, says that: "spoken words (*ta en te phone*) are the symbols of mental experience (*pathemata tes psyches*) and written words are the symbols of spoken words" (Derrida 11). Derrida cleverly projects such assumptions into the situation of hearing oneself speak (*s'entendre-parler*), an experience that provides the basis for logocentrism: "that experience lives and proclaims itself as the exclusion of writing, that is to say of the invoking of an 'exterior,' 'sensible,' 'spatial' signifier interrupting self-presence" (98). When you hear yourself speak, it is easy to assume that the language issues directly from the realm of thought without loss of immediacy in what is analogous to the supposed closed circuit or perfect self-reflexivity of consciousness, where consciousness in language becomes pure self-consciousness, a transparent self-relation of unalloyed self-presence. According to this metaphysical picture: "consciousness is the experience of pure auto-affection," and the logos "can be *produced as auto-affection,* only through the *voice:* an order of the signifier by which the subject takes from itself into itself, does not borrow outside of itself the signifier that it emits and that affects it at the same time" (98).

Derrida's line of argument assumes tacitly that post-Cartesian philosophy always considers subjectivity as "self-presence" or self-reflection. He is then able to diagnose the overvaluation of speech at the expense of writing as a result of the way speech appeared to be a natural extension of thought itself, because such experiences as hearing oneself speak seemed to offer a confirming, experiential image of the reality of subjectivity. Language appears to the unreflective observer to be a phonetic structure for which writing is an incidental addition, a mere system of marks transcribing its sounds. Derrida shows first of all that writing cannot simply be the direct expression of thought, and that this is why most thinkers have set it aside from their deliberations, and then after a deconstructive move of the kind he has made his own, he claims that the characteristics of writing cannot be a direct transcription of speech either. Writing cannot be self-identical and produce fixed, clear meanings, but this must be true of all language because all forms of language can be redescribed as writing, and hence the "différance" of writing, its imbrication of absence and deferral, must be generally true of speech as well as of writing. Therefore no language, not even the speech that hears itself, can be the matrix of transparent self-consciousness, and certain concepts like "subject" and "meaning" are revealed to be metaphysical, despite their apparent tangibility. The term "subject" for example: "will refer, by the entire thread of its history, to the substantiality of a presence unperturbed by accidents, or to the identity of the selfsame [*le propre*] in the presence of self-relationship" (69). These arguments assume that experiences (however abstract and hypothetical) of hearing-oneself-speak actually can occur and result in (mistaken) conclusions about the relations between thought and language, and this invites the speculation that certain rituals in everyday life might in part be attempts to stage such experiences in order to sustain or challenge the crucial metaphysics. Derrida's own presentation of the argument seems to tacitly expect that, at the very least, the actions of analytic argument will take place, as can be seen in his discussion of literal meaning when he points out that the experience of hearing oneself speak functions as an anchor to the supposed capacity for literalness of language:

> The literal [*propre*] meaning does not exist, its "appearance" is a necessary function—and must be analyzed as such—in the system of differences and metaphors. The absolute *parousia* of the literal meaning, as the presence to the self of the logos within its voice, in the absolute hearing-itself-speak, should be *situated* as a function responding to an indestructible but relative necessity, within a system that encompasses it. That amounts to *situating* the metaphysics or the ontotheology of the logos. (89)

The exposure of this creation of the literal is an action, the action of philosophical argument, as the verbs "analyzed," "situated," and "situating," as well as the injunction "should," all attest.

If we don't assume that philosophical action is the only possible response to such experience, then other kinds of action might also create similar critical effects, and one of these could be the public performance of writing as speech, in which the "metaphysics of the logos" is situated in a specific history, place, and intersubjective relation. A wider narrative in Derrida's discussion places deconstruction in a history measured in self-important millennia and uses the word "logocentrism" as the name for a historically locatable activity associated with Western thought. It follows that the "experience" referred to could itself be undergoing change and, more significantly, might be capable of acts or occasions of self-examination that create and test such experiences within delimited discursive events.

Poetry readings can be historical dramas in which the history of language, poetry, and its performance are shady protagonists. They can dramatize such anchoring experiences as hearing-oneself-speak, and by demonstrating pertinent complexities of language, subjectivity and intersubjectivity may provide experiences that don't necessarily support the local metaphysics of the day. The poetic text in this situation sometimes exceeds existing explanations of its functioning and significance, and this excess provides one of the main reasons for the continuing success of readings: the performance of the poem compels recognition of the limits of our understanding of language. Poetry readings present problems of contemporary language and communication in manageable but unresolvable form, problems that, of course, are often also active in twentieth-century philosophy, amongst other venues. In the following sections I shall sketch a history of these occasions before returning to look in more detail at how these intersubjective dramas take place.

THE SILENT HISTORY OF READING

What is the history of poetry readings? The conventional view seems to be that the proliferation of readings since the fifties is an entirely new response to the long established constriction of poetry diagnosed by Charles Olson: "What we have suffered from, is manuscript, press, the removal of verse from its producer and its reproducer, the voice, a removal by one, by two removes from its place of origin *and* its destination" (Olson, *Human Universe,* 57). Poetry readings of the kind offered by universities for several decades were much too "podium oriented" (Economou 655), too formal and too closely linked to the lecture format to offer any opportunity to radically enact the wider possibilities for poetry. Poets took poetry readings out of the universities into diverse urban venues where they could mingle with other arts, politics, and forms of leisure, stimulated by widely reported events like Dylan Thomas's tour of America and readings by Beat writers. Expectations of performance have been written into poems composed in a context characterized by an extraordinary and increasing amount of activity and interest in the public reading of poetry. George Economou's evaluation of the reading series he helped organize in New York, at which he and other poets read medieval poetry to a Jazz accompaniment typifies the accepted history. According to Economou:

> It was to my knowledge, the first time that translations of medieval European poems and original Middle English lyrics were read with jazz accompaniment, that a group of poets was concerned with the problems of preparing for performance the work of old and, in some cases, anonymous poets rather than their own. (656)

A widespread resistance to any claims for the importance of recent tradition led these poets to acknowledge only Dada and the oral poetics of nonliterate societies as precursors, and as George Quasha makes clear, Dada's influence was felt to be only indirect, even on a poet like Jackson Mac Low. To appeal to Dada, says Quasha,

> does not help us to enter the necessary relation to the text either as written or as performed, since it draws us away from a *radical particularity:* the freedom of the performer and audience to originate an unknown state of attention or to enter an "anarchistic" social relationship through language. (488)

Poets who gave this any thought at all linked their oral practice to preliterate cultures where poetry was performed as an ordinary part of the culture's business, and they elided modern history altogether. Jerome Rothenberg's remarkable work on oral poetics understandably led him to downplay the pertinence of recent history: "The Renaissance is over or it begins again with us. Yet the origins we seek—the frame that bounds our past, that's set against an open-ended future—are no longer Greek, nor even Indo-European, but take in all times and places" (Rothenberg 165). In his interview with William Spanos he more explicitly sidelines the recent past by invoking a "*mainstream* of poetry that goes back to the old tribes & has been carried forward by the great subterranean culture."[7] The contemporary poetry reading seems to stand clear of history altogether in a thoroughly modern fashion.

There is another, less romantic, oral tradition however. Poetry readings emerge from a long history of the oral performance of written texts that reaches back through the Renaissance and medieval cultures to the classical world. Until the advent of the new forms of leisure after the First World War, ordinary experience for almost everyone, whether rich or poor, included participation in groups listening to texts read aloud. The reading aloud itself was not merely taken for granted either. Many rigorous forms of pedagogy under a range of nomenclatures from "rhetoric" to "elocution" have taught people how to read texts aloud, including poetry. Only in the decades immediately prior to the emergence of the contemporary poetry reading did this training really falter, for reasons I shall examine in a moment. So that when Quasha says that "there has *always* been been more oral than written poetry," and that "there is clearly a gain in seeing both oral and literate in the same transcultural and synchronic context—as *synchronicity* rather than literary history" he is accurately describing a history that his other statements seem to belie. Silent reading and reading aloud have been part of a single economy of reading throughout history. The difficulty for poets wanting to extend the poetics of orality has been that the shift from oral to written culture is usually portrayed as a gradual, irreversible change from reading aloud to silent reading, one that happened gradually over centuries until its completion in the Renaissance, and eventually led to the utter ascendancy of print at least four centuries ago. It is a history with no place for the poetic virtues of orality, which assumes that such change is inevitable since silent reading is wholly preferable to the cumbersome demands of reading aloud to a group, and only took so long to develop because of illiteracy, the scarcity of texts, and a general lack of privacy. Recently there have been signs that historians of writing and reading are finding evidence that supports the idea that orality and literacy are much more interdependent than has hitherto been supposed, and poets have become less inclined to polarize orality and literacy in such value-laden terms. The intense preoccupation with the history of texts, language, speech, and writing in recent French thought has overthrown many unexamined prejudices, although some of these ideas have themselves created new dogmas about writing and communication.

The history of reading is still full of puzzles. We know much less about the extent and emergence of silent reading than we might wish, and we still don't know enough about the complex social conditions and consequences of oral reading. Scholars dispute when literacy emerged in ancient Greece and whether Chaucer wrote his poetry for oral performance. Surprisingly little information has been collated about reading aloud even in the last century, despite innumerable references to domestic practice and its importance. Henry James attributed his interest in the dramatic possibilities of fiction to the experience of listening to Dickens read aloud. Even contemporary poets occasionally offer glimpses of the continuing importance of reading aloud, like Susan Howe's remark that it was hearing poems read aloud as a child that stimulated a habit of thinking within patterns of rhythmic phrasing.[8] Two important conclusions emerge from recent research into this history of oral reading for the understanding of the sudden explosion of poetry readings in the past half century. One is fairly obvious.

All the essays on contemporary poetry readings stress, with varying degrees of approval, that the poetry reading "brings together an audience which wishes to participate in consuming poetry with others who also wish to do so, to acknowledge poetry, and to feel part of a community" (Stern), and in doing so they are recognizing what readers have always known. Reading aloud is a form of sociality. When Augustine recalled in his *Confessions* his mentor Ambrose, he particularly remembered the bishop's ability to read silently, but instead of seeing the future he saw someone resting from social contact:

> We wondered if he read silently perhaps to protect himself in case he had a hearer interested and intent on the matter, to whom he might have to expound the text being read if it contained difficulties, or who might wish to debate some difficult questions. . . . Whatever motive he had for his habit, this man had a good reason for what he did." (Augustine 93)

You needed a good reason, a good excuse, to read silently. A historian of medieval reading habits, Joyce Coleman, cites Robert Manning saying that he wrote his history of Britain:

For to haf solace and gamen
In felawschip when thai sitt samen. (Coleman 130)

Chaucer offers a satirical self-portrait of himself as a silent reader in *The House of Fame* as a "heremyte" who sits "dumb as any stoon," implying that this is a peculiar and unsociable activity for his contemporaries. By the mid-sixteenth century, reading was becoming much more private, especially amongst the cultural elite, for whom it often represented a desirable form of withdrawal from the demands of the world, yet reading aloud remained a widespread means of sustaining sociality. The historian of books and reading, Roger Chartier, who believes that "reading is always a practice embodied in acts, spaces, and habits," cites a very moving account of a man on military service between 1635 and 1642 who dragged around with him nearly a whole cartload of books. Henri Campion explained in his memoirs how reading them sustained his friendship with fellow officers: "l'un de nous lisait haut quelque bon livre, dont nous examinions les plus beaux passages, pour apprendre à bien vivre et à bien mourir, selon la morale, qui était notre principale étude" (Chartier 107). For Samuel Pepys, reading aloud was part of other social activities, whether an attempt at flirtation with a strange woman in a coach, or part of his relationship with his wife, or simply using his servant to read to him—an early equivalent of listening to the radio. Reading aloud was deeply embedded in ordinary social relations of every kind, from court to the domestic world.

The vicissitudes of a lost poem by James Boswell underline how embedded in everyday life, and how interconnected writing, silent reading, and reading aloud really were. In his London journal for January 5, 1763, he records how he sent a poem (since lost) to his friend Lord Eglinton saying: "You know we have often disputed whether or not I am a poet. I have sent you an ode. Lord Elibank thought it good. I think so too" (Boswell, 124–29). Eglinton writes back the same day with a wonderfully ambiguous response: "I like your ode much. There was no need of that to convince me you had genius. I wish I was as sure of your judgement of men and things." Eglinton interprets the poem as a display of intelligence, as if that is what a poem is ordinarily for. That evening Boswell goes to Lord Eglinton's house and joins a group of clever men who talk about a whole range of things upon which he has no judgment to make at all. Suddenly Lord Eglinton produces the poem claiming that he has just discovered it in his pocket where it has lain for such a long time he doesn't recall the author. One of the other guests takes the paper and reads the poem aloud, and then criticizes it, especially for the very lines that Boswell is most proud of. At the end of the evening Eglinton takes Boswell aside and says, "I hope we are very good friends," in case the young man has misinterpreted events. On the way home Boswell projected his sense of having been robbed of his poetic dignity onto a fear of street robbery and "determined against suppers" for the sake of his health. This little game is Eglinton's answer to Boswell's original question, partly to avoid a direct written response that might wound his friend, but largely because reading aloud and the resultant discussion are an ordinary form of criticism. Subterfuge helps to displace any formality attendant on an author reading a poem in public, as well as shielding the young man from exposure.

In the nineteenth century, performance became more and more formalized in public settings. Alongside the nearly universal domestic readings of poems and novels, there was a new interest in public readings by actresses like Fanny Kemble and writers like Dickens. Working-class men organized themselves into groups to read aloud in public, notably in the "Penny Readings," meetings where the audience would each pay a penny to hear selected audience members read aloud from texts that tended to the comic or the emotional, so that any impetus toward self-improvement behind these reading groups was kept in check by the desire for entertainment. Factory workers might pay someone to read aloud to them from a book or newspaper while they worked, and in the coffeehouses (which frequently had libraries attached), people would often read aloud to a group.[9] Local clubs and reading circles existed everywhere and made singing, reciting, and lecturing a part of the entertainment they provided to people looking for a mix of education and fun. Such clubs persisted into the early twentieth century.

A comparison of two clubs inaugurated in the same year, 1916, both successful on the terms they set themselves and both carrying on this long tradition of clubs organized around participant performance, summarizes the consequence of these changes. In October 1916, William Carlos Williams helped form the Polytopics Club in Rutherford, New Jersey, where he practiced as a doctor.[10] Its members, twelve lawyers, doctors, and businessmen and their wives, wore tuxedos to their fortnightly meetings at which they often had an outside speaker as well as discussion, reading aloud, music, and singing. In March 1921, Williams read to them from *Kora in Hell,* and the secretary afterward noted that the usually calm discussion became unusually heated. It was too much for Williams's wife, who pointed out to him that the audience had laughed at the wrong things, and she made him promise not to read his poems to them again. Even a profession and a dinner jacket were not enough to make modernism palatable for oral performance. The incomprehension and laughter that greeted *Kora in Hell* also mark a sociable antisociality that another club started the same year as the Polytopics Club began to aim for. The Cabaret Voltaire is usually treated as if it were a world away from the bourgeois suburbs of places like Rutherford, yet what often goes unnoticed in accounts of its Dada performances is that alongside the radical verse and the simultaneous readings were readings of Rimbaud and Apollinaire, Russian poetry, and music that was recognizably music. The radical material emerged from and counterpointed the more familiar activities. Moreover the Cabaret Voltaire was a hybrid, part club, part café, and part music hall. One historian of the influence of popular performance on modern art argues that it was music hall that most influenced the artists because it was so modern, or as Marinetti said, had "no tradition, no masters and no dogma" (Weiss 5). The Polytopics Club was tame by comparison and took place on the boundary between private and public spheres, yet some of its entertainments sound close to cabaret: in the thirties there were plays, some written by Williams, in one of which he wore shaving cream on his face and his wife wore mud, and they played husband and wife. Another play was set in a Paris café as if aspiring to some of the ambience of a Cabaret Voltaire.

What were poetry performances at the Cabaret Voltaire supposedly aiming at? Hugo Ball's account of his performance of sound poetry taken from an account translated in *Transition,* shows that one aim was precisely to elicit reflections on the history of performance and ritual. Ball's costume was a bizarre transmogrification of two just barely recognizable traditions of clothing, the theatrical and the priestly, that conventionally signal the authority of the wearer's speech. His trousers were encased in a blue cardboard buskin, and he wore an enormous red and gold collar that could be flapped like wings, evoking both a chasuble and an angel's wings. On his head was a large top hat in blue and white (in Hans Richter's account it is a "witch-doctor's hat" [42]). The upper part of the costume was also a parody of bourgeois male smartness, represented by top hats and wide lapelled coats. Hugo Ball likens the cardboard boot to an obelisk, an inorganic shape that contributes to the effacing of his human presence, which was then further undermined by the lack of meaning in the syllables he was chanting. A typical line of this poem called "O Gadji Beri Bimba" reads "gadjama bim beri glassala." These were phonemes that a listener would not be able to interpret as words, although he tells us that his tone was recognizable as similar to that of "the age-old cadence of the sacerdotal lamentation, like the chanting of the mass." It had the form of sacred authority without the meaningful words to support it, and instead a series of syllables combining a heavy use of metallic consonants /b/, /d/, /g/, with a preponderance of front vowels (a, e, i). According to the cognitive linguist Reuven Tsur, a front vowel is perceived differently from a back vowel because although the lowest frequency element, or formant, of the sound is of a similar frequency in each case, the upper formants, or overtone structures, which create distinctions between the phonemes on which their linguistic significance is based, are very different. Front vowels have high formants, whereas the back vowels have formants close in frequency and therefore more readily merged with the lower formant. Experiments with the effects of the sounds of these vowels on listeners show that people can more easily notice the sound element in front vowels than in back vowels, a finding that is very significant. A front vowel with its formants widely spaced across the frequency spectrum enables the neural system to exit from the speech listening mode more easily (23).

Sounds like those used by Hugo Ball are not neutral. He introduced these sound poems with a polemical injunction to poets to "withdraw into the innermost alchemy of the word," even if this meant actually renouncing words themselves, thus "conserving for poetry its most sacred domain" against the contemporary destruction of language by what he calls "journalism" (xxvi). The sacral dimension of language was evoked by his costume and delivery, while at the same time its usual mediators, the priests and their rituals, were mocked by the costume, the delivery, and the apparent vacuity of the language. Sixty years later the poet Jerome Rothenberg is still struggling with the same terms in an interview with William Spanos, the editor of *Boundary 2*. "I would like to desanctify and demystify the written word. . . . I don't have any use for 'the sacred' in that sense—for the idea of book or text as the authoritative, coercive version of some absolute truth . . . & I'm saying that the domain of poetry includes both oral & written forms" (10–11 in *Prefaces*). Rothenberg is as reluctant as Ball to expel the sacred and simply renames it shamanism in his interview, placing it opposite theology in one of a series of paired binaries, poetry/philosophy, oral/literal, and individual/state.

Sound poetry has provoked revulsion as much as awe ever since the time of Dada. Andrew Duncan's recent dismissal of British sound poetry in *Angel Exhaust 9* for its ugliness, infantilism, and, above all, its failure to communicate has affinities with the hostility of the members of the audiences for Dada poetry readings.[11] According to Hans Richter, the audience for Hugo Ball's poem was initially stymied and then "exploded," although this was mostly laughter and applause rather than the riots that occurred on other occasions. Richter's account of a performance in the Saal zur Kaufleuten on April 9, 1919, reveals that the interruption of speech perception was one of the most provocative acts of the Dadaists, one that Tristan Tzara excelled in. After a simultaneous poem had been read, the audience became almost riotous; Tzara had cleverly arranged an interval, not so that people could calm down but just the reverse. It was "an animated interval, in which the inflamed passions of the audience gathered strength for a defiant response to any new defiance on our part." Then Walter Serner, seated and wearing wedding clothes with his back to the audience, offered a bouquet of flowers to a headless dummy to smell then recited from a work called "Final Dissolution." By placing himself facing away from the audience and making the gesture with the headless mannequin, Serner was both implying that the audience lacked a mind to hear what he was saying and deliberately impeded its audition. His violation of the communicative contract provoked catcalls, then the "noise almost entirely drowned Serner's voice, which could be heard, during a momentary lull, saying the words, "Napoleon was a big, strong oaf, after all" (78). At this the men in the audience leapt onto the stage, ripped out pieces of the balustrade from the balcony, and chased Serner off the stage. Richter was convinced that this was a moment of general madness by the behavior of a journalist sitting near him, who seized him and kept yelling the same phrase in his ear. These experiments with impeded communication, using poems with unrecognizable phonemes, simultaneous readings that overloaded the listeners' ability to process speech and produced noise, and violations of communicative ethics, provoked uncontrolled cathartic reactions.

The sacred domain was extremely powerful but was it really no more than an invitation to regression? Linguists have pointed out that children seem to be able to make all the possible verbal sounds before they learn to speak, and then quite quickly narrow down their repertoire to the requirements of their own language. Verbal gestures that are not in the language are often used by children for expressive purposes, especially when the sounds themselves carry particularly strong suggestions. The taunting children's repetition "nyah, nyah," for example, uses the palatal sound gesture that involves an increase of the contact area between the two surfaces of the mouth that produce the sound, compared to the simple /n/ (48). Andrew Duncan's mockery of sound poetry as being composed of sounds like "yibble yibble nee nee nana nunu" seems to echo this children's chant as well as one of the first words to be learned by children, mama. Many listeners to sound poetry are likely to hear it as if it were a language of the prelinguistic child and may be powerfully disturbed by it.

The disappointing reception of *Kora in Hell* showed that a reading circle could not provide the kind of relation with his readers that a modernist poet needed. Some new kind of performance space was needed. In 1919, Williams went to Chicago for several days at a time when he was feeling exhausted by his medical work and family life to give a talk and a reading to an audience that included Carl Sandburg and Ben Hecht. Feeling reinvented as a poet, he was emboldened to sleep with a woman who was the assistant editor of *Poetry*. A few weeks later he wrote to Harriet Monroe, the editor of *Poetry*, and half apologized for his behavior, saying, "I had never in my life before had an opportunity to be just a poet, the one thing I want to be. I was, to the vulgar eye at least, a poet! I was at least as near to being a poet as I had ever been and it was as if new bones had been put into me" (Mariani 160). It took the emergent college reading platform to provide the social energy he needed to sustain himself as a modern poet. A revealing comment by a young woman interviewed by Robert and Helen Merrell Lynd for their follow-up study of "Middletown," confirms Williams's sense that reading aloud in everyday groups was an increasingly unviable partner for modernist writing:

> My mother belongs to a little group who are reading together such things as Hart Crane, E. E. Cummings, Gertrude Stein, and Vincent Sheean. They steer clear of most of the poets tinged with economic radicalism, but are well read on the symbolists. Yet I don't think they derive a great amount of personal satisfaction from their reading. (Lynd, *Middletown Transition,* 282)

The Lynds' research confirms that reading aloud disappeared rapidly after the First World War in the face of new forms of public entertainment, more educational opportunities, mass journalism, and the automobile. "Middletown" in the 1890s loved reading circles, yet by the twenties they had almost disappeared: "No longer do a Young Ladies' Reading Circle, a Christian Literary Society (of fifty), a Literary League, a Literary Home Circle, a Literary Fireside Club meet weekly or bi-weekly as in 1890, nor are reading circles formed in various sections of the city, nor does a group of young women meet to discuss the classics" (Lynd, *Middletown,* 233). The diverse cultural effects created by public oral reading were increasingly segmented into more specialized leisure pursuits, eventually including the contemporary poetry reading.

A second, less easily comprehended, element of this history of oral reading is the relation between the different forms of understanding active in silent and audible reading. Medieval authors and readers were, according to Joyce Coleman, part of a performance economy that worked "synchronically to shape a mutually satisfying performance text and diachronically to create a shared vernacular of vocabulary and significance" (Coleman 126). A man like the medieval miller, Menocchio, merged oral and written culture together, as Carlo Ginzburg's rhetorical question indicates: "To what extent did the prevalently oral culture of those readers interject itself in the use of the text, modifying it, reworking it, perhaps to the point of changing its very essence?" (Ginzburg xxii). Reading aloud and the ensuing conversation were integral parts of the text, in a way that Ginzburg insists is utterly different than that of a modern "educated reader." But is it? Recently a strange debate has broken out amongst Chaucer scholars about the value of reading Chaucer's poetry aloud with a supposedly authentic pronunciation. One line of argument against it offered by Michael Murphy is that the poetry is too complex to be assimilated aurally and deliberately uses ambiguities that are ruined by a speaker's choice between them. Alan Gaylord makes a comment that is of particular relevance for understanding the economy of the poetry reading: "one *says* the verse in order to find those places that *will not be said;* which is to say, performance is a propaedeutics to contemplation" (Gaylord 109). Gaylord can only imagine the interjections and modifications in terms of the social sphere he knows best, the academy, but in effect he is admitting that the different forms of reading together still constitute an economy of reception.

Scholars working on the emergence of writing and reading in Ancient Greece provide useful insight into the interdependence of reading aloud and silent reading, because this highly articulate and self-analytic culture only slowly embraced reading, perhaps not until the end of the fifth century B.C. Most reading was done by specialists, the scribes and others who recorded information and read aloud to the rest, and so people were acutely aware of the implications of this relation. Jesper Svenbro believes that reading felt invasive to these Greeks because they imagined that to read was to lend one's voice and become "the instrument necessary for the text to be realized" (Svenbro 46) in what they sometimes understood as an almost sexual penetration of the self. Inscriptions on the base of early funerary monuments are often written in the first person ("Eumares set me up as a monument" or "I am the memorial of Glaukos" [30]) but this did not imply that they believed that the statues had an inner being of some kind, simply that the writing would remain mute until a passer-by lent it a voice and read it aloud. Such inscriptions therefore anticipate and control a reader's relation to the text. A memorial verse for a man called Mnesitheos uses two different words for reading and both refer to it as a vocal act, not as an act of semiotic decoding, as we might expect. One of these, the verb "ananémesthai," which means literally "to distribute" and was used ordinarily to mean to read and recite, is used in this context to ask the passer-by to distribute the memorial verse by reading it aloud, and in doing so to distribute the meaning to him or herself (48–52). "The reading aloud is a part of the text, an integral part of it" (45). Reading aloud was often left to slaves, because during reading it was felt that someone else's words took possession of a passive reader, like a male lover approaching a boy, and so was given to people whose self-integrity did not matter. Svenbro even claims that "pederasty was one of the models the Greeks used in order to think about writing and reading" (198). This ethnography of reading in a very different culture from the contemporary world encourages two lines of enquiry into the poetry reading. It shows that a culture may try to comprehend reading according to dominant forms of affective relationship, and it suggests that for Greek culture, at least, silent reading would have been incomplete reading, not because its acoustic properties were left idle but because the distributive power of the writing would remain inactive.

I think that some limited evidence of uneasiness about poetry readings evident in the biographies of writers whose careers either spanned the decades between the demise of the reading clubs and the emergence of contemporary readings, or began during that phase, supports Svenbro's speculation about the projection of dominant forms of desire into acts of reading. Some very obviously male ego anxieties were generated by the situations in which these poets sometimes found themselves. Williams became a regular on the college circuit but often experienced a degree of alienation. "It makes me weary for some instructor at Columbia to come up to me after a reading and ask why I put a certain verse in the form which I put it in" (Mariani 369).[12] After a reading at NYU in 1949 when he had read one or two confessional pieces that he had not intended to read, he told the friend who had arranged the reading that he felt like he had been "talking into a felt mattress." Confessing in public felt as if you have pulled "back your foreskin (if you have one) in public" (589). The castration anxiety suggests how threatening reading could become. Williams was usually more sanguine about readings and never shared Wallace Stevens's chronic hatred, expressed in a letter refusing to read at the Museum of Modern Art in 1943. "I am not a troubadour and I think the public reading of poetry is something particularly ghastly" (Richardson 225). This is a trope that the next generation would actually find quite congenial as Economou's account showed. Charles Olson seems to have imagined that readings were like formal political speeches in their defining impact, if Tom Clark is to be believed. Robert Duncan told Tom Clark that Olson had to be reassured before a reading in San Francisco that this was not definitive performance. Duncan reportedly said to Olson, "Charles, you're just reading your poetry among friends, it won't have to last four days" (Clark 263). I wonder if Duncan also meant that the reading's impact was not intended to be a policy pronouncement intended to last "for days." These three stories all remind us that the contemporary poetry reading has had to develop its own social relations.

What we can conclude from this history is that written poetry has always been read aloud by both authors and readers, long before the advent of the contemporary poetry reading, which is now such a dominant feature of poetic practice. The contemporary poetry reading is an attempt to reintroduce features of the reading economy that have been lost, just as the growth of fan conferences for genre writing, especially science fiction, obviously results from the desire of readers to take an active part in the shaping of the texts themselves, as well as a desire for that sociability mediated by texts that was such a distinctive feature of earlier forms of reading. The precise nature of that loss can only be grasped if the poetry reading is placed in another history that has shaped it, the history of public speaking. Sometimes called rhetoric, sometimes elocution, oral reading, and even orthophony, the training of public speaking with written texts, including poetry, is the missing ancestor in the history of poetry readings. When George Economou said that he and his fellow poets were the first to read aloud the medieval poets, he was forgetting the work of the verse speakers of the early twentieth century. Writing as late as 1951 on "The Audible Reading of Poetry," Yvor Winters felt the need to begin with a disclaimer: "My title may seem to have in it something of the jargon of the modern Educationalist" (Winters 433)—but by the sixties most poets (Denise Levertov is an interesting exception, although she is entirely dismissive of what she remembers of prewar public verse speaking [Levertov, *Light Up the Cave,* 46]) seem to have forgotten entirely the importance attached to public verse speaking by teachers and social reformers over the past two centuries.

VERSE SPEAKING

The Popular Elocutionist and Reciter comprising Practical Hints on Public Reading and Reciting and An extensive collection of speeches, dramatic scenes, dialogues, soliloquies, readings and recitations selected from The Best Authors Past and Present with Original hints on elocution by J. E. Carpenter, published in 1906, devotes an entire chapter to "readings in poetry" and anticipates many features of the contemporary poetry reading. Poetry recitation is a problem he blames on the intersubjective demands that easily exceed an ordinary reciter's powers.

> There are many excellent readers of prose who entirely fail to distinguish the equable and harmonious flow of sound which distinguishes poetry from ordinary unmeasured composition. . . . Unless the author be thoroughly appreciated and his intention, not only expressed but implied, mastered, the natural emotions (and consequently the proper inflexions and varieties of voice) cannot possibly arise, and, if not, how can they be expressed save by a studied, stilted, and artificial style? It is, perhaps, not saying too much to aver that only a poet can read poetry properly: at any rate only those who are perfectly imbued with the poetic feeling can do so. Given all these qualifications, and action, voice, and gesture will follow naturally and spontaneously; the electric fire will flash from the speaker to his audience, enthusiasm will be kindled, and a result that only true genius can achieve will be accomplished. The great secret in reading poetry is to exercise the art that conceals art, or rather the art that seems to heighten and improve nature and to subdue it, so that it is never apparent that the speaker is delivering the words of others. To the hearers it should be as though the speaker were giving the utterances of his own heart, and his own brain, an impulsive and involuntary outpouring excited by existing and surrounding circumstances.

This forgotten advice bears repeating because it encapsulates beliefs that are still active in poetry readings today, even though no one links them with elocution and the author is almost always the reader (as if audiences have decided that only the poet who composed the lines is capable of sufficient "poetic feeling" to do justice to the work). Many poets read as if they were uttering the lines for the first time in "an impulsive and involuntary outpouring" and try hard to make that electric fire "flash" in what Olson called the "energy-discharge" of the poem (Olson 52). This continuity between 1906 and the present is no accident. Poetry readings draw upon a long history of training and practice of formal oral performance whose history is ignored, as much because such analysis as Carpenter's makes too explicit the artifice behind the spontaneity, as because elocution is now hopelessly associated with training in correct pronunciation of the kind needed by aspirant middle-class children or actors trying to improve the projection of their voice. In Carpenter's time elocution had far more ambitious aims than these. Its history helps explain both the implicit agendas of contemporary poetry readings and why it has become so difficult to justify the claim that the semantic repertoire of the poem is significantly extended by oral performance.

Rhetoric was a part of the training of an educated young man from the time of Socrates until the Renaissance. It simultaneously provided the necessary basis for participation in public life, where effective public speaking was essential, and a training in the varieties of argument. We have no modern counterpart because we subdivide our knowledge, politics, and arts very differently. Rhetoric's organization of thought helped shape education and, by molding reasoning into its forms, provided the means to comprehend writing, speech, and language. The oration largely played the part that the essay does today in our educational system. Performance, which included everything from voice and emotional influence to the structures of reception, was integral to logic, the consequence being that actual voice production was usually, in Aristotle's words, "not regarded as an elevated subject of inquiry."[13] All this changed at the end of the seventeenth century once logical argument was prized away from its association with certain features of rhetoric, notably the studied use of tropes as a means of making ideas persuasive and accessible. The Royal Society advocated a plain style for scientific writing, and the arts of persuasion were treated as, at best, ornaments and, at worst, distortions of well-argued evidential prose. In all this ferment the actual business of delivery seems to have gone uncriticized by the reformers, and perhaps for that reason, eighteenth-century critics began to talk about it with a new zeal, as if the lack of criticism proved its continuing validity (Howell 153). It seems likely too that this very continuity enabled its proponents to imagine that a training in oral rhetorical performance would somehow re-create a bond between ethics and cognition that had been lost to the public sphere. Thomas Sheridan, father of the playwright, justifies the importance of a training in elocution on the grounds that without it "how many well instructed minds, and honest hearts, furnished with the means, and most ardent inclination to serve their country, have sat still in silent indignation, where her interests were nearly concerned, for want of a practised tongue to disclose what passed in their minds" (Sheridan 52). He internalizes an imaginary unity of moral purpose, argumentative accuracy, and clarity and represents its public absence by this muteness, which he wishfully attributes to a fault in the engineering of voice. He is therefore able to assume that the existence of what has disappeared from the public sphere continues in a series of lost private worlds.

The continuing interest in elocution, as it came to be known, depended upon a conjunction of such elevated ambitions with much more pragmatic, self-interested concerns. Young people from the upper classes needed to be able to read aloud reasonably well because this was one of the cultural accomplishments that distinguished a young person, along with music, singing, dancing, and drawing. Speaking well became the sign of good breeding, and this added to its importance for those aspirants less sure of their class position. Books and teachers of speaking aloud became very popular, and they used both prose and poetry as material. According to Mary Robb, two theories of elocution came to dominate the field. One emerged directly from the Enlightenment commitment to scientific rules and method and was promulgated in such books as James Rush's *The Philosophy of the Human Voice,* and later in Alexander Melville Bell's *The Principles of Elocution* (he was the father of the inventor). The creation of a physics of the voice is captured in this passage from Bell:

> Expression may be defined as the *Effective Expression of Thought and Sentiment* by Speech, Intonation, and Gesture. Speech is wholly conventional in its expressiveness, and mechanical in its processes. Intonation and gesture constitute a Natural Language, which may be used either independently of, or as assistant to, speech. . . . The student of Elocution, then, should be made acquainted with the instrument of Speech *as an instrument,* that all its parts may be under his control, as the stops, the keys, the pedals, and the bellows are subject to the organist. (Bell 157)

It is not hard to see that this approach could lead to a mechanical, artificial style of speaking and that in turn might eventually elicit a reaction toward a more natural one. Aided by the growth of psychology, elocution gradually shifted the emphasis away from physiology to the mind behind the voice, and it became possible to claim that sound was a systematic vehicle of expression: "particular sounds or elements are uniformly used to express particular emotions . . . tone-colour is the avenue along which the emotion passes in its progress from within outward, or from the poet to his hearer. The mere fact is expressed by the words; the emotion is expressed by the various qualities of the voice" (Robb 176). This theory of William Chamberlain and Solomon Clark's is an ur-theory of sound symbolism limited by the way the adjective "uniformly" reveals that this is also a prestructural theory of language, and it goes too far in assuming that sounds themselves form a fixed code of affects. Nevertheless, Clark's emphasis on emotion points the way forward to the emerging "naturalist" school of elocution, which argued that voice production depended upon aesthetic and interpretative criteria and could not be reduced to a system of rules.

A final flowering of elocution took place in the twentieth century and found many surprizing supporters early in the century. In his commencement address to Bryn Mawr in 1905, Henry James recommended a diligent study of good speaking to the graduating class, as if this were the most effective means he could imagine for these young women to engage in social reform. His argument, although more sophisticated than Sheridan's, still assumes that clarity of articulation will facilitate the communication upon which society rests:

> [A]ll life comes back to the question of our relations with each other. These relations are made possible, are registered, are verily constituted, by our speech, and are successful (to repeat my word) in proportion as our speech is worthy of its great human and social functions; is developed, delicate, flexible, rich—an adequate, accomplished fact. The more it suggests and expresses the more we live by it—the more it promotes and enhances life . . . it is very largely by saying, all the while, that we live and play our parts. (H. James 21)

The same aspirations that animated Sheridan are still evident here, and they similarly lead to the seeming bathos of a call for better pronunciation. James was not alone in his convictions. The leading teacher of speech in Britain in the first decades of this century, Elsie Fogerty, founded the Central School of Speech Training and Dramatic Art in London the following year, 1906, and a few years later also helped found the new medical field of speech therapy. Fogerty trained several generations of actors and speakers of verse, teaching them that written words were the record of "audible movements translated by visible signs" (Sivier 296). Like earlier elocutionists, she believed that "the knowledge and practice of written speech in all its mental and physical forms represents for us the lifework of prophet, poet, and philosopher, of thinker and fool alike" (Fogerty 73), and in her textbooks, as in her teaching, she brought together an extraordinary synthesis of Bergson, anthropology, physiology, linguistics, and aesthetics under the rubric of rhythm. She may have been influenced, like John Masefield, by the style of W. B. Yeats, whose oral reading, according to Masefield, "put great (many thought too great) yet always subtle insistence upon the rhythm; it dwelt upon the vowels and the beats. In Lyric it tended ever towards what seemed like Indian singing; in other measures, towards an almost fierce *recitativo*" (Masefield 130). Later still in the twenties, Fogerty collaborated with John Masefield, Marjorie Gullan, and others in the development of public displays and competitions in verse speaking.

This final fling of the elocution movement in Britain led to some extraordinary attempts to re-create the performance of verse. The poet John Masefield founded a verse-speaking competition in Oxford in 1923 and later, in 1929, helped found the English Verse-Speaking Association. His aim was to sweep away the artificiality that had resulted from methods of teaching elocution that "had concentrated on acquiring an equipment of tricks and recipes for delivery that should fulfil their every requirement," failing to recognize that "the sound of a poem is part of its meaning, and needs a vocal cultivation for its revealing that shall be as exacting as a great singer's, and as undemonstrative as the singer's often is demonstrative" (Sansome 138). In his autobiography, he recalls ironically that in his youth, popular stage reciters of verse were "at their best in works dealing with the murderous, the mad, and the drunken" (Masefield 132). In an address to the Scottish Association for the Speaking of Verse in 1924, he talked eloquently of the role of poetry in national life:

> The arts of speech and creation seem to be linked together, as of course they must be: the breath is the life. When poetry is good, speech and song are good. . . . I have watched the effect of poetry upon many audiences, on audiences of savages and of the civilized. It seems to me to excite the savage and to hypnotise the civilized,

> but it moves both so powerfully that I feel it to be irresistible. (Masefield, *Living Voice,* 11, 30)

He goes on to argue that early poets took for granted that they would speak or even sing their poetry, but since the Romantic period, poets have been "shut away from the life of their time," and the main cause of this has been the material conditions of publication: "the printing press stood between them and their audience" (21). As a result, he adds, he and his audience "have seldom or never heard a poet making his work under the influence of those excited to hear him" (28). Masefield's solution was choral verse speaking and education. He strongly supported the work of Fogerty and Gullan, whose pupils aimed for "natural voice habits" in all their work, some of which even included choral verse speaking, surely one of the most peculiar developments in poetry performance. Several of these choirs were formed in the twenties and thirties and practiced group speaking in unison, not, as one might imagine, aiming for clever part harmonies as in the singing of a madrigal. Yet neither of these solutions turned out to be as effective as the idea of hearing the poets themselves reading their work, or improvising it, aloud to an audience, and Masefield's contribution to that development and to the prevalence of readings today is largely forgotten.

In America, voice training was now widely taught in higher education but was undergoing a rapid transformation signaled by the way the terminology changed. The Emerson College of Oratory became the Emerson College of Liberal Arts in 1936, and the word "elocution" was used more and more rarely. College catalogues for 1929–1931 listed more than two thousand courses in oral practice, but the favored term now was "interpretation," and increasingly these courses were being tied to specialisms, notably linguistics and drama. Academics could still claim, like Clarence T. Simon in an essay called "Appreciation in Reading," that "muscles, nerves, glands, all do their part in our reaction to literature . . . it is this 'doing something' which is the appreciation," but increasingly the passage from glands to literary criticism was Balkanized by incommensurable and noncommunicating sciences and arts (Robb 199). It seems reasonable to assume that the young Charles Olson was trained in these traditions as a successful school debater and then drew on them unacknowledged in his "Projective Verse" essay, which is why the continuities mentioned earlier can be found.

The history of elocution and verse speaking is a history of an attempt to restore a diremption of cognition, ethics, and art that developed during the Enlightenment; a futile attempt because it was forgotten that "pronuntiatio" once meant much more than the mere shaping of vocal sounds by the body. The deliberate amnesia about the importance of the elocution movement for shaping our current experience of verse speaking in the contemporary poetry reading probably derives from the unwillingness to recognize this failure for what it is. Certainly the primitivism of much discussion of oral poetics would confirm this because it so evidently represents a similar aspiration for imagined pre-Enlightenment unities.

COLLECTIVE EVENTS

The UK Poetry Society's 1987 pamphlet on how to promote poetry offers strong advice to novice organizers of poetry events about audiences. Treat them well! "A warm, crowded space is preferable to a cold, half-empty hall," the would-be organizer is told; the pamphlet then gives strict numerical guidelines on the number of minutes a poet should read for: "The importance of these timings cannot be over-emphasised: listening to poetry requires great concentration; an audience still eager for more will return, a bored audience never" (Clunies-Ross 30). The relation between the audience and the poet is at the heart of the event, yet at first sight seems to be merely a matter of such managerial pragmatics, not the space in which the poem's meaning is negotiated and possibly extended. The eager audience may be suffused with empathy for the poet and interest in the work, but have they really extended their comprehension of the work itself? Like the inscription from ancient Greece, the poet has distributed the poem to the audience, but what does it mean to say that this is an integral part of the poem itself? For some readers Maggie O'Sullivan's poetry seems to require oral performance as well as silent reading, but this doesn't prove that the meaning of a particular poem is actually extended or transfigured by performance. To do that it is necessary to take seriously the Poetry Society's advice and think of the audience.

Audience and poet collaborate in the performance of the poem. The audience is not simply a collection of autonomous individuals whose auditions of the poem are entirely independent. During performance, the audience is formed by the event and creates an intersubjective network, which can then become an element in the poem itself. Intersubjectivity is only partially available as an instrument for the poet to play and is an ever-changing, turbulent process that can overwhelm or ignore the poet, yet it is far from passive. Both the author poet and the listening audience are performances, not static phenomena. The audience effectively stages its own reception, allowing the poet to script its semantic adventures as participant witnesses, and all this takes place beyond any individual will and largely beyond the capacity of any recording technology to reproduce. What we can do is to consider the metaperformative strategies in a particular poem read at a particular venue and speculate on the kinds of intersubjective formation that might be at work.

Poetry readings demonstrate that there is no Other—only others sustaining the textual economy. In all of the poetry readings I have described so far, the audience has played a part in generating the poem in performance. Unlike the "reader" of a text in literary theory, this audience is irreducibly plural. When a poem is read aloud at a poetry reading, an intersubjective network arises that can become an intrinsic element of the meaning of the poem. The effects of this are already evident in my previous examples. Shouts of encouragement at Ginsberg's reading acted like a collective "amen." Levertov's anecdote (discussed in the previous chapter) about other listeners leaving forced the listeners who remained to reflect on why and how they were listening and on what commitment they were collectively forging as an audience capable of remaining to listen and participate in the project proposed by her poetry. Fisher's audience at the Langton Street reading (also discussed in the previous chapter) became partially resistant to a demand by the poetry to take part in a large scale evaluation of contemporary knowledges, and that resistance tended to reify the poet. Poetry readings are inherently collective events during which a text is the simultaneous object of attention by many participants. I have already considered some features of this process: the allegorical transformation of the venue and the tension between poetry and the surrounding reminders of what resists poetry; the intersubjective drama of authorship centered on the deceptive presence of the poet as origin of the poetry; the challenges to self-reflexive subjectivities maintained by the oscillations between speech and writing; and the kinesthetic, material relations created by sound waves. It is now time to consider this intersubjective drama as a whole. To do so it is necessary to discuss what is meant by intersubjectivity and to delineate the problems of discussing it within frameworks derived from Saussurean linguistics.

Agreement that intersubjectivity is the relation between different subjects as subjects hides largely unarticulated disagreements about what exactly is related and how. Is intersubjectivity conscious or unconscious, and is it a form of self-consciousness or not? How does it occur: through language, affect, recognition, imitation, or some other form of connection? Is it the result of subjects interacting with each other or is it a prior condition that makes individual subjectivity possible? Is it a conceptual delusion?[14] Anglo American philosophy has found the term useful to describe forms of collective agreement that are conscious but not necessarily arrived at by means of deliberative argument. Philosophers as dissimilar as Donald Davidson and Thomas Nagel recognize the importance of what Davidson calls "a largely correct, shared, view of how things are" (199), and Nagel calls the "view from nowhere" (14), for making sense of objectivity. Edmund Husserl's late work was devoted to the problem of intersubjectivity and has been developed into various theories of the lifeworld. Intersubjectivity is also a key term for Jürgen Habermas's theory of communicative action: "To the extent that language becomes established as the principle of sociation, the conditions of socialization converge with the conditions of communicatively produced intersubjectivity" (Habermas 93). This is a history still in need of its historians. My brief outline is only sufficient to indicate that although no working theory of intersubjectivity commands general assent the question of how people interact as conscious beings has been widely explored in modern thought, and that it is not an adequate response merely to dismiss the term on the basis of one specific interpretation. Derrida's often cited, confident assumption that intersubjectivity is always assumed to be an "intentional phenomenon of the ego" (Derrida 12) and to amount to no more than "the co-presence of the other and of the self," simply doesn't answer to the range of philosophical discussion beyond Husserl. Nor can intersubjectivity be dismissed because some linguists have understood it to mean a kind of pure communication.[15]

Derrida's dismissal of the term has a counterpart in Saussure's linguistics and its inability to represent communication adequately. For that reason, the intersubjectivity of a poetry reading is hard to place within a Saussurean linguistics and the literary theory that springs from it. Roy Harris claims that the problem arises because Saussure has a mistaken concept of linguistic value. Saussure tries to find a material embodiment of his key insight that language is a collective institution that is outside the control of the individual speaker, and he does so by inserting a cognitive rule system, "la langue," into the mind of each individual speaker. Several philosophers and linguists have argued that this model itself is deeply flawed because it imagines communication as rather like a transfer of something tangible, as if communication were a "conduit" channeling materials from one person to another or a telephone line delivering packets of electrical information. Speakers supposedly understand one another because they have the same inner programming for dealing with what is sent. This model of intersubjectivity effectively sidesteps the problem by covertly assuming that everyone is the same on the inside and therefore intersubjectivity is inevitable under the right conditions. Communication is demonstrably unlike this, however, as even Saussure admits at times in the *Course.* Speakers infer what one another are saying in ways that inevitably result in misunderstanding, however limited or innovative, as many commentators have observed.[16] The idea that communication takes place within a perfect circuit also gives a peculiar interpretation to his key theoretical proposition that "language is a system of pure values, determined by nothing else apart from the temporary state of its constituent elements" (Saussure 80 [116]). The values must be fixed because otherwise communication would be impossible, a travesty of the working of values in an economic system. Harris argues that Saussure fails "to see that values are subordinate to transactions, not transactions to values" (Harris, *Reading Saussure,* 232), whether in monetary exchange or language. The value of something is determined only by what value is attached to it in a particular transaction. "Transaction" is a pertinent term for poetry readings, where linguistic transactions occur in public situations capable of self-referential feedback about just such values. These are not primarily judgments of success or worth, as the term "value" might suggest, so much as self-reflecting investigations of the semantic values, or meanings, possible within this particular group of language users consisting of audience and poet. Such transactions are a form of freedom, a "poetic interaction" in the words of the philosopher John McCumber, and Saussure's description of them is remarkably relevant to the way poets create opportunities for interpretation to flourish. Discussing what he calls "associative relations," Saussure admits that "any given term acts as the centre of a constellation, from which connected terms radiate *ad infinitum*" (Saussure 124 [174]). The problem with Saussure's general system, as Harris points out, is that it tacitly admits that speakers are not bound by fixed values in such cases. If this is so it is hard to see how *any* word can be said to have a fixed value, since under certain conditions at least, such as those occurring in the reading of a poem, all words are opened to infinity.

The intersubjectivity of the poetry reading offers important resources to poets, (especially some contemporary avant-garde writers), although the actual reading is as much "uninterruptable discourse" as written poetry is, according to David Antin.[17] The utterances made during a poetry reading occur in a highly abstract, reflexive mode of speech that lacks the more direct answerability of ordinary dialogic speech and permits the saying of utterances many of which would not ordinarily be intelligible or even sayable in conversation. As public utterance, it sustains a reflexive intersubjective drama of central importance to the event that makes visible the readership of the poetry to itself, including the relations between readers. The audience experiences itself as not just the group of people present in the space, but as a group (not a singular) listener brought into being by the performance of the poem, an audience created by the poetry, and it can therefore also, at least potentially, imagine how this might happen within individual acts of private reading.

A good example of the intersubjective transformations of a text during performance occurred when Susan Howe read *Thorow* at Southampton University in 1993. Susan Howe read her poems with a tone that conveyed suprise, wonder, sadness, nostalgia, and careful thought. One section that indicates the possibilities she could realize is the following:

> The Source of snow
> the nearness of Poetry
>
> The Captain of Indians
> the cause of Liberty
>
> Mortal particulars
> whose shatter we are
>
> A sort of border life
> A single group of trees

Sun on our back

Unappropriated land
all the works and redoubts

Young pine in a stand of oak
young oak in a stand of pine

Expectation of Epiphany

Not to look off from it
but to look at it

Original of the Otherside
understory of anotherword
(Howe, "Thorow," *Singularities,* 50)

In the taped record of the reading she enunciates individual words with extreme care, because these, rather than sentences, are her primary unit. The collective pronoun used in the presence of the audience includes her listeners, who become the "shatter of mortal particulars." For a moment it is the audience's back that feels the sun, feels lost in the unmapped America of the early settlers. The audience is offered a position of identification as a collective subject undergoing a disorienting exposure to a landscape whose meaning is not properly articulated and struggling to fix its significance with abstract ideals such as Liberty. The slight fall in her voice in many lines suggests that this character she has put on by reading this section is not optimistic about our enlistment. The words speak of exploration, of being unsure of location, of having the sun behind some collective identity. This collective she speaks for, this audience as it identifies itself in the collective pronoun, does not quite know where it is, but finds itself being spoken for by a visionary leader who for a moment articulates expectations of epiphany. Listeners wonder what enlightenment they can hope for, what understanding of their condition. A British audience is also aware of an imaginative distance distorting its participation because it is not American and hasn't absorbed years of American patriotic history, years of images of discovery, exploration, and settlement in a new land. A few pages later in *Thorow,* the text is scattered over the page, lines run off at skew angles and even lie upside down, as if the text had just fallen there, and she reads it with vigor, with a zest and light staccato emphasis that seems to indicate more freedom and hope, especially as she says "cannot be everywhere I entreat." The "everywhere I" of the audience, the collective brought into line behind the poem earlier, is mirrored and scattered for a moment. Always the poem invites the audience to take compass bearings, to share in the search, not for a meaning denied by the performer, but meanings the situation seems to make stumble. Hearing the poem at the reading was to become a different kind of reader than the isolated private self who reads the published text in a journal or book.

Intersubjectivity can be too ready to join in and empathize, and some poetries exploit this, notably the poetry of John Ashbery. He read with Denise Levertov at the 1985 Cambridge Poetry Festival to a large, respectful audience in the Cambridge Union debating hall. The venue was a strong reminder of undergraduate political debate, and the polished wooden paneling and seating evoked a feeling of permanence at odds with the event and even more with Ashbery's preoccupation with the evanescence of experience. He looked a little frail beside Levertov, and his poems sounded almost evasive compared with her firm self-assertions. On the BBC broadcast recording of his reading of "Vaucanson" from *April Galleons* his voice is quiet, very slightly elegiac, unemphatic. There is no hint of chant or rhythmic pulse, just the clear enunciation of a man speaking in a reflective manner about some unidentified writer who feels "relaxed and singular" and mistrusts the mood, convinced that he ought to be striving for understanding.

Vaucanson was an eighteenth-century inventor, most famous for his automatic duck that could eat, drink, and even excrete, but he was also, like his contemporaries, fascinated by the challenge of designing a machine that could speak recognizable words.[18] Such a machine would demonstrate the power of Enlightenment science, and would also have represented a challenge to its beliefs in the relation between the voice and reason. Ashbery uses the title allegorically, as if a useful adjective to describe the plight of a poet, and his poem enables the audience to perform itself with a set of cues that work almost as stage directions before turning an unflattering mirror on its alleged self-indulgence toward both self-knowledge and art. From the start, Ashbery's presence offers a contrast to the scene depicted by the poem, a poet writing in a gray room, not a poet standing, talking, in a debating chamber. The first two lines are descriptive, but the third enacts a metadiscursive change of state: "But no one, of course, ever trusts these moods." Phrases like "of course," so ready in conversation, are rarely used in poetry, and commonly red-lined by editors and teachers, because they are redundant appeals by someone who is not sure enough of the argument to present it directly and falls back on an appeal to a putative consensus, which it would supposedly be absurd to question, so that the audience's complicity in this judgement is both taken for granted and shown to be a source of unease. This third line's direct proposition is given the full weight of the poet's authority by his presence, and it brings the audience in on the wider argument, because presumably they too will want to affirm that they don't trust "these moods" and require "understanding" as well. We have been set up by the performance to demand understanding, and it follows that we even want to understand this poem, this very demand for understanding. Then the poem goes on to a larger proposition, which is offered as an apparent explanation of this will to knowledge:

> We are creatures, therefore we walk and talk
> And people come up to us, or listen
> And then move away

This is offered as if it were an explanation of why the writer in the gray room, and readers of the poem, and, indeed, people in general, all want to understand the relations between people, ideas, and things. In the recording, Ashbery pauses for longer after "creatures" than he does for the stanza breaks, allowing this word maximum air time to push listeners into a momentary contemplation of its resonance with the near homonyms "creators" and "created," as well as the implications of this fact. Standing there in front of his audience he models a bare account of human life as no more than a series of utterances and motions, colliding and rebounding. He himself is surely one of these creatures and we, the audience, "listen and then move away," figuratively through inattention or resistance and literally by leaving at the end. The poem performed in this manner neatly places the audience in a narrative of its own making, and it makes a prediction whose accuracy will soon be proven and therefore confirm the conclusions of the poem itself.

The poem then builds further on this foundation. Having taken over the broad outlines of the event with its proleptic narrative, it proceeds to imagine its relation to the space: "Music fills the spaces / Where figures are pulled to the edges, / And it can only say something." This admission of weakness, its inability to do more than "say something," is deceptive, as if more were somehow possible, and invites listeners to switch off all hermeneutic functions at once. It is deceptive because "saying something" is all that the poem can apparently do and would usually be taken to be an achievement. To say something is to say something worth hearing. The result is a kind of throwaway irony, as if to say that all communication is a waste of time, and at the same time, as if it were boasting by understatement, in the way people say "it was nothing" when praised for their actions. Ashbery's line "it can only say something" also reverses Freud's dictum "where id was there shall ego be." Has the "it" finally found a voice in the person of the performer?

The final section invites the members of the audience, who have abandoned hope of understanding and hearing "something" said, to indulge in imaginary bodily sensations, of sun on one's shoulders and thinking "good thoughts," only to reveal immediately that this would be self-deception. It is the sun that is doing the writing, "completing its trilogy," not the writer, poet, or listener. Enjoying the exalted mood leads immediately to absence, even of life, for if "life must be back there," someone is dead, or at least lacking in vitality. The listener who has been completely wrong-footed is offered a refuge in childishness, the whole performance to be ended in pretense, like a play, "by ringing down the curtain." The listeners in the poem, with whom the audience is encouraged to identify, would think that it had ended perfectly, wouldn't even notice because they would not feel the guilt, dismay, or tragedy they ought to, "only the warm sunlight / That slides easily down shoulders / To the soft, melting heart." Thus the poem ends up enacting in an imaginary register its own staging and climax and is able to underline this imaginary work it demands of the audience by the contrast with the absence of actual curtain and staging at the reading. Its allusion to the stage here, and the organization of performance by such external devices as the curtain, which functions as a period to the sentence of the drama, reflexively stages the adventures of the argument.

This authorial prestidigitation and the intersubjective coaxing into imagined moods extends the significance of the poem from its opening lines:

> It was snowing as he wrote.
> In the grey room he felt relaxed and singular,
> But no one, of course, ever trusts these moods.

The identity of the poet in the gray room—who may or may not be Ashbery because he may be referring to himself in the third person, or to someone else, or perhaps to a generic poet—becomes a question that the performance develops into a debate about the value of the activity itself. Perhaps being singular in the room rather than plural in the performance space is not the value it seems, or perhaps the testimony of the performance is biased. It surely depends on the work done in such rooms. "Vaucanson" anticipates performance and incorporates previous experiences of public reading as it stages an intersubjective melodrama in which the audience members are constantly caught trying to indulge feelings they should not. It is a poem whose semantic range is extended by performance and, when read silently, gestures at this absent occasion of its possible realizations. Much of this would escape most listeners who had never heard the poem, but typically the poem is then broadcast on the radio, remains in the memory, and is reread silently from a book so that it becomes something larger than any single reading.

What these examples cannot show is another dimension of listening that all poetry readings anticipate. Reception is not simply an addition of individual receptions, each autonomous from the others, because the performed poem both modulates existing networks of intersubjective relations and articulates new ones, so that the aggregate reception of the poem is not purely a series of independent auditions all directed only at the poem. If intersubjectivity were thought of as a field, it would be neither uniform throughout its range nor continuous, but such metaphors distort the activity of intersubjectivity. Intersubjectivity is only partly under the sway of the author and poem and is turbulent, unpredictable, and capable of warping as well as amplifying texts. But this too could be misleading if it implied that the poetic intersubjectivity of performance was passive, and this is not the case.

Just as the poet/author is a fiction actively performed by the reader, so the audience too is a performance, a staging of itself as an audience. Poetry readings delegate some of the constructional authority for this process to the poet at the front, whose poetry choreographs the semantic adventures of the listening witnesses and contributes something as well.

This process takes place largely beyond singular articulation and can only be inferred by the consequences of readings and such reflexive images as those provided in some poems.

Poetry readings are part of the long biography of poems, part of the distribution from poet to readers, and readers to readers, which takes place through silent reading, memory, active analysis, discussion, performance, publication, and all the many processes whereby thoughts, feelings, and knowledges circulate. The poem (like all texts) is a multidimensional entity, not reducible to one act of reading, one set of marks on one page, nor one poetry reading. J. Hillis Miller half perceives this feature of texts when he says that, once written, "the book is detached from its author and wanders here and there by itself in the world, having such unpredictable effects as it does have when it is read or misread, and even when it is not read at all" (Miller 106), but this whimsical image of the wandering book is misleadingly singular. A better image is that offered by Bruno Latour for the "quasi-object" or extended network that forms around a feature of the physical world, like the laser or gravity, so that an object, a social tie, a text, and Being itself, can all be indistinguishably intertwined: "This liaison of the four repertoires [i.e., material world, social world, discourse, Being] in the same networks . . . allows us to construct a dwelling large enough to house the Middle Kingdom, the authentic common home of the nonmodern world as well as its Constitution" (Latour 89). It exists in multiple locales at once and has simultaneous receptions that develop both in and out of sync.

A similar understanding of literary practice can be discerned in the work of some poet-critics. Michael Davidson's distinction between Language Writers and the New American Poets displays a similar understanding to Latour's: "Whereas gesture for the generation of Olson and Ginsberg implied single expressive moments, recorded spontaneously on the page and realized in the oral performance, for writers of a more recent generation gesture refers to the interactive, social web in which language exists" (Davidson, "Skewed," 45). And I would add, the poem itself. Instead of thinking of the poem as something that moves around being variously interpreted, read aloud, published in different forms, and generally provoking distinct interpretations, we might be better to think of it all as a large heteroclite entity that mixes texts, people, performances, memories, and other possible affines in a process that engages many people, perhaps only briefly, over a long period of time, whose outcomes are usually hard to see and that has no clear boundaries, not the page, the reading, the critical study.[19] Then it is possible to say firmly that the poetry reading does change the meaning of the text because the poem is the totality of the field of these elements in time and space. That is its possible politics, its middle, that it shares with all texts and that some contemporary poetries, especially the avant-gardes, have investigated with great care, persistence, and intelligence.

Performance is a moment when social interaction can study and celebrate itself, and the poet is given significant new materials with which to extend the signifying field of the poem. Authorship and intersubjectivity collaborate with the implicit allegorization of poetry's potential and actual place in everyday life. The unstable balance between the mimicry of expressive utterance that occurs when a poet reads a poem as if it were only then being spoken for the first time and the self-alienation of reading a text written at another time as if by another self offers a wide field of social and semantic significance for active poetic construction. The dramatization of the moments at which subjectivity is generated in the relations between a speaker and an audience opens into a qualitatively different effect. The presentation of the poetry in a public space to an audience that is constituted by that performance for the time of the reading enables the poem to constitute a virtual public space that is, if not utopian, certainly proleptic of possible social change as a part of its production of meaning. Part of what the poem means is what it means as an event in which individual identity is set alongside the group identification of an audience. Poetry readings foreground the ordinary processes whereby meanings are produced within linguistic negotiations between speakers in a textual culture, by balancing on the knife-edge boundary between two signifying media, sound and writing, at the moment of reception. Reading is made aware of itself as an activity organized by and within communities that calls for a locally civic virtue.

Chapter 4
Anonymous Poetry

The event has now dispersed into engrams, conversations, the anonymous kipple of cultural memory.[1] The organizer has returned to his own nation, the listeners are now themselves speakers and actors, inheritors of what they amassed then. These notes have no tendons to pull, no body to perform, no staring audience, no unlit late afternoon indistinctness to gray the paper and spread a thin murk over corners that need not be seen. No silence leaks with slushy distance around the clear enunciations of a central voice, no you and you to stand for the occasion. Even the note of melancholy is silenced. And yet inexpressible loss is a phrase that one would never use to mark where the event has been; talk of the inexpressible is reserved for those times when irreversibility wipes out catharsis. This is the everyday disappearance of a hearing into the spreading anonymity of the past. The event is now conjugated as the said, the unsayable, the readable. Is writing then the future of speech? Who was it who said that all writing continually aspires to the condition of speech? If only we could find an author for this assertion an entire lifeline would be available to give the words history and cosmos. Or is this retrospection mistakenly thinking that there is a voice in the text because the text says that there is a past in this voice? Perhaps the voice that has been found by so many authors of contemporary lyric poetry is a defense against the erasure of identity by the production of temporality, more than a claim to be authentic enough to be a poet? Or is it just the winning sincerity of remembered suffering and out of sight insight?

"Evanescence" and "charm" are characteristics of the genre of the talk on poetics, at least according to the organizer of the talk series where this was performed, the poet Bob Perelman, who for a time was based at King's College, London. I am not sure about charm, in my talk or others, although rhetoric's charm was once believed to be more leadership's magic ability to talk collective activities into being out of disorganized listeners than mere stylish fascination. My dictionary says that charm can be a "metrical form of words." Perhaps the talk retains a prosody that the essay lacks? Perelman speaks with some authority on these matters, having organized talks (and they are "talks" not performances or papers) since the nineteen-seventies, when he first began arranging conversations about contemporary poetry at his loft in San Francisco. His description of talk could be the definition of a public sphere: "Talk is the most mixed of media: social, bodily, clichéd, spontaneous, conflictual, identificatory . . . the tone and rhythm of culturally perspicacious speech make for an effective token of the possibility of individual agency."[2] Or it could be a description of the dominant form of contemporary poetry. I am constantly brought back to one particularly unabashed summary of what the avant-garde, the headbangers, and the deconstructionists treat as the bad Other. Mary Oliver, a Pulitzer Prize–winning poet, and therefore a poet whose work presumably speaks for the opinion formers, says that much contemporary poetry has a tone of "natural and friendly intimacy," which projects a "perfectly *knowable* person, behind the poem," and she is entirely comfortable with this, not least because the idea of the neighborly poem encourages writers to "speak out about their personal and community life, to reveal themselves, as it were" (77–79). What sort of consonance is this between the talk and the personable poem? Bob Perelman is a Language Writer, and these poets are distinguished in part by an avoidance of voice and its ghostly presences, as well as the use of what has been felicitously called "diminished referentiality," as if it were a diminished responsibility for bourgeois law. In his recent work, Perelman has clearly become uneasy about the belief that the author is dead in avant-garde poetry, and when he writes about Barrett Watten's poem *Progress* (1985), he says that "impersonality is built into the poem" (123), because after all, radical poetry should not be providing podia for even tokens of agency, yet "built into" makes it all sound like the incorporation of something that was previously optional and remains just one feature for the realtor to talk up. Perelman has begun to want those nonlinguistic features of bodily existence and its socialities, such as are inadequately called agency, body, identification, and society, to move from the talk into poetry, and he finds them even in Watten's poetry. *Progress* reveals the "author's emotion" and "a great desire for power," as if behind the impersonality were a perfectly knowable passion for justice, perhaps. Why can't the self in the poem be large enough to contain impersonality and personality, along with multitudes, bodies, and communities? I and I might make out in the poem, or, as in a recent poem of Perelman's, arrive at "a general agreement to differ from ourselves" (*Future*, Perelman, 61).

This pointing out of an authorship winking from the ruins of narrative and referentiality in formalist catachresis was the occasion of the talk below. Why did the author have to disappear not only from academic literary studies but the writing spaces of avant-garde poets too? Seán Burke argues that literary "theory became possible with the exclusion of the author" (191), but he blames it on the academic reception of Barthes, Foucault, and Derrida. Why then should radical poetry also want to see the author dead? Is it just because the poets who are taken to represent the dominant political ideologies of our time apparently believe that the equivalent of a poetic hello is enough to sustain a communicative ethics? Their advice to the poet to listen to "spoken language" carefully and "aim to capture some of its directness and naturalness in the language" of the poem (in the words of *Teach Yourself Writing Poetry and Getting Published*, Sweeney and Williams, 34) certainly presupposes that there are person standards, and these products of personhood understand one another. "Is there no one," one is tempted to ask, as Kenneth Koch's disenchanted poet does, "who feels like a pair of pants?" (32) Or is the problem elsewhere than the defense of academic professionalism and the need to distinguish one's literary radicalism with an antiemotional textual rigorism? Are the poets responding to social conditions of recognition that make "the performance of a subject within his text" (191), in Burke's words, a problem somehow synchronous with the culture of anonymity and celebrity commodity in which we live?

What follows is an assemblage of a script that attempted to begin thinking through these issues in a form suitable for talk, where agency could show its tokens and a subject perform. The "social, bodily, clichéd, spontaneous, conflictual, identificatory" occasions imagined by the text in stage direction italics have a temporality of their own and are one of its limits. Perelman's praise of the talk genre makes it sound almost as if it is the space where avant-garde poetic imagination can "act out" the repressed person behind the radical constructivist poet. Or are the referentially challenged poetics of risk-prone writing developing a poetics of thaw for the cryogenics by which ordinary autobiographical verse chills what it perceives to be the dangerous democracies of conversation?

I could stop there [*long pause*], seeming to stutter, I, I, yes, yes, this is me, I, [*gesture toward chest*] I, I. The stutter makes tangible the physical formation of the word in my throat, locating the word's origin inside my body, as it speaks of the psychic interiority of my person. "Every respiration proves the discontinuity of spoken meaning" (Appelbaum 40). Sounding like a sharp exhalation, a counter-breath, this vowel [*heavy mouth*] *I* marks out whatever will follow, which has not yet happened, suspending us all in an awkward temporality of incompletion, where the interiority has as yet only the tangibility of these sounds from a hole in the body to signal with. And instead of finishing what I have, or should it now be *has*, begun, a metalinguistic turn instead. Is it too uttered under the sign of the *I*? Does this word turn every immediately subsequent word into a consequence of its action and being, as if it were a bracket whose circumference lay at infinity? [*sigh*]

Here is the sentence that should have occurred. [*new tone of voice*] I will talk today about first-person poetry and some current debates about its opportunities, delusions, and addictions, especially the hostility of the avant-garde, which has been persistently suspicious of first-person poetry since the early seventies, unless it dresses in ironically exposed personae, metacritiques itself to the point of dissolution, or justifies its appearance with a political passion that requires its forceful agency. [*said with the voice of the international avant-garde*] No confessions, no sincere admissions, no more anecdotes with a concerned moral purpose. [*the tone of a situationist struggling with a complex aleatory method*] No childhood memories, no short narrative epiphanies, no day residues worked into poetic dreams. Show me a self in poetry and I will show you ideology interpellating a language worker blacklegging on the production line of capitalism, [*cozy inclusion of audience*] they say.

My opening closure of the first-person sentence attempts to use this occasion to begin to reflect on the authorship at work in the use of the first person. When you hear my use of the first person doesn't this reassure you that the person you know as Peter Middleton, [*make sure of rhetorical avoidance of the literal*] with whatever information about his appearance, history, writing, habits and shortcomings, anecdotes and impressions, you attribute to this person, warrants these words? What is going to be said will not be anonymous, it will be Middletonly said, whether the words are my arrangement or sampled from elsewhere. Looking over here you will assume, and why not, that this collection of pinks and blacks [*waves* Agnes B *black cotton jacket*], this assembly of movements, from which intelligible sound issues, is a person called Peter Middleton, not some hologram recording, simulacrum, or experiment in artificial intelligence. [*assess response*]

And after all, even the most ascetic, impersonal, constructivist of poets allow time for their first person. When Jackson Mac Low writes in the appendix to *Stanzas for Iris Lezak,* a book of poems written according to strict chance formulae for choosing words from existing texts, that "the type of word string I used most frequently was one beginning with the next word in the source text having the required initial letter," the personal admission seems acceptable. He is [*italicize in tone*] offstage here, the poems are ego-free, now he can relax and reveal intention and authorial history, telling us about subway rides and how "after a while, I got tired of the frequent recurrence of the same structure words" (402). [*world weary pose of language scientist who has single-handedly deciphered the unsayable*]. Does the off-duty poetic ego have any poetic relation to the poems at all, or is the poet never speaking off the record and able to carry only limited liability for her or his assertions?

Consider another form of the first person—the plural, inclusive, cooptive word *we.* Is *we* any different from *I*? The Berkeley Six—Ron Silliman, Carla Harryman, Lyn Hejinian, Steve Benson, Bob Perelman, and Barrett Watten—in a "manifesto" (the title was given by the magazine's editors) in *Social Text,* suggested that the collective first-person pronoun was okay if it referred to an actual set of persons. When they say "we" they mean the six of them, not a collectivity that would include readers and unidentified others, and this "we" is an intersubjective authorship: "If there has been one premise of our group that approaches the status of a first principle, it has been not the 'self-sufficiency of language' or the 'materiality of the sign' but the *reciprocity of practice implied by a community of writers who read each other's work*" (Silliman 271). This fine phrase, "reciprocity of practice," is, I shall suggest in a minute, key to tracing the enormous success of the first-person lyric in dominant contemporary poetry. The Berkeley Six are explicit about their dislike of such poetry for its "pseudo-intimacy of an overarching authorial voice" and the "transcendent elevation of carefully scripted incidents" (266). Such condemnation has become widespread. Jed Rasula's brilliant polemic against the hegemonic institutions of American poetry, *The American Poetry Wax Museum,* singles out poetic "voice" for a harsh rhetorical acid-bath: "The voice remains a calculus of the speaking subject" in the dominant paradigms of contemporary American poetry, which therefore "seems piloted by the capital 'I'" (38). This craft of poetry credulously believes the superstition that "a humanoid unit called The Self has its natural corollary in an aesthetic unit," the poem with a personal voice.

This humanoid unit [*joke about avoiding Turing tests*] Pdot Middleton at Unidotacdotuk, [*point to self as if about to utter a proper name*] and its corresponding aesthetic unit, the talk, will now try to investigate these charges of superstition and the rituals that attach to it. Similar judgments have been made by many other avant-garde poets whose work appears in the anthologies *In The American Tree* and *From The Other Side Of The Century,* yet the voice and its license, the first person, remain vocal in these collections. Even if we set aside poets like Robert Creeley and Alice Notley as writers whose practice was formed by an earlier generation of "New American" poets, there are recently emergent poets whose first-person narratives have been consistently published alongside the poetries of diminished reference, nonnarrative, and dispersed subjectivity [*joke about recycled subjectivity*]. Fanny Howe is one of these. Pressed by an interviewer to measure her relation to Language writing, she first expresses admiration for it and then says that she is still committed to the "charged vocabulary of a Romantic" (Brito 102). "My expressive impulse is direct—to the world right after I experience it" (99). Rasula doesn't mention her, but wouldn't she fall foul of his strictures for her willingness to let her poems be piloted by the ego? Or are there different ways in which the first person is manifest in contemporary poetry like Fanny Howe's, which require us to rethink our current discourses of poetic subjectivity and especially the reasons why some of the widespread uses of the first person in the short poem now seem unacceptable to innovative writers and their readers while others are quietly admitted? What is this world to which the expression is directed?

Let us look at a few examples of the first-person lyric [*overhead pro-*

jected verse] taken from all sides of the poetry scene. First a poem that a diagram would place somewhere between avant-garde and mainstream practice, a designation that at once disturbs us and undercuts any sense that this is a self ready to market its finished product. [*here a little nostalgic pedagogic play with blackboards*] Andrew Crozier's poem "Poem Of This Poem" in *Pleats* (1975) might seem a direct outcome of the aesthetic Rasula deplores. Climbing into bed in a dark room where his partner is already asleep [*barest mime*], his growing awareness of space and distance provides a moment not of transcendence but embeddedness [*does this pun need me to make a face*] once his own intrusive entrance is stilled: "Hearing such space / that slowly stills into an ambient / jointure of being" (176). I like the felicity of the phrase "jointure of being" better than Edmund Husserl's algebraic assertion that "the only conceivable manner in which others can have for me the sense and status of existent others, thus and so determined, consists in their being constituted *in me* as others" (128). Although the poem traces the repayment of the work of sensory attentiveness to light and sound, space and time, by the achievement of momentary self-consciousness of inwardness with the existence of the world, it doesn't imagine anything has been abstracted permanently. But what interests me here is that its use of the first person and present tense appears to affirm a formalism that makes it the kind of poem the poet Douglas Oliver endorses, the autobiographical lyric. In the lines, "I create darkness / and enter closing the door behind me" [etc.], the present tense can stand for several different temporal relations, and the ambiguity that would be erased by the determining context for a speech act allows for a complex of relations. "I create darkness" [etc.] is at once a happening in process and its transformation into a generic, timeless assertion, whose assertive authenticity derives from its claim to be the narration of actual incident. The event stands as its own outcome instead of requiring a narrative closure appearing as the consequence of a causal series of steps. The expression "I create darkness" need not defer its meaning until some narrative climax. The [*hands of a creator scoop the air*] "world" that "rises into" them is a world that does not depend on shared acts of reflective consciousness (the partner is asleep), but on the commonality of a life history and the trusting proximity [*intimate gaze*] signaled by a prelinguistic gesture as the speaker enters the space.

Such subtleties are not common in most of the well-marketed poetry of today. Poetic formalism of the first-person present-tense narrative is a standard. Here are a few examples from *The New* [*avoid wincing*] *Poetry*. Eavan Boland writes: "The radio is playing downstairs in the kitchen / [. . .] Don't leave, I say."[3] John Burnside reports: "I dream of the silence / the day before Adam came." Michele Roberts says, "I carry your dying / inside me." Peter Didsbury says, "I look out of my window." Lavinia Greenlaw narrates both physical activity and mental process in her use of the present tense: "I drive back along the river / like I always do, not noticing."[4] In these poems self-consciousness is imagined to be available to report on the activities of the self as they happen, as if one side of the self were surprised by what the other side is doing and yet easily finds words to name the actions. This gives the narration a compulsively consumable mixture of spontaneity and reflectiveness that is even more able to dissolve the resistances of careful thought. The self that is announced by the *I* is master of its actions in a static present so that the *I* is forever about to speak, dream, carry, look, and drive, its agency at full strength. Hannah Arendt discusses a related form of illusory self-understanding in her account of "action." Action is the distinguishing feature of human beings, the capacity to emulate the endless inventiveness of time and innovate, create, make something new happen. To will. But she is wary of this will, unsurprisingly, wary of the pride of intention in its capacity to control outcomes. "Nobody is the author of his own life story," she says, because "stories, the results of action and speech, reveal an agent, but this agent is not an author or producer" (184). She has several reasons why there is such a limit to the linguistic self-consciousness. Actions have boundless consequences so that their actor cannot know them sufficiently to represent the action; only historians can do that, and self-awareness is limited; "nobody knows whom he reveals when he discloses himself in deed or word" (180). Who one is will always be unfinished while alive, so self-description is always undone. The autobiographical lyric that presents the author's self in a present action assumes that this simple act of recorded specularity can readily emulate self-consciousness's report on itself under the conditions of late modernity. It is the action that is the problem. Action takes it out into the world of recognition and Arendt's storytelling, or later theorists' symbolic.

This is an *I* that doesn't recognize the others it has constituted in its narrative of self-conscious action. It stays there in its "specious present" [*William, brother of the more famous Henry*]. This perpetual motion of self-consciousness is evident in an interesting poem by Raymond Carver selected by Jo Shapcott and Matthew Sweeney for *Emergency Kit*, another anthology broadly representative of tastes and expectations for poetry at present. "I go to sleep on one beach, / wake up on another. // Boat all fitted out, / tugging against its rope."[5] That is all there is of this bedtime poem. Hard not to see early Imagist petals, hear crowds in the Metro, feel instants of time. No "temporal community of the constitutively interrelated monads" (Husserl 128) here despite the evidently "primordial temporality" of the sleep cycle. I still like this poem [*be sincere—or is it impossible to intend sincerity*]; it evokes some of the risks of the involuntary amnesis that sleep's unconscious brings, and the fear that more than a single night will elapse, which can prompt that second's dizzy uncertainty about where it is one is waking up. But hear this poem more strongly as speech than philosophical rough trade—hey, you know what happened to me, I go to sleep on one beach, and guess what, I wake up on another—and the present tense of the spoken utterance will be interpreted as referring to a past event, not a present unfolding tense [*enact a poet talking to the camera of time*]. It might be a dream, it might be a smart analogue for some recent adventure, yet whatever happened, it is still authentically, individually contingent and assumes that there could be such an utterance that would be of interest to someone who already shares some background knowledge with this speaker. What does the stranger who reads the poem make of it? The poet knows that this linguistic form could also infer a *habitus*, project everyday nomadism through this postmodern Robinsonade, taking us on tour, or simply into a daily restlessness, waking each time to a world that demands new actions. It is not uninteresting as an idea.

In written narrative, the past tense is what linguists call "unmarked," not just past but also capable of referring to the moment of utterance, as well as past, future, recurrent, general, norms, and timelessness. In speech, it is the present tense that works like this. Carver's poem, like so much other contemporary poetry, takes advantage of the curious effect that results from the written representation of a spoken narrative. The marking becomes undecidable, creating an instability that enables it to step aside from problems of temporality and recognition. A confessional poem by Sarah Maguire, also in *Emergency Kit*, called "Spilt Milk," takes full advantage of this. A woman narrator takes us moment by moment through a painful involuntary recollection of her lover's semen cued by the sight of aspirin dissolving in a glass. "I twist," "I imagine," "I sit here," "I write," "I drain the glass." The temporality of this is too complex to unravel here,[6] but surely one reaction to such poems would be to ask why I as a reader should be interested in the experiences of a total stranger. Why are you telling me this I might say? Why should I care that you had to take aspirin after seeing your lover and it reminded you of him in such an intimate manner? [*the interrogative is one of the most affect-laden modalities*] Why might we want to read about the personal habits, families, loves, and fantasies of complete strangers who don't try and reach us by universalizing these intimacies and thereby making them pertinent to many readers, as nineteenth-century poets would have done, or providing a theoretical frame for the empirical presentation?

Consider by contrast the *I* in the lines "I lift a tract from the shelf / and weigh it" (A. Fisher, *Future,* 100) from part 6 of Allen Fisher's "Bel-Air," in which the divulgence of the personal narrative is outweighed by the generalizing framework of speculation about mass and interpretation [*palms enclose the generalized universe*]. The *I* does not imply any self-consciousness when it imparts this report to the reader. This is not an author telling his story (and this conclusion is irrespective of whether this *I* is a fictive persona as might be the case in Fisher's South London comedy of art).

You hardly need to be told that contemporary poetry competitively divulges. But why do we need to know that Robert Lowell's father had oil central heating, or that Allen Ginsberg's mother was photographed playing a mandolin, or Tony Harrison's father went on putting a hot water bottle in the bed after his wife died? And as the mention of Ginsberg might indicate, it is not just the poetries that command mainstream publication that thrive on personal revelation and insistent contingent detail of private life. Look [*look*] at the work of some of the less prominent U.S. avant-garde poets of the past three decades. Joanne Kyger begins "October 11" like this: "Oh well, it's a gray day. I paid all my / bills. I'm not in debt to anybody / Little birds rustling but I can't see them / Huh! what's wrong / On October 11, 1977, with me this heart" (83). The poem goes on to say that she is waiting for a moment (like Crozier?) "to be called up in the fire / of the new season" [*Remember how in Buffalo, at Allen de Loach's reading series, she arrived flustered, uncertain, admired*]. Or a favorite poet of mine, Philip Whalen, telling us about his bath: "I'm really going to take a bath now. I split wood (gift of the landlord) while water / Plooshes into iron pot" (7); or telling us that he can imagine living in America like his grandmother "gathering wild blackberries" (13) in the Northwest [*Whalen's* Scenes of Life at the Capital *may need introducing as Kyoto Zen memoirs—check quizzicality*]. Both these poems bring into being a somewhat comic version of the humanoid unit of authenticity inflected by Buddhist practice, which treats the pretensions to self-founding subjectivity as a clumsiness of self that deserves to be seen for the comedy it presents to the enlightened. Does this suggest that all uses of the first person might be moments of perspectival cohesion in a wider process of deferral and disjunction explicable within a variety of ideologies, sacred and secular, or are these special cases?

In the present tense, the poem interrupts the drive of narrative toward furtherance, causality, and consequence, trying instead to maintain a temporal suspension that results in a half-narrative, half-timeless [*in a voice without temporal burden*] mode, in which the coexistence of these tendencies suspends judgment on either. The mode is a method of disavowing the responsibility of the subsequent judgment nevertheless implicit in the act of its construction. Such advanced poetic technology creates intense identification and leaves no place for the outside observer [*over the shoulder*], no third person to form a triangle, no later time for more considered hindsight. The missing standpoint is the place from where the discursivity, the significance, and the transmissibility of these informations might be subjects of talk, negotiable, a polis, a democracy, a place for a point in space. Instead these standardized poems direct the readerly gaze away from off-screen activities that keep the set working.

In such poems the present tense is in part a past tense, a means of providing a temporal separation from two moments of consciousness, the moment of acting and the moment of becoming conscious of having acted. The *I* in the poem reports on itself as if the reporter were outside the self and its language. What such poems offer is not just the possibility that self-reflection can take place with beneficial consequences, as if to demonstrate the efficacy of the injunction to "know thyself," but also the actual experience of self-knowledge as bounded articulation. They do this by placing the reader firmly within the moment of specularity in two positions: first as the I with whom any reader is compelled to identify initially by its placement of identity once the words are uttered (however silently) by the reader; and second through the position provided by its second-person address. Pronominal indeterminacy permits the second person *you* [*stare/don't stare at a person opposite*] to provide a capacious position for the person whom the poet once embraced, the same person to whom this poem is subsequently addressed with a display of intimacy, and a reader who supplants this individual recipient through the reiterative performance of the poem as it extends itself through many printed copies and readings. The proleptic reader is there in the room [*in the room you will be there, don't dream, try to mean what you are saying*] and there in the recollected self-consciousness of the poem. Readerly absorption into the poem's performance of self-consciousness curiously allows the poem to be less individualized, less located in a specific voice than it would have been if its distinctiveness had been less easily merged with that of any reader, because the act of self-reflection is generic, universal.

The default form of the personal lyric is a performance of hyper-authenticity, a clever formal means of abstracting a supposed essence of personhood and holding it up as a major source of cultural value for which authenticating detail is the gold standard underwriting the scrip of the name as the poetic texts circulate in the economy of readings, publication, and recognition. My [*palatal cavity resonating with the diphthong*] contention is that we need a better understanding of how this and other poetic economies operate, and not least to acknowledge that just abandoning the standard may not be the answer. It may not be the problem that there is too much first-personal emotion, memory, and opinion in verse, but actually too little, that the paranoid vision of the majority of poems as replicants dressed in verse might also reveal a partial truth of modernity.

Many of the "New American Poets" were committed to an ethics of attentiveness, an almost scientific belief in the importance of accurate observation of both the objective and psychic worlds (Robert Duncan's "responsibility is the ability to respond," or Charles Olson's "that it all start up to the eye as if it had never happened" [Olson, *Maximus*, 111]). In an interview with Linda Wagner, Robert Creeley outlined his poetics with the term "attention": "the organizations of poetry . . . are very, very articulate and if much attention isn't given them, they don't just fall simply to hand. It's a highly articulate craft which is accumulated with many hours and years of attention" (113). He praises Franz Kline and claims him as a model for many writers because of Kline's "lovely, uncluttered directness of perception and act" in his paintings (Creeley 79). This ethics of attentiveness could range across material phenomena, people's incoming embrace, one's own thought process, and language. It could also divide up the tasks, as writers within the group responded to each other's practice as coworkers mapping another part of the same landscape. The complex history of the first person in recent poetry ought to make us cautious about abandoning the first person or treating it as only possible when given a transcendental turn, Buddhist reflexivity, or ironizing performance, because it might also mean the abandonment of the conditions for challenging existing knowledge and finding out new features of the world.[*Remember that "on the kinemorphic level, stance serves to mark the beginning and end of action sequences*" (Birdwhistell 200)] Not all first-person poetry is branded intimacy—the unknown is also on the inside.

Imagine a world of anonymous poems. Those troublesome first person pronouns in poems no longer have any identity-card proper names to show to the reader. Normally things are very different. Whereas most of the social world provides itself as the anonymous product of human creation so that we can at least temporarily assign it our own individual or locally collective significance as commodity, gift, tool, or memorial, poems are different. They arrive with names, and those names are commonly keyed to minibiographies, chronologies, bodies of work, opinionated readerships, and possibly to economic calculations of sales. What would change if all poems were anonymous? Is it just copyright's economy that would falter? After all, much text already meets us without an individual author's handshake in newspapers, advertising, reports, and information handouts, buoyed along in the continuum of texts in which we live by the name of the newspaper or organization that presents it as cake mix in a box or adventurers in polygons, and poems without authors would surely sail along with the rest, even if part of the poem would sink below recognition, edges merging with the continuum, losing definition and clear connections. The more fluid anon poetry runs the risk of not always being noticed as poetry, affinities between poems would depend entirely upon the value given to features by readers, and sometimes a scrap of print unintended as a poem would slip by too.

The world of humanly produced objects in which I sit rewriting this article, feeling that it needs to say more about the social need for the personable poem, is a room full of objects, most of which affirm their identity handsomely with logos, pictures, designs, typefaces, and at the very least, with names: JVC, Oxford, Princeton, Mustek, Centurion, Bantex, Golding, and Nature. Not all the objects are openly identified however; some are generic, anonymous. The lamp, the carpet, the shelving bear no identifying marks that I can see, although I know where they were purchased, and close examination could possibly reveal manufacturer's marks. The walls, the flooring, the mouldings, and the window glass are more anonymous still. Yet these contrasts between Princeton and linoleum are deceptive, for the distinguished identities name an unnamed, which has been rendered as unforthcoming by these loud logos as the reflective black surface of my old floor covering. When I was a child living in Maryland in the nineteen-fifties I used to think that a woman called Betty Crocker mixed together cake ingredients, which were put into the boxes that my mother bought in the supermarket, and I am tempted to say that I once believed that a saint had somehow overseen the production of my underwear (the St Michael of the retailer Marks and Spencer's brand name), although this is a memory that surely must have emerged entirely from secondary revision. Even now, as I guess is intended, I can easily forget for a moment that the University of Oxford did not collectively authorize the companion to twentieth-century poetry. These names are identifying references for companies whose collective efforts are bleached of all fleshed-out history of the actual people whose skills, thought, physical effort, and care were necessary, despite whatever help from tools and machines they had, to produce the furnishings for this room, of which they had no anticipation. As an owner, I keep company with a friendly fiction endowed with a new identity that I am encouraged to think of as a personalized location. They are commercial, corporate names and no single body is referred to, even when Betty Crocker, Paul Hamlyn, or Paul Smith appear on commodities, and in the latter two cases are indeed historical beings with a special legal relationship to the item. Part of the work involved in manufacturing these objects is the production of their anonymity, their conformity to a company standard, and the labor that produced them loses any trace of an individual or collective history associated with the laborer's history.

It doesn't end there. This empty space where once a history unfolded is not simply dominated by the company's substituted authorship staring down from its walls; now that these objects enter the space of my room, they begin to bear my face within them as my history, my memories of the time of purchase, the uses to which I have put them, the events and people that have been in this room, like traces of perfume on a letter, forms associations, as we call them, with the masks that hide anonymity. A company of producers has become a company of cues to a cultural memory. Marantz, Penguin, Casio, and Rey have all allowed me to make them part of my tradition and identity, free from the burden of other histories and the recognition of other intersubjectivities.

With one apparent exception: in the midst of this field of consumer resignification a different category of name can be glimpsed. John Rawls, Marilyn Strathern, Lorine Niedecker, Douglas Oliver, Maggie O'Sullivan. But I have to stop because I would simply begin listing the poets and other writers on the shelves around the room and piled on the desk, authors whose names seem to have survived this continuing nomocide that I live quite comfortably with. All trace of who operated the printing machine, typeset the book, placed it on the bookstore shelf, or posted the information about it may have gone unrecognized in my appropriation, but here is one clear sign of authorial activity in my hand, an anthology edited by Ric Caddel and Peter Quatermain. I have met them, I know they exist (no Albert Caeiros here); they are not imaginary figures like Crocker or Lara Croft; they live (or did—Richard Caddel, sadly, died in 2003) in worlds that are, at points at least, both coeval and sometimes coterminous with mine—this book represents Caddel and Quatermain knowledge and the research, reading, and selecting of recent British poetry. Inside are more names attached to short pieces of book, poems that often retain the letter *I* for the author's affirmation of experience and opinion. Or are these names so wholly different to the centurions of commodity identity? Has the transformative power of commodification turned the labors of Lee Harwood or Tom Raworth into the Harwood that you too can own, or the Raworth, an upmarket vehicle whose very name is indicative of value?

This is one way of describing the current textual condition of poetry, in the would-be critical language of commodification, that should provoke unease—the writing itself a Middleton that you may now also own, as well as a potentially judgmental discourse of commodification that is accurate enough about the nexus of exchange relations, fungibility, and ownership and yet misses this masquerade of introductions (my name is JVC) and anonymity passing itself off as part of the company of memory. This writing itself seems guilty of what it may be criticizing, for who was that who was speaking just now? A place (but where, in what economic, spatial, interpersonal geography?), a person (but on what authority, from what identity, for what occasion, and with what mediation between utterance and print?), an act of witness (but with what perceptual, ethical, or psychic modality?), a time (but is this chronometric or subjective time, a time of legitimation or a disembedded temporality?), a language (but why does it assume recognition from its readers, and why does it have confidence in a form of argument based on an appeal to common reasonableness and the use of familiar inferential sequences?). It is not a problem of familiarity; its spokesplace in persontime is more recognizable than any portmanteau words that try to home in on it. Its personalizing style may seem excessive, but without any such equivalent Middletonness at all would you read it?

A likely response to the excessive pliabilities that make the personal tone unable to prize loose the certainties of friendly asseveration is to wish for the greater anonymity of a more disciplinary abstraction with proven, and timely, directives on the salient issues. Why not a more conceptual systematics of this dialectic of reentry for the text or linoleum after production? Would a culturally responsive sociology help? Ethnomethodological study of both ordinary and exceptional social activities shows how pervasive are the background knowledges and expectancies that form the unexamined commonalities that grease the freedom of action necessary to speed business and intimacy in modern life. Living in extended spheres of operation in which most of the people and objects do not share the history of a small closed community—who laid the linoleum in my house, indeed who built it—creates new needs for the visibility of history. Sociology is not alone in its proffered diagnoses. Ethnographers have reported on cultures where persons are names imposed on anonymity instead of unique individualities whose namable distinctiveness might be suppressed into anonymity. Philosophers and cultural critics have sought to locate the imaginary moments when the anonymities of writing become the amities of textuality's authorship. American poets of the past three decades have written extensively about the problems of expression and voice as markers of authenticity and symptoms of ideology, and in less manifestoed conditions the British avant-garde poets have asked similar questions. A quiet theme in Caddel and Quatermain is whether, say, the name Tom Leonard at the head of a poem is part of the poem, is its frame and condition of possibility or not? Who says "if you dribble past five defenders, it isn't called sheer prose": Leonard, Caddel, Quatermain, Wesleyan, or none of the above?[7] Could there be poems without names, anonymous poems?

There is nothing strange about anonymity—it's intimate, familiar. A walk or a drive are reminders of "the anonymity characteristic of the everyday social world" (112) as Paul Ricoeur reminds us. The difficulty is to understand how the immediate sphere of direct intersubjective engagements merges with the wider world in which the people encountered are entirely subsumed for us in their functions as other drivers, shop assistants, bank managers, clients, or the even more anonymous role of people whose teeming presence makes the landscape visibly urban. To phrase it like this is to make it sound synonymous with the alienation of objectivity, but this might be misleading. This anonymity is the social unconscious, the collective to which we feel we belong because our interactions with it ordinarily work. Cars stay out of our path, the shop assistant exchanges goods for money that the bank teller gives us, management issues instructions, and clients expect us to provide whatever service it is we offer. Anonymity doesn't usually feel a burden or a threat, but why not? Ricoeur, following Alfred Schutz, renames anonymity as "symbolic mediations" that take the place of the more direct interinvolvement possible with people whose histories of mutual recognition we share in our immediate circles. Generic forms stand in for the more specific interchanges laden with affect and demanding of recognition. The unknown contemporary world that surrounds us with anonymities we confidently believe we could convert into knowable and nameable persons given the desire and opportunity, and which communicates through commodities, the media, the arts, and even sometimes poems, imperceptibly shades into the facing world of here and now where the unknown is hard to notice. The generic forms stand in for a possibility, as forms of trust and risk, of what could be named and done if it were to be necessary, a virtual future that underwrites the present's absence of name. The names on the poems are such symbolic mediations.

It can be hard to be a person, let alone an author or a poem. Anonymity of the physical body, whose characteristics may distinguish but not confer individuality, anonymity of numbers (there are so many of us), or the discontinuities of action, of consciousness, of multiple identities. This is in part because what is ordinarily understood by the person is itself an unattainable abstraction. The anthropologist Marilyn Strathern has compared Western senses of person with those held by groups of people in Papua New Guinea and suggests that our own idea of the person as an individual who enters into relationships with other persons, or with an environment, or society, or history, is very different than what is meant in Melanesia. In the West, a person elicits from someone who meets them the assumption that this is an individual who moves against a backdrop called society. Persons in company make up societies. Listen to their accent, look at their clothes, check out their use of the first person in their poetry, and you know their relation to the social environment. People in Melanesia, Strathern tells us, experience persons very differently. They feel that they begin as part of a continuum of relations; individuality is something that only sometimes emerges as the result of effort, rather than being what one starts with. Strathern found that "the fact of relating forms a background sociality to people's existence, out of which people work to make specific relationships appear." To be a person is to be a dimension of relatedness. Another anthropologist, Roy Wagner, has actually suggested that in Melanesia the person has a fractal social dimension: analogous to the geometric figure of a fractal, their social compositeness remains the same whatever the scale of social activity. Individuals and relations can be made to appear momentarily from the less differentiated background of relative anonymity. The distinct person is elicited by means of ritual and the construction of visible forms of division and specific relation. "Melanesian accumulation is tempered by the fact that acts, like relations, work to substitutive effect . . . relations are either made to appear or appear in their making; every new relationship displaces a former one" (Strathern, "Partners," 594). These anthropologists are professionally careful not to extrapolate to Western society. I would nevertheless like to suggest that Strathern's contrasts between the two cultures is as much rooted in a contrast between methodologies of anthropology as in the practice of cultural difference; her Melanesian identities could be discerned as less developed possibilities in Western cultural practice. What if print and personhood are actually more like the Melanesian experience than our dominant ideologies of individuality claim?

Instead of thinking of a spectrum of commodified identity along which poems with authorial tags, clocks with manufacturer's names, and even humble linoleum are ranged, we might trace the commodification of anonymity instead. The poem that tells us about its author's personal memories is doubling up on the naming process to make more sure that another kind of specific relationship and personhood does not appear, and what we witness is the fractal sociality of a certain generalizable intimacy already familiar from the small talk of the anonymity of the everyday. Strathern argues in her study of English kinship, *After Nature*, that the "hyperindividualism" (150) of the late twentieth century is paradoxically a sign of the demise of the individual, because the individual no longer makes visible, or helps elicit, society. The first-person lyric demonstrates a similar paradox. Reader and first-person poem together work hard to manifest a social tie made visible as a relation between the named voice of a poem and a reader who knows her own name, and yet this relation depends on a prior anonymity.

Poems are not the only products that present the history and distinction of specific persons when others gaze upon their magnificence. In a study of the complexity of so-called gift economies, the anthropologist Annette Weiner noticed that there were objects in these economies that did not circulate in the ordinary fashion because they had a special function: they helped legitimate the social and cosmological status of their owners. "What makes a possession inalienable," she writes, "is its exclusive and cumulative identity with a particular series of owners through time. Its history is authenticated by fictive or true genealogies, origin myths, sacred ancestors, and gods" (33). What we should also notice is that this identity only makes sense as a version of the collective one. These objects help make an otherwise hidden history visible, but they exist under a certain economic pressure; recognizably valuable within the system of values and yet not subjected to the tests of exchange, they often merge with the gift economy as temporary loans or publicly displayed reminders of the prestige of their owners, who have to work hard to appear individual against the inherent sociality of their culture. First-person poems are simulacra of inalienable possessions; they authenticate their author's status through the public display of a personal history in a form that carries with it the high status of poetic art. The problem is that what readers elicit is this anonymity of function.

Poets have worked through these issues in various guises. One is to let individuality manifest its complex conditions as a realization of sociality—it would be possible to read poets as different as John Ashbery and Maggie O'Sullivan like this. Another would be to follow the ruses of the name as the anonymity it represents performs all the persons of conjugation. In the new anthology from Richard Caddel and Peter Quatermain, for example, Douglas Oliver is represented by a poem that makes voice an issue of national identity: "Instead of that well-gnawed British despair / [. . .] these words are angry, in a flood of lyric feeling: / I return the black jacket, put on the frayed tweed."[8] And the tweed is the British stereotype, the self of homespun mingled threads of Celtic and English heritage that need the remaking, like the selves that lie so frozen in time in these mass-produced lyrics of the name. Is this Douglas Oliver or does the "middle-class tie" signal the "word knots of Celan?" Is the image of his trousers and under-vest as lily and moon being written by Heinrich Heine? Although the poem puts on the first person, it is a jacket over an angry dreaming breakfast-eater who might be any poet of the "red heat, a tiny furnace" inside the word, whose anger is the fractal political emotion engendered by injustice that works in the body politic toward emancipatory social change. Oliver's poem is a talk poem with its own kipple of crumpled clothes and phraseologies, and not surprisingly ends with an effort to tidy things up: it is time to "replace the tie, still knotted, in the cupboard." Other guises proliferate, too many to enumerate.

Putting the first person and its social tie back in the closet also takes us back to the opening of this essay. This essay has plenty of transcendental credit to support its cumulative identity if its ties to authorities and salient histories are not enough to overcome the ambient anonymity. It is after all written on a "Vision Master," the saint's label rubs its reminder of support, and the page is Wesleyan, although now I see that the paper is reflecting light across Oliver's poem so that it is no longer readable in the illumination of this late night room. Or is its anonymity another ruse of history?

Chapter 5
The Line-Break in Everyday Life

What
poetry do meanings
experience readers
This line-break the in
symmetry and order of estrangement
out find and try to experiment an of part is
most is What
much how is visible immediately
the in occurs meaning
syntax backward
Do line-break the of influence the under acting
line-breaks
backward words of dream
see to way better What
to than
and world verse familiar the invert
the of practices poetic contemporary all of radical most the study
stop line
(BILE) Ending Line Idiophonic British The
practice distinguishing a is
rush broadband whose poets of
registers of
idioms dissonant and metrics homophones allusions concepts
cognition vertiginous its concentrates
line-break every at

you remind already may this Reading
is usually line-break the invisible how just of
catches BILE how and
out you
labor is this Reading
uncertainty semantic new induces ending line Each
suprasegmental this of modality predictable No
verse free most in as poem single a of words the codes entry
interrogative an is break Every
column or block visual a create to ended line the Has
words of unit distinct rhythmically a mark it Does
sentence quasi a line the Is
altogether ignored be left to right from drop and scurry the Should
enjambment called familiarly and
intake breath's and pause thought's of analogy corporeal mimetic a Is
line-breaks Creeley's Robert in be to seems there as work at
uncertainty Perhaps
for stands line metrical the that all to allusion an to emphasis lends
to mistake a it is Or
BILE this read
all at interpretation for demand renewed repeatedly a as
poetry UK of metabolism the of part been has BILE The
now decades two than more for
noted barely yet
acronym appropriate an is BILE
injustice at anger because
poems these of argument and form the motivates
Traditionalists
The ear the to discordant and bitter intellectually poetry this find
BILE of semantics complex
choler beyond far extend
humors four the of one was which
(perhaps poetry *bad*-humored a of think)
deconstructive be may role biochemical bile's medicine modern In
construction cell to preliminary a as only but
liver the by produced cocktail digestion This
action detergent whose acids cholic esterified includes
vitamins some and cholesterol fats digest helps

androgens and steroids contains also Bile
or fats Digested
lipids
ATP of production the for reservoir essential the are
triphosphate 5′ adenosine
organisms in energy of source main the
phospholipids of form the in membranes cell of and
proteins and lipids of consisting LDLs or lipoproteins density Low
bloodstream the in body the around cholesterol take
throughway the jam traffic don't they as long as well goes all and
long too for diet rich a eaten has consumer the because
intimal the in parked up end they Then
artery the of wall cell
there trapped and squashed
travelers fat these of suspicious become macrophages so
attack
tissue fat spongy into turn themselves then and them absorb and
artery the of outside the overstretches that
If pipeline the of inside the on membrane the weakens and
and clot mix fat and blood tears this
attack heart with consumer the kill
poetics oppositional an for metaphor extended an like sounds this If
accident no is this
science's Contemporary
plasm political and social with glints often rhetoric
diverges BILE
line-break of types familiar two from
inspiration of enactment mimetic the and stave metrical the
"Wind" Fenton's James of stanza first the In
Each caps initial the by reinforced is line-break the instance for
end-stops line

This is the wind, the wind in a field of corn.
Great crowds are fleeing from a major disaster
Down the long valleys, the green swaying wadis,
Down through the beautiful catastrophe of wind.

Rhythmic
poem the of half second the in cæsura the of side either repetition

syntax the of voicing everyday pressurizes
the calls Wesling Donald what creating
"scissoring of grammar and meter."
"catastrophe" with conclude to tries Syntax
pattern the complete to iamb more one on insists meter whereas
of consideration the in up set is tension a so and
be might catastrophe a what
plot poetic this in
An
affairs of states existing to end absolute
construction odd the through or
"of wind"
a than more no as interpretable
back dying of cycle seasonal
periodicity the repeats poem this in ending line Every
conclusion sentential potential a of
sentence extending the whatever
The otherwise doing be might
line-break first poet's
sentence the of force propositional the to adds further
reinforcing
syntax and stop full of combination authoritative already the
two line in stop full no is there Although
of sentence end-stopped an be to it allows syntax the
compared two force
line opening the in line-break three force the with
single The
endings line his of modality
word citizen each of monoculture the advertises
"A dish of aloes"
"dish of helloes" a as heard be to meant apparently not is
"sentimental trash" as "corn" nor noun a as "rose" verb the nor
"beautiful" in idiom sales fashion nor
"wadis" in hiding squaddies or wads nor "sword" in sward nor
unavoidable pun a makes compression poetic When
some or ending line the
up lights sign neon other
"Like chaff we were borne / In the wind"
nation one—be words shall so ends line the As

nations colonized formerly of histories the imagining of capable
nature of control own our in implicit destinies as
authority propositional a assume also line-breaks skilful
Fenton's
irony self-inflicted a against off played is which

I saw a thousand years pass in two seconds
Land was lost, languages rose and divided

poet's fanciful the at directed is Irony
see can that eye
the of history the
field farmer's a in Mediterranean
idea the of assertability the at not
writer this by said and said be can it that
"lost" was "land" that
riven languages
Indeed
sentence the to opposed as line the of force propositional the
claims knowledge of policing institutional evades
a only be to appearing by
certainty such of simulation
judgments such make to authority poetic Fenton's
the by supported also is
the of tone emotional standard
line-break
although
verse recent other much in than here evidence in less is it
performance in especially
verse contemporary of writers Most
aloud read
catalexis aural special a with
Longley's Michael In
The Ghost Orchid of recording
of ends
pitch and volume of alteration without read are lines enjambed
muttered almost are lines end-stopped but
the produces that volume and pitch in fall the is such

mix emotional
sadness and longing awe regret of
"poetic" the of expect audiences
"Autumn Lady's Tresses" of lines four last the are These

Or the aftermath of lit thistledown, peacock
Butterflies above marram grass, lady's tresses
That wind into their spirals of white flowers
Cowrie shells for decorating your sand hair?

final The
"flowers" of syllable
disappears almost
catalexis of form a it call I why is which
The familiar be will reading of mode Longley's
poets other many so and Longley and Fenton of line
calls Jarvis Simon what produce to designed is
"a pattern of collectively preformed expectations"
and are these what Just
is them to rise gave politics and history what
elicited are expectations those when understood easily most
a of detergents the by emulsified then and
androgens and steroids acids whose poetry
a from secreted are
line-break similar seemingly
sort the of nothing is that
Wilkinson's John
is *Torn off a Strip* from "Flowers of Nationhood"
couplets nineteen in out set
page the of wall left the against neatly stacked
right the on length word's long a about by varying irregularly
couplets of series a like looks it Visually
an in Longley or Fenton alongside appear might that
verses like-minded of anthology
chapbook this in poems other the of Most
way this arranged also are
line a of end the at stop full one only is there poem this In
the is that and

poem whole the in line last
and midline stop full a with end sentences some although
letters capital
the at sentences new introduce
Wilkinson's lines some of beginning
orderly visually appear line-breaks
different very are they syntactically and orally but
to as varied so
random first at seem
stops full of force the have few A
exclamations reinforce some words isolate some
(gilly) morpheme a highlights one
indefinable are some enjambment is one
ending this of effect the is What

Bring us your mortality list, statistics for output,
break them down, before they turn to ashes truly

skills no sensible disputes, the team as a whole's
raring to get cracking. Mass to take what's feasible (104)

possible seem phrases the of dispositions linear Other
phrases unsyntaxed of intrusion repeated the given which
citational sound
"This is a disclaimer masquerades as inevitability" line the In
"This is a disclaimer" treat to is it read to way obvious an
A marks quotation in were it if as
the argue might prosodist hostile
cannot poet
all at line-break the handle
say to tempted be might readers Sympathetic
tradition of trivia such to indifferent is poet the that
mistake a be would This
His properly tradition hate does Wilkinson
poem
cognitive of self-consciousness and intensity the up scales so
reaction emotional and
line-break the of device prosodic the to

that
role its from change qualitative a undergoes significance its
Fenton's like poetry subservient metrically more in
line-break of type specific a of think to not important is It
for quantity fixed a as be might meanings its complex however
readers historied differently
Wilkinson of Readers
moods and dispositions ideas habits with begin
outings poetry previous by formed
difference the with familiar be will readers all Almost
text unjustified and justified between
variations local many lie this beyond but
of publication BBC the in poems the from judge To
100 Popular Poems From the BBC Radio 4 Programme
More Poetry Please!
endings line defined strongly
by marked
resolution syntactical of degrees and completion metrical rhyme
familiar most the are
childhood from them of many
associated and
nostalgias compensatory and loss of senses desires the with
with drug memories childhood
affects repeated few a to counterpart the are endings line These
wonder beauty in delight existence at joy mortality of fear
Wilkinson of readers sophisticated more Slightly
experience such to added have will
Longley and Fenton by those like poems of readings
resolution emotional meter of scissors a offers line the where
and resignation enlightened in
The statement of authority reassuring a
Wilkinson of readers experienced most
will
a breath a is that line metaphysical the encountered also have
its in away blows and endures emerges that thought
a moment separate and clear phenomenologically
The voice to language from back speaking
mode idiophonic the headline lines ten first

the that admit should I And
abreactions linguistic other and semantic of metonymic is phonic

Let's understand this body controls world athletics,
bale out, bring a near miss, revile a new manager

professes continuity, favors cold authentic choice
This is a disclaimer masquerades as inevitability

stage a ceremony to aid tripwire migrants; whomever,
definitively ID'ed, come to heel with that *the*

whose screeds of sweat perforate the immortal dolls,
on smooth desktops, families of rouged dolls nest,

statements snake out from their abdomen, "we have
been led to believe, we have been struck to stumble"
(104)

stimulate to bound is form Verse
regularity of expectations
less the and
read to trying be will they more the reader the sophisticated
active scissors the make to meter for
to is effect one So
reader of circles outer and inner separate
tradition verse of simulation Visual
rhythm of structures internal the of perception with interferes
syntax and repetition
Suprasegmentals
divisions segment the hide
that
The assembled fully be can it before proposition every fracture
four first the that so relineated be instance for could poetry
read lines

Let's understand
this body controls world athletics

bale out
bring a near miss
revile a new manager
professes continuity
favors cold authentic choice
This is a disclaimer
masquerades as inevitability

the as much so nothing resembles it way this in out Set
like books in used form verse
Raworth's Tom
Eternal Sections
a does then What
Instead BILE using by gain poet
and clauses well-formed to line the linking of
the disjunction and parataxis mark line-break the letting then
disjunction
end line the at occasionally as well as lines inside occurs
tends Poetry
phrases recognizable stack to
them with bricolage speculative invite and columns in
uncertainty with charged neither is ending line The
force assertoric any if much have line the does nor
authority no sentence No
the and reaction of wariness the both keeps BILE
active assertion of possibility
Unanswering Rational Shore poem recent Prynne's H. J.
a in line-break the practices
manner similar

On the track the news radiates like a planet auction
for the best rates hard to chew. If it seems too good,
sucker, the pap is surely toxic, unless the glad
hand goes your way, soft as velvet. The strokes
of the palm not even touched, a waft of livid air
gives the take its donation, sexual preening overtly
lavish in symmetry; your flicker goes to mine and
(no page no.)

verse stanzaic traditional be could this appearance visual In
and frustration rouses therefore expectations such with Reading
and disorientation even
can this
I Here with work to able be will poem the that emotions elicit
detour a take to want
the studies Katz Jack
everyday through performed emotions
interactions social
when rage road their for notorious are L.A. in Drivers
automobile another by off cut

> Drivers usually do not *perceive* themselves being cut off *and then decide* to construct their anger; rather, it is in seeing themselves cut off that they first find themselves angry. What makes the self-conscious nature of emotions difficult to see is that the turn on the self is done sensually and aesthetically, through a kind of living poetry, and not in the form of discursive reason that commentaries about 'reflection' have traditionally evoked. How does becoming angry when driving bring previously tacit, transcendent dimensions of action into vivid corporeal awareness? First of all, driving is itself essentially a means of transcending space, of getting from here to there. When traffic or a "rude" driver cuts one off, the experience is of falling out of a flow and being stuck or held back . . . for each participant what is collectively treated as locally transpiring will have unshared, transcendent implications in the form of sensed relevancies for other encounters in some other time and place. The emotional meanings of everyday life are naturally and necessarily hidden because selves, although they are always presented in forms that are tailored to a social time and place, are always produced by bodies, and what having a body most fundamentally means for a person is that he or she lives an ongoing continuity beyond the social situations passed through in everyday life. (34, 37)

induce reading and driving Both
the which in being of states
the world material the into out flows self

text of lines the road
forward and backward extends consciousness while
lines time extensive along
driving like skill learned a is prose justified Reading
be can that
and movement eye the of awareness conscious little so with done
letters printed the of decipherment
the that
interaction the from arising story ongoing an with merges self
with
line the than horizon longer much a has usually that narrative a
by motivated are that cuts with poetry Reading
only that means voice or metric
and instability momentary produce will enjambment
reverie the on in cut to enough not usually
The again and again reader the on in cuts however BILE
is BILE possibilities two suggest would driving with analogy
unpredictable semantically and predictable visually
a as experienced is line-break the that means which
the by off cut sudden
is which body reading phenomenological
awareness into startled
and shape verse a to conformity visual inexorable the of
of interruption the at angered be to likely
the
line the reading of work perceptual the of transcendence self's
text this with problem a be to likely not is That
to enough long not fortunately is that
of anesthesia habit's create
labor eye's the
BILE into initiated already those for that speculate would I
anger any
verse contemporary conservative at directed be will generated
layout visual the by represented
denunciation ethical of subjects target the at and
Prynne's In
toward desire of manipulation media's news the are these stanza
ends political and economic

reader A
these at anger direct well may poetries such with unfamiliar
themselves line-breaks unexpected
poem the by offered direction the in not and
could BILE
of iconic is form verse where culture a in arisen have only
of all above and authority tradition order
affects public legitimate
alter-soma fleshy its as complex as is BILE
responsibility ethical and skill poetic great requires
its of effects shear the if
verse of view exploded
readership off cut to simply not are
uneven is poetry BILE Although
texts subtle politically and brilliant some produced has it
because
emotional the and cognitive the both addressing of tactic its of
line-break the of resources
national the on founded as
verse standard in encoded passions social and ideology
risky also is It
because
of remediation the toward anger elicited direct to needs it
it of symbols convenient at not injustice
like causes eccentric into overflow to it allow to nor
revolutions prosodic grand
one uncomfortable an is acronym My
criticism or ridicule as read be could that
the as about talking am I what is risk that just but
itself poetry the of risk
a is It
still may poets risk
take to need

Chapter 6
The New Memoryism

Reading Poetry in the Nineties

I don't remember the nineties.[1] The invitation to speak at a conference entitled "Remembering the Nineties" would seem to rule me out from the start. When I perform an act of introspection and try to find memories of the nineties, all I find are disordered news images and traces of personal memory: incinerated Iraqis outside Kuwait City; John Major's grin and Bill Clinton's grin and hugs; my children in different sizes and degrees of emotional command; or a computer that has just lost what I was writing. Are those years themselves already lost, the engrams too faint, just a vast scrap heap of sensed moments, tags of speech, comings and goings, passions and research exercises, pages and tele-news-websites of faded insights? Is this a fault with my own brain, with the medial temporal lobe perhaps, which neurologists believe links the amygdala and hippocampus, structures in the brain that together consolidate memory? Perhaps enough time has not passed. Neurological research suggests that some memories improve over time; hypermnesia is a result of regular rehearsal of memories and the accompanying biochemical factors that require the passage of time. But maybe my problem is the demand to remember the nineties itself. What would such an act look like? It would surely not be a matter of looking up what reference books there might be—that would be simply the conscious synthesis of existing knowledge. This remembering ought to be a purely reflexive internal act of consciousness going behind itself to its inner sources, since memories have the distinctive quality of belonging to oneself and have, since the nineteenth century, been considered to be the core of the ego identity. It would seem as if remembering the nineties would be a paradoxical act: both confirming identity and learning the history of this recent decade for one's own memory to internalize. The idea of a collective memory of recent history, of remembering the nineties, does appear to assume that individual memory and social history are somehow integratable into acts of memory, even if there is no cultural hippocampus or political medial temporal lobe.

Memory is the new sexuality: we are our truest selves when we remember, we experience the sharpest passions through recollection, and we celebrate its erotics of delay and reenactment. Just as Lacan said there was no sexual relation, and Derrida has persistently questioned our unexamined concepts of intersubjectivity, so we should ask of these mnemics, is memory really a historical relation? As Tim Woods and I argued in our book, *Literatures of Memory*, if memory is to continue to be a useable analytic concept, we need to listen to the research of both psychologists as well as psychoanalysts, poets as well as literary theorists, while remembering that memory work is itself done according to cultural codes, and that these theories of memory are articulations of these changing codes rather than laws of a mnemonic physics. Memory might be better thought of as the work of a network of cultural practices in history than as a set of material entities or singular acts of consciousness and the unconscious. The work of Mary Carruthers and others on memory in the medieval period could be extrapolated into the much more complex worlds of contemporary practice, in which the literary text has a long biography intrinsic to its work as cultural memory, extending from composition to diverse reading uses, to performance, to cultural and economic value, and to intertextualities.

The New Historicism was a dominant force in literary and cultural studies in the eighties because it recognized that the importance of power and representation as enabling forces in the construction of subject positions made it possible to read literary and cultural texts as an important means of subject production. During the past decade the rapid growth of interest in suppressed histories of oppressed, colonized, marginalized, and annihilated peoples led to a new method of cultural and literary study that could be called the New Memoryism. Recovered histories of individual and collective self-representation make ethical and political demands that require the recognition of the different temporalities at work in recovery, atonement, trauma, and forgetting. Such history's common-sense tie to the singular personal ownership of memory, as well as the effect of influential theories of the temporality and identity formation of trauma, offers a valuable and ethically sensitive new methodology for the cultural sciences. That the New Memoryism is not already so-named may be because to do so might call too much attention to certain conceptually unjustifiable blurrings of social and individual memory, to assumptions about the subject's integrity that would embarrass a cultural theory that claims to have accepted the deconstructive critique, and to the role of communications technology in the workings of our concepts and metaphors for memory.

The New Memoryism has been made possible by this surge of general interest in memory but has yet to reflect on the consequences of its indebtedness. Memory's seductiveness as a libidinal home ground is due to the alienations of sociality and culture that are being brought about by the widespread commodification of certain new technologies and the improvised politics of resistance and reconfiguration that they have elicited. The mobile phone, the internet, the personal computer, and digital image processing have had a greater impact on the way we live than any new set of technologies since the arrival of the motor car, telephone, and radio a century earlier and are genetically modifying the ways we remember and the ways we read.

What nineties text had the most influence on the way we read now? *Gender Trouble*? *The Black Atlantic*? *Cultural Capital*?—or *Trainspotting*? *Beloved*? *The Satanic Verses*? *Bridget Jones's Diary*? I think it would be more plausible to propose a software manual for this honor. Who would have imagined that we would be reading these turgid and often impenetrable books as we struggled to make word processors, spreadsheets, databases, printers, and latterly, web pages work? Text was suddenly elusive, machine dependent, futuristic, and even uncanny. At the beginning of the decade it was still something of a novelty to see a computer on a desk, whereas now a desk without one is naked, and passing an open office door one is almost certain to see its occupants reading a screen and typing away on a keyboard. Many people more used to reading literary works than operating machinery found themselves trying to understand the puzzling machinery on their desks and how they could use it to communicate with others, all the while struggling to formulate images of social interactions it might make possible. We all had to read in new ways in the nineties, not just manuals, but computer languages and the screens themselves, newly conscious that printed material was merely "hard copy," and wondering if it might soon be superseded altogether.

The nineties were a period of constant and often uncomfortable readjustment to the rapidly changing field of technology we loosely call the computer and the internet, and a detailed history of those years would show that writers and readers were increasingly dependent on computers for word processing, archiving of drafts, data analysis, bibliographic information, communication, debate, criticism, the maintenance of most literary institutions, and eventually for the formation of new readerships through online communities. This all happened haphazardly. Nobody knew where computer technology was going, many technologies into which we put a lot of time learning their uses turned out to be turkeys, it was expensive and therefore our use of it often lagged behind market availability, and it was often time-consuming to master. Old metaphors for writing, reading, interpretation, and the circulation and reception of texts all had to be reconfigured in ad hoc ways just to enable us to comprehend what was often highly abstract or technical, however well concealed behind the walnut veneer of GUIs and flying toasters. A few constituencies of writers and readers did take to the new medium with alacrity. Hypertext novels (see Janet H. Murray's work), fan fiction, and HTML poetry (discussed by Loss Glazier in the first book on the subject) were early adopters who took advantage of the programming itself, as well as the new communications links, but if we look at the wider field of literary activity, the effects of the computer are harder to describe. Some commentators read too much William Gibson and began to talk about the virtual imaginary, losing sight of the person at the terminal and, in effect, as James Slevin puts it, "extricating human interaction in 'virtual communities' from the contextuality of time-space" (106). Such speculation also lost sight of the phenomenology of reading, which was merely subsumed into accounts of the liminal landscapes of information.

One of the best discussions of the effects of the internet on the reading of literary texts can be found in Jerome McGann's *Radiant Textuality.* He does believe that a fundamentally new modality of the text, a "quantum poetics," has emerged with computer use: "aesthetic space is organized like quantum space, where the 'identity' of the elements making up the space are perceived to shift and change, even reverse themselves, when measures of attention move across discrete quantum levels" (183). Although the scientific terminology is no more than a clever metaphor in this context, it does help illuminate features of the passage to digitization. McGann's work has focused for many years on the significance of the material text, its many manuscript and printed variants as well as their visual appearance, and to this he has also increasingly added attention to what he now calls the "rhetorical scene" (102), the whole history of readings, interpretations, and misinterpretations of a text ("we don't want to discover what the texts mean but what they might be imagined to mean or to have meant" [152]). Computers and the internet, he believes, make it possible to meet both the demands of the requisite critical analysis and the bibliographic and archival consequences of this project.

One of the basic ways this can happen is via the logics of programming itself: "the executable codes (algorithms) of computational devices have much to tell us about the functioning structures of traditional textual devices" (19), because the computer is able to manipulate and display the interdependence of markers that guide reading and semantic layers. Such work reveals that the page is a much more active generator of meaning than is usually recognized:

> For the truth is that all textualizations—but pre-eminently imaginative textualities—are organised through concurrent structures. Texts have bibliographical and linguistic structures, and those are riven by other concurrencies: rhetorical structures, grammatical, metrical, sonic, referential. The more complex the structure the more concurrencies are set in play. (90)

As his citations attest, he draws on many avant-garde writers for inspiration and then reformulates their insights in the terminology of computation, sometimes proposing new software that would assist the interpreter of literary works at the level of interpretation rather than of mere data analysis. His many examples of what a new use of computers might achieve in the interpretation of texts all share a common feature, they subject texts to procedural transformations that act like a cutaway drawing of subsystems of a three-dimensional structure (think of medical figures of the human body) and give new salience to features of the poem that were hitherto subordinated to a few critically valued dominant features. These transformations are effectively stripped of their presumptive intentionality by the mediation of the software algorithm and invite a reader of these textual conversions to project a new set of meanings, emotions, and intents from them that act rather like a directed beam of light casting strong shadows and highlighting contours of the initiating poem, making more evident the concealed harmonics that compose its tone.

McGann's discussion reminds us that we ought to have been more prepared than we were for recent changes in reading. A long revolution in reading has been underway for at least the past century. Literary reading material has enormously increased in quantity and accessibility over the past century due to the increasing cheapness of books relative to median incomes and accumulated investment in public and institutional libraries; readers with literary interests have potential access to extensive archives and are likely to own what would have seemed an exceptional number of books for a home library belonging to their counterparts a century earlier. Owning books, or being able to access them easily in a library, makes a qualitative difference in the capacity to be attentive if one wishes, to read with care and insight, just as the video makes it possible to review films to a degree once only possible for a few professionals. The context of reading has changed too. A hundred years ago, before radio and television and other widely accessible leisure entertainments for all ages and classes, reading aloud as entertainment and support for the nonliterate was common. Just as the arrival of photography radically altered painting because it rendered many former expectations and uses of painting, notably the portrait, less compelling, so too has the spread of cinema and television changed the reasons why people read and also acted as a pressure on the forms of literary text produced. Readers have changed too. In an age of widespread literacy in which almost everyone is adept at reading newspapers and magazines, substantial numbers of people are also expert readers of one or more additional categories of specialist discourse required for their job or hobby (and these texts can be so difficult to read without training as to be nearly incomprehensible to an outsider). The rapid increase in the numbers of university graduates in the humanities also means that the typical reader of a sophisticated literary work is quite likely to come to it with some training, possibly in the criticism of literature and certainly in the study of complex texts. Literary texts are therefore able to anticipate advanced levels of reading skills, including those directed at nonliterary specialisms, and skills of selective attention developed for negotiation with the myriad texts of the mass media, commercial advertising, and government agencies. Ambitious literary texts make good use of all these transformations of reading and even the most market-oriented have to take them into consideration.

A typical novel of today is white page fiction—much more a script for the mind's cinema than one of a hundred years back; today it will present actions with little or no comment, dialogue will be highly salient, and what representation of thought process there is will usually be in the form of free indirect discourse.[2] Poetry too has achieved similar virtualities and economies of expression: more white space in the line and the whiting out of discourse that would once have been expected for intelligibility. But literary texts are not just aping film and television in an attempt to be noticed, they have also jettisoned some of the purposes that earlier literature assumed: there is less need to guide the reader's attention, less need to provide a densely referenced world, and less need even to construct reading networks through the workings of the text itself if it is marketed heavily enough to create that readership. Change does not all go in one direction. At the same time, literary texts need to insist on their distinction in the face of so much media artifice, and the simplest means is to manufacture authenticity, through such strategies as those of realism, the thematization of memory, and the performance of the individuality of authorship. Poems become personal, confessional, and tell their author's stories.

Global news networks, mobile phones, digital imaging, the computer, the internet, and the many ancillary technologies—these can appear simply to be new tools for doing what we did less well before, rather than step changes in the economic, political, aesthetic, or cognitive spheres; but thinking of them as mere extensions of existing human capacity is misleading. What is changing is the character of the intersubjective and social interaction associated with speech, writing, and reading. Nor are the new technologies necessarily working in the manner that their designers intended and their proponents expect; the evidence is that people persistently transform them into forms of communication by which new forms of intimacy, friendship, and community can be evolved. With the mobile phone it is possible to talk to anyone at any time if their phone is accessible, yet text messaging has been an unexpected success for the phone companies and accounts for much of their income. E-mail is even stranger.

E-mail is successful partly because the internet lets users regulate intimacy, and this may be why no one predicted that telephone calls would be replaced by short typed letters. E-mail's current hegemony of communication would have seemed implausible to futurologists and science fiction writers who expected us all to go for some equivalent of videoconferencing and were not thinking about the social need to manage degrees of anonymity. Explanations for the success (and burden) of e-mail stress its speed, simplicity, and user control; another less well recognized cause points to much of what has happened to reading in the nineties. A different protocol governs the use of e-mail from the letter, which is now considered paradoxically both much more formal on the one hand, and more personal (a thank you is usually best handwritten for instance). It is a paradox explained by the diminished affect of e-mail. The absence of familiar nonverbal guides to interpretation, such as facial expression, voicing, handwriting, and in the case of the letter, its appearance as an object (highly formal or casually scrawled), which are replaced by what are likely to be (for most users) the presence of mildly alienating effects of the standardized computer interface itself, contribute to a flatness of expression. This neutrality of tone makes certain types of communication easier by eliminating many markers of difference that might otherwise impede the creation of networks of informative exchange across distances that are as much created by age, class, gender, religion, ethnicity, and culture, as by geography. Some of the changes in recent literary texts can be accounted for as a response to a shift of readerly interpretation of affect in text after years of immersion in e-mail production and reception.

What other changes in reading that have, or are likely to have, impact on poetry, have been brought about by the computer? Start with the screen on which text is displayed either as if it existed on a long scroll or in nonsimultaneous layers. You can't see much text at once, and it seems to be hiding just out of sight above, below, or behind the visible words, a physical condition that feels very different to printed text, which can usually be held in the hand while you flick through its rectangular frames of text or hold one steady in front of your eyes for close attention. Not much of an advance? Mouse and keyboard automation remain much more awkward to control than manually-operated bound paper. It is computer memory that starts to make a difference, whether in the ROM used for correcting, cutting, and pasting text, or the hard and floppy disks used for filing multiple drafts, semidetached versions, spare phrases and paragraphs that might come in useful later, alongside other writers' texts for sampling. Marks of mental and physical effort are erased by conversion to these digital media—no need for visible crossings-out or expressive handwriting. Each time you write a text and save it, or import someone else's composition, the text reserves accumulate, and writers become text-rich. The line between writers and readers can blur because readers themselves can easily annotate, revise, or simply rewrite others' texts (and much software ingenuity has been put to work avoiding crises in the process of doing so) becoming cowriters along the way. The metaphor of a reservoir of text, and the image of scrolls, might seem to point to the new phenomenology of reading as an immersion in a textuality without end, akin to breathing omnipresent air, but this is not yet the full story. Computer text is constantly broken up into short elements separated by usually hidden codes that will make the text break apart if it is shifted from one site to another (perhaps from e-mail into a word processor then into a web page). Mention of code is a reminder that sometimes computer text belongs to a special lexicon even though the words themselves are familiar, one in which most of the words have special meaning for a particular programming language. Finally, the page dependent markers of semantic value that so interest Jerome McGann become increasingly open to manipulation through the flexibility and visibility of this code and its mechanical operators.

The result of these demands to develop new habits of reading is an altered perceptual and cognitive relation to computer text that easily transfers itself to other practices of reading. Like driving, these practices of reading soon fall below the ordinary level of awareness. The phenomenology of reading that emerges from them shifts away from the sense of reading and writing as the only two directions of a highway into and out of the soul, and adds a very tangible third person plural. Constraints of keyboard, mouse, and screen are experienced as resistances from a machine intelligence governed by a social network whose horizon is out of sight, and these resistances are felt as both gateways and interfaces between body and machine. Text is no longer projected as a bounded material object; it is more like a landscape of which only part is visible due to the limits of the gaze. Text unrolls down the screen in a manner not unlike the road or track unrolling before the gaze in a computer simulation of driving, and that is based on the framing of landscape by a windshield, so we might be tempted to wonder if the experience of reading has more affinity with driving than before. I don't know if we should take this further. What the comparison does emphasise, besides making the point that different technologies for mediating experience may converge in surprising ways, is that computer text is presented in such a way that an area of text comes under the glare of an attention strictly bounded by the perimeter of the screen now live with potential. A book by comparison allows the dexterity of the hand to create senses of simultaneously looking at several or many pages, and the solidity of the object reassures us of its relative permanence.

The computer also foregrounds the device of mediation more than a book, which for most readers has become so easily set aside by the mind that as the eyes scan words a quasi-sensory internal experience unfolds. The computer's resistances to instant assimilation of text and its new saliences of text marking, result in many more rapid shifts back and forth between awareness of perceptual/cognitive activity and imaginative transcendence. Maybe this estrangement effect will diminish rapidly as time makes us familiar with the machines, but it seems likely that traces of the computer's mediation will remain prominent in the ordinary experience of computer reading.

These are effects of the stand-alone computer; connect it to a cable network, and e-mail and internet bring a further transformation of the phenomenology of reading. Flowing into the reservoir of text conserved in files on permanent media is an even vaster reserve of text that appears to exist in some in-between realm. My metaphors are an attempt to offer images for an experience that lacks the sort of culturally embedded guiding images of the ontology of texts that reading printed texts does have (a void into which all kinds of fantasies of virtuality rush). Most readers are aware that this half-way world engenders a new intensity, both as speed and quantity, of response to new and old texts. All reading is an interactive process, yet despite the long history of a provision of margins for notes, the printed text is ill-equipped to record responses that have developed as far as an urge to write further than the text goes, and there is rarely any means of circulating one's marginalia to other readers or to the writer (think of how much we now value the marginalia of great writers). The literary book as a singular object also hinders recognition of the workings of readership because it acts as an obvious icon of both autonomous authorship and autonomous reading, the latter a strong illusion despite the fact that there are usually many other coeval copies, some even being coevally read, so that the text's cultural work can take place only in isolated pockets that become aware of each other over time, if at all. In practice, the encompassing literary field or movement can partially function like this—one novel is answered by another, magazines provide reviews and letters that can at least represent aspects of collective response—a process that is rarely representative or democratic.

There is one last aspect of the phenomenology of internet reading that has helped give rise to the New Memoryism. The success of the printed book depended on several interdependent features that all ultimately tie into the workings of memory: ease of deciphering letters and scanning the words and pages; ease of rereading and rechecking what was read in order to be clear and certain; compression both cognitive and material that writing makes possible compared to oral presentation (so much information can be carried in a portable form); record keeping and reference; the transmission across time and space of human knowledge and insight in an enduring form; the lightness of physical and perceptual effort required to call out its pleasures, emotions, and memories. Books in any quantity are cumbersome, however small, and an individual reader can only ever hope to have ready access to a tiny percentage of the texts that exist, meaning that the support for memory that stems from the culture of the book is dependent on contingent factors largely irrelevant to what it might wish to establish. The internet, although at an early stage, appears to be on the way to offering an archive of all extant printed texts as well as accompanying commentaries, and however far short it falls of this expectation, it already creates a phenomenological strain on the individual's capacity to work with it as a form of memory. A rhetoric of memory that is used to name the handling of electrical charges on which much of the power of computers depend, and the similarity of reading on screen to the reading of printed texts, creates a new and tense phenomenology of reading. The internet appears to carry over the book's mnemic functions and become one vast undifferentiated memory, out of which individual identity has to struggle to hold its own. It is from this that the extraordinary passion for personal memory has arisen, as much as from the political goals of disenfranchised groups.

A new phenomenology of reading will always be registered most quickly by linguistically sensitive genres like poetry, a highly responsive seismograph of changes in communicative interaction, especially reading's interpretive responses to speech and writing. We would expect to see the effects written across recent poetry with particular sharpness, and two very different bodies of recent poetry suggest themselves as evidence of the transformations that have been occurring: first, winners of the UK literary prize the Whitbread prize for poetry, which is an acknowledgement of wide sales and readership, and second, avant-garde poets whose work explicitly critiques economic, political, and environmental crises of late modernity. How, if at all, have they registered the new habits of reading produced by the phenomenology of computer-driven communications, and how do their forms and themes add detail to the kind of speculations I have offered on changes in the self-representations generated by our literary reading practices over the past decade?

The Whitbread prize for poetry, established in 1971, is one of a group of literary prizes awarded under this name (a prominent UK company) to different categories of book each year, and is a good index of popularity for poets. Its explicit commitment to "identifying and celebrating some of the most enjoyable books published in the UK each year" (see www.whitbread-bookawards.co.uk) suggests how it goes about this. The prizes for the last decade went to the following books of poetry:

1990	Paul Durcan	*Daddy Daddy*
1991	Michael Longley	*Gorse Fires*
1992	Tony Harrison	*The Gaze of the Gorgon*
1993	Carol Ann Duffy	*Mean Time*
1994	James Fenton	*Out of Danger*
1995	Bernard O'Donoghue	*Gunpowder*
1996	Seamus Heaney	*The Spirit Level*
1997	Ted Hughes	*Tales from Ovid*
1998	Ted Hughes	*Birthday Letters*
1999	Seamus Heaney	*Beowulf*
2000	John Burnside	*The Asylum Dance*

Here are some of the leading names in British poetry for the past quarter century, poets studied by several generations of schoolchildren, Harrison,

Heaney, and Hughes; some currently high-profile poets, Duffy, Fenton, and Longley; as well as three slightly less well-known figures, Burnside, Durcan, and O'Donoghue. It is in no way representative of poetry in the round, of course: only one woman, no immigrant writer, and none of the modernists. Nor is this a poetry whose topics and tropes could be said to represent the texture of the history of this decade—there is almost no new technology evident, and not much contemporary history outside Fenton's collection. These are books in which the classics loom large, the landscapes are rural, and the relationships familial.

Look more closely, however, and the impact of the internet computer is there like stage machinery behind the poetic flats and the pastoral-lite. It is there first of all as the shadow against which the poems insist on the endurance of poetry's civilizing mission and its transcendence of local historical change. Tony Harrison can write as if classical Greek culture were simply extending itself in contemporary verse and begin the poem "The Pomegranates of Patmos" (from *The Gaze of the Gorgon*) in the persona of a sensualist whose brother is studying chiliastic dogma with St John of the Apocalypse. Seamus Heaney introduces his translation of *Beowulf* by claiming it as "one of the foundation works of poetry in English" (1). Ovid, whose narratives have hardly ever been out of the poetry lists in some form or other, is brought to popular attention yet again, this time by Ted Hughes. Such worlds are attractively simple compared to ours, as Heaney tacitly admits in his translation: poets are appreciated for their "clear songs" as they sit on the "mead benches" of a hall from an earlier age. This all seems the antithesis of silicon chips and coded electrical messages, but such renewed popularity for writing in the margins of the classics is actually part of a much wider literary development for which the internet has been very important. Many websites now host what is popularly known as "fan fiction," narrative fiction written by fans of well-known stories (ranging from epics to classic novels and television series) that extrapolates or interpolates its own subnarratives like a virus within the urtext. You can write back to the text, either metacritically, in your judgments, or by inventing new episodes, or even by seducing the characters of well-known novels, films, and television series in paraplots.

When poets write back to the classics they are readers who are becoming cowriters, just as computer users begin to find themselves coauthors of the fabric of the web, and these seemingly very traditional poems are signs of a growing trend, stimulated by the phenomenology of reading toward the blurring of reading and writing. One popular website, www.fanfiction.net, listed sixty rewritings of Homer when I looked in October 2002. Most of this marginalia fiction is short and semianonymous: a new ending in which Odysseus arranges to marry his son to Princess Samean from Crete; an episode in which Telemachus is made spellbound for a month by the beauty of a sea-nymph; and another new ending in which Odysseus and Penelope reconfirm their marriage vows and, more importantly, are reconciled with the parents of the dead suitors, all done in a skillful pastiche of Homeric rhetoric. An interactive facility on this website enables anyone to offer a review of the fiction, and one commentator (more popular rewritable texts will have many of these) has taken advantage of this to say that the confirmation-of-vows ending is "extremely creative and well-written" (note the insistence that such work can be "creative"). Homer is not the main topic of interest—popular novels and movies are the most written over. The same thing is going on in literary fiction too—sophisticated literary authors are writing sequels and interpolations for everything in the canon from Robinson Crusoe to Sherlock Holmes and Marcel Proust.[3] Poets have always been interested in translation and sustaining a tradition through the use of prestigious forms of prosody, layout, tropes, and reworkings of established genres like pastoral or ode. The popularity of this poetry in the nineties suggests that the internet has indeed transformed the phenomenology of reading into a practice that is more liminally compositional than ever before. A classic narrative is one that lots of readers know and can be treated not as a complete text that is fixed beyond refurbishment but more like an evolving house and grounds onto which more text can be added, reshaping existing plots and leading characters into new sequels, not only in the manner of the television series, but as a form of even more direct participatory production.

This Whitbread-prize poetry also shows the influence of the internet and the computer in its pervasive emphasis on the sustaining and guiding power of memory. John Burnside, a poet who had worked for some years in the computer industry, returns again and again to the attempt to capture the significance of memory in daily life. In one poem, "The Singer," the confusion of feeling "all at sea" in one's life is the cue for this concluding anamnesic sentiment:

At sea
the stillness thickens, charged with idle boats
and schools of fishes swimming in the blur
of memory, or joy, or what it is
to happen in the hurry of a world
that ebbs and flows like song, or given light,
against the random static of the dark. (59)

The threatening conditions of late modernity are summarized by the image of "random static," a form of electric charge that is the enemy of the precise manipulation of current on which computers depend. Engineers repairing computers have to watch out for static carried by their bodies as they touch delicate components. In Burnside's complex image, however, the static is also metonymic of the entire phenomenon of electronic technology that, it is suggested, is part of the darkness that threatens organic life and its vital memory. Reviewers were very drawn to the appeal of this message. One said: "Such poetry is badly needed in an age when religion fails many, its language polluted and stale. An age when the ocean of science weighs heavy on our hands—the weight of logic that says there is nothing sacred" (Taylor 99). The book has an epigram from Martin Heidegger (a philosopher who was deeply skeptical about an earlier phase of technology that now looks primitive when compared to computers) on the theme of "dwelling," and this points to the modernity-averse tone of the book. It represents modernity only indirectly through the borrowed poetic forms of free verse, much of which owes its stepped shapes to the poetic line developed by William Carlos Williams. This turns out to be largely a visual and therefore empty form of modernity and furthers the overall theme: the triadic tiers and short lines are only partially active as markers of emotional and enunciatory stress, and often merely indicate syntactically defined clauses or phrases.

Anecdotes whose authenticity is carefully maintained are refracted by Burnside through what another reviewer called the "prism of memory" (Wardle), and transmuted into a guiding value to be set against this dangerous static of late modernity. A poetic strategy familiar from a hundred other volumes of contemporary poetry unfolds in the central long poem "Fields": a remembered image of his father cleaning a mower ("a man in an old white shirt / a pair of jeans / some workboots he'd bought for a job"),[4] is followed by an elegiac account of taking these clothes out into a field where he buried them and was left with a tantalizing hint of promise ("the pull of the withheld"). This is a poetry of memory as nostalgia for childhood and lost loves, as well as a nostalgia for Romantic visions. His poem "Blue" might be a seaide postcard rewrite of Wordsworth's meditation on memory and change "Lines Written Above Tintern Abbey," when it notes:

> The way some towns would change under a rain
> in childhood
> and how they no longer do, or are never quite
> as blue as they were (45)

Memory is insistently personalized in Burnside's book in ways that invite the reader to share the pleasures of familial recollection. This is from part 4 of "Fields":

> Be quick when you switch on the light
> and you'll see the dark
> was how my father put it:
>   catch
> the otherlife of things
>   before a look
> immerses them. (42)

Does the way this passage and the previous one, with its image of memory as a sea, both conceptualize memory owe anything to the experience of computer reading? The poem's content avoids technology, but I think the way the poem enacts memory is homologous to the computer's treatment of its archive. Memory of his father's wisdom is made available the way a computer file is accessed, and in this instance the narrative itself could be reread as an allegory of the phenomenology of reading on the computer: switching on the internet produces a sense of darkness, of the invisible but seemingly infinite resources and lives out there on the net that have to be channeled through the gaze of the user, until eventually a corner of the text that represents this "otherlife" can be lit by our gaze. Such poetry of memory strives for an authenticity capable of resisting the dissolution of identity that would supposedly follow the loss of acknowledgement of one's own personal memory in the vast anonymity of new communications technology.

The work of a somewhat different Whitbread poet, Bernard O'Donoghue, suggests that the New Memoryism is an attempt to reenchant everyday life. He writes poems in which his identity as an Irishman in Britain is the theme, either told in a series of self-deprecating anecdotes of present-day encounters in which his background is highly salient or through memories of childhood that outline the implications of such a history: photographs of Canada provided by the Sun Life Insurance company that contrasted with the wet Irish landscape of childhood, the empty shell cases his father used to leave lying around, or road signs for places with exotic names. Catherine Fisher's review in *Poetry Wales* shows why the New Memoryism is so valued:

> Bernard O'Donoghue's second collection of poems is a delight, a book with a quiet charm and a beguiling often wry, simplicity. His poems deal very much with the minutiae of life, sparking quiet musings and ponderings, coming to no overt conclusions, but offering glimpses of truth, glimmers of understanding. . . . The collection is full of memories . . . a series of poems that reveal more than they tell, and which are entirely memorable. (C. Fisher 64)

Poems full of the author's memories that are also readily remembered by the reader doubly confirm that memory's support for identity continues.

Similar sentiments can be found in the work of other poets on the Whitbread list. One critic cites James Fenton defining of the lyric poem in a manner that makes plain just how slant from history poetic memory can be in practice (although many of Fenton's own poems, not surprisingly given his success as the writer of lyrics for musicals, belong more to a tradition of ballads and songs): "A lyric is about a particular feeling, not a particular person, it's about a moment either in your own life or in the life of somebody else. What you do is truthfully to represent the moment and that's the thing that will stand out of the lyric, the truth of the moment" (Norman). Only moments matter, and poems file the experience of them. When the Whitbread prize judges looked for terms in which to praise John Burnside, they said that *The Asylum Dance* is "a sensory delight with an epiphany on every page."[5] "Epiphany" has become a synonym for intense personal memory.

These reviews indicate the poetic effects that made this prize-winning poetry: authentic memories, cues that elicit complementary eidetic responses from the reader, and the creation of an archive of memories significant for their capacity to speak from the local to the general or from the private reader to the public world of the readership. The growth of computing and the internet have played a part in making these features seem highly significant as signs of poetic value, and all of them are aspects of the presentation of identity. Many commentators have noted that the internet fosters extemporized identity. Participants in discussion lists, for example, can hide their gender, age, and other forms of identity behind pseudonyms and verbal formulae. Computing always requires users to muse, ponder, and respond, however superficially, and a poetry that also invites such participation at this level is likely to fit with readers' changing habits and expectations. The computer and the internet create the impression that they contain vast archives of cultural memory, everyday trivia, and crucial data, and that to work with a computer is to link one's own local context with this spanning memory. The most successful recent UK poetry clearly knows this and offers popular solutions that appease the desire to put a familiar, traditional face on this disturbingly unprecedented phenomenon.

The Whitbread poets rarely mention the new technology and have even less to say about its impact. Poets whose work appears in little magazines and other low-budget and noncommercial publications have been much more ready to investigate the computer as a phenomenon. Some, like John Cayley, have produced work in hypercard or hypertext, or work that otherwise makes use of the possibilities of using the computer to animate text as it is read, and others have written poems that enact the thrills and linguistic excesses of the video game (Douglas Oliver's "The Video House of Fame" [*Arrondissements*]), exploit the graphics and printing power of the computer (Caroline Bergvall's *Éclat*), or take up the metaphoricity of the jargon (J. H. Prynne's "Select an object with no predecessors" in *For the Monogram*). These poems make the new communications technology part of their field of reference, semantic, visual, and lexical, all broadly at the level of content. Other changes are taking place in which reading becomes more reflexive and more aware of its intersubjective project, treating text as an active archival spreadsheet of textual possibilities waiting to be assembled locally for the specific reading.

One text that demonstrates both qualities is Drew Milne's *The Gates of Gaza.* Like Prynne's *For the Monogram,* it employs many computer terms ("tortured armies leased to / light-weight image editors") as it moves between the scene of Samson's capture, the modern Gaza Strip, and the media of late modernity, a jargon that is consonant with its style. Like many contemporary British avant-garde poems, it takes an apparently traditional form, four stanzas of three lines of equal length, and then breaks the syntax into a series of disjunct phrases that spill across the line-breaks, creating uncertainty each time about the line's value.

IV.
the cloth options out just to drop
and drag, processing straight on
back as if to a file shrunk fresco

of its miraculous trigonometry on
one stilling pleonasm, dark night
withstood, a lunch-break backslash

then simply beds down the paving
for domain values of the mandate
a wild fling through clogged rota

let fall the haughty moon to loaf
as each casual battle has a furry
idol bouncing off the windscreen
(no page nos.)

The poem has epigraphs that offer two apparently opposed views of what constitutes essential humanity, one from the Dead Sea Scrolls, which talks of human "clay," and one from Galen Strawson, which says that "one could in principle create a normally experiencing human being out of a piano." Instead of offering explicit opinions on these issues, as the prize-winning poetry tends to do in its striving for an explicit wisdom language, this poem offers instead a peregrinating narrative located in an environment changing as rapidly as a fast-cut film, and whose narrative elements need to be treated metaphorically if they are to produce cognitive and affective cohesion. Guidance for the reader's interpretive agenda is not signposted in large letters. It is a text that already takes for granted a reader who is used to selecting a section of text and manipulating it according to protocols embedded in the text as it is rendered by the computer and internet. Janet H. Murray, in her study of computer narrative, *Hamlet on the Holodeck,* calls the computer "the most powerful representational medium ever invented" (Murray 284), because it enables the user to push the construction and presentation of fictional narrative much further than the printed novel or even television serial drama could ever manage. "On the computer we can lay out all the simultaneous actions in one grid and then allow the interactor to navigate among them. We can have the expansiveness of the novel with the rapid intercutting of the film" (157). Each stanza of Milne's poem might be a frame or screen page of text whose order, whilst significant, does not restrict the cross-combining or even wholesale reconfiguration of its immanent semantics.

Two other poets whose work is intelligently responsive to shifting conditions of readership, Rob MacKenzie and Helen Macdonald, both have interests in science that may well account for their willingness to accommodate rather than resist. MacKenzie is a research scientist, and these lines from "Taliban Lamp-post" (Johnson 128) (written before the recent U.S. invasion) show just how integral his knowledge can be to his poetics:

> The crystal grows; fault remains the same.
> Archimedes 'n Escher laugh uncontrollably,
> but only if the playground's bigger than the game
> an' the rain's a drizzle. Simple
> in the lab, but in the earth's sense?
>
> Here flux's are 'n flux
> waves dissipate
> an' all our measurements ask
>
> should gaelic live?
> Kirk aye, toun no, schule tint.
>
> Duendishly prepositional, spectral,
> more regular'n english,

though there's no length of learning
let's you talk with your parents.

Chan e "Dè gaidhlig a th'air x" ach
"Dè a tha gorm'sa bheurla?".
Teip gu teip.

This complex and witty meditation on various sorts of fundamentalist belief and the extremes of social oppression they can lead to, emerges from an interest in the interdependence of different cultures and knowledges. Its globalist poetics offers world images such as the Taliban hatred of beardless men (strung up on lampposts) as metaphors for the dangers of cross-cultural hostilities, and also allows the swift transition from one register to another ("The phase space dells're filling up," or "The stoor, enjambement, drug n'shop"), by which this poetics can absorb concepts from physics, street talk, Celtic myth, and Gaelic slang, to host questions about its own assumptions. A globalist poetics could not avoid risks of imperialism and misrepresentation. In the section I have quoted, which asks difficult questions about the value of Gaelic today, the rapid shift of register is also a way of hyperlinking the contexts of the words together, and of signaling the paths that responsive discussion might take.

Helen Macdonald, an expert on the rearing of birds of prey ("a hawk / rousing one's mind from safety and tameable illness / to beautiful comprehension in the form of a hunch / as patience directs" [22]) and on the history of falconry, writes a poetry that anticipates a reader who has developed the special readerly competence to employ types of transformation made current by the computer and the internet. I quote the entirety of the first, short poem to show how this works:

Taxonomy

Wren. Full song. No subsong. Call of alarm, spreketh & ought
damage the eyes with its form, small body, tail pricked up &
beak like a hair

trailed through briars & at a distance scored with lime scent in
the nose
like scrapings from a goldsmith's cuttle, rock alum & fair butter
well-temped

which script goes is unrecognised by this one, is pulled by the ear
in anger the line at fault is under and inwardly drear as a bridge
in winter

reared up inotherwise to seal the eyes through darkness, the
bridge speaks
it does not speak, the starlings speak that steal the speech of
men, *uc antea*

a spark that meets the idea of itself, apparently fearless.
Ah cruelty. And I had not stopped to think upon it

& I had not extended it into the world for love for naught. (7)

The poem goes through a series of transformations, from headword to subheadings to shifts of linguistic temporality ("spreketh"), to narrative of memory (but whose is not clear), to metapoetic reflection, during which the wren, at risk from starlings, becomes a sign of hope and danger. Each shift could be imagined as a hyperlink. Click on "wren" and you reach "full song" and see that there is no further link, "no subsong." The linear continuity of a text that juxtaposes distinct sections of syntactically defined meaning simulates the scrolling continuous text of a computer whose proximity is no guarantee of affinity and similarly invites a cut-and-paste reader response. Authorship shifts from anonymous ornithological reference to early modern authors, to the apparently authentic memory of this author, to what might be processing instructions. Just as the off-rhymes draw attention to the residual nonrhyming phonemes that might otherwise be out of earshot as it were, the entire poem invites the reader to follow the *subsong* of the words themselves, from the title onward. "Taxonomy" can be heard slowly as a series of phonetic elements making up the phrase "[at]tacks on oh me," and many of the more salient words in the poem invite similar disarticulation, whilst not necessarily endorsing all consequences ("And I had not stopped to think upon it"). It is a poem that is used to the ceding of absolute authorship during computerized reading.

In the poem "Earth Station," Macdonald looks across a rural landscape dominated by radio telescope dishes and recalls an inexplicit dialogue between author and an unnamed man, whose final comment resonates with my discussion of the New Memoryism: "speech in wires he laughed and returned the compliment / because they were speaking for him, as they had always done" (58). These poetic strategies that I have demarcated as ones that anticipate a readerly expertise imposed by the phenomenology of reading that is still emerging from the use of computer and internet as a new mode of textual communication may not seem new in themselves. And this is part of my point. They "speak for us as they had always done" because what is happening is not that some alien system is demanding that we learn an entirely new language of reading; the computer and internet are enabling long-established constituents of textual activity to be developed much further than hitherto, creating new possibilities of meaning and compression and making demands on our capability as readers. None of my "avant-garde" poets regard this simply with equanimity, but they don't deny that these changes are occurring; they go ahead with explorations of the new passages of intersubjectivity, wondering all the time what the ethics and aesthetics of this condition might be. The New Memoryism may become a powerful critical method if it reflects on the paradoxes of its genesis in individual history, cultures, and the machine-coordinated writings by which narrative is increasingly mediated. Whatever memory will become, it will have to incorporate the mnemic filestores spread across the internet as well as those waiting among our neurons.

Chapter 7
Dirigibles

The first successful dirigible flight was made by the Brazilian aviator Alberto Santos-Dumont in Paris in 1901. "At about midday, on October 18, he suddenly decided to start. At half-past two the balloon rose and, with a gentle breeze astern, headed for the Eiffel Tower at a good pace" (Williams 52). This was his third attempt to win the prize (of 100,000 francs) announced a year earlier for the first person to make a journey from the Aero Club to the Eiffel Tower and back in thirty minutes (Nancy Winters says it was October 19 [46]). Things soon began to go wrong. "The guide rope caught on a house and pulled the balloon up with a jerk, causing it to swing in an alarming manner. People rushed up and unhitched the rope, allowing the airship to resume its journey. Rising to a height of about 800 feet, Santos-Dumont circled the Tower at a respectful distance, and 9 minutes from the start was heading for home in the face of the breeze" (Williams 52). A photograph shows the dirigible looking like a pair of giant pursed lips passing surrealistically above the girders.

> The motor now began to fire irregularly and for a time things looked as if the airship would be swept backwards against the Tower with disastrous results. At the critical moment the engine picked up again till the danger was past, though soon it recommenced misfiring, with the result that the balloon lost height quickly, and narrowly escaped hitting the grand-stand of the Auteuil racecourse. As the balloon approached the Aero Park the motor got into its stride again, and some of the time lost was made up. Great excite-

> ment prevailed among the spectators, for it had now become evident that, if the prize were won, it would be won by seconds only. With three-quarters of a minute in hand the airship crossed the mark, but at such a height that the guide rope was just out of reach, and a minute and a half more elapsed before it could be caught. (53)

The outcome was disputed; it took two weeks of deliberation about the timing before he was awarded the prize. "Man flies," his childhood friend Pedro wrote to him (Winters 55).

The words uttered by cartoon characters in comics are usually presented in white ellipsoids held in place against some anti-gravitational force by a downward tethering nipple pointing at their speaker. These are the descendants of the speech "balloons," which began to appear intermittently in the new color comics included as supplements to New York newspapers in the eighteen-nineties (their antecedents go back to political broadsides and have even been traced to Renaissance experiments like those of Bruno di Giovanni reported by Vasari [Carrier 41]), and first became a consistent convention for the representation of utterances in Rudolph Dirks's "Katzenjammer Kids" of 1897 (in the early frames they look uncannily like children's party balloons with long strings attaching the smallish print zone to a point near the mouth of the character).

Balloon flight was an increasing preoccupation of the eighteen-eighties and -nineties, and navigability was the goal that remained elusive despite Henri Giffard's invention of a steerable balloon as far back as 1852. It was the well-publicized experiments of Alberto Santos-Dumont with petrol engine airships filled with helium (later known as blimps) between 1898 and 1905 in France, and the initially less-successful attempts of the retired Count Von Zeppelin in Germany, that made balloon transport a possibility and also made "the distinction between *ballon spherique* (the ordinary globular, drifting balloon) and *ballon dirigeable* (the elongated, power-driven balloon or airship)" (Stubelius 171) of general interest. Reports on these successes introduced the word "dirigible" into English where it became well established until the First World War, when the navy, which in those days was responsible for aircraft and had always preferred the term "airship," ensured that this more nautical word gained ascendancy. In any case, once the steerage of a lighter-than-air craft could be taken for granted the emphasis on control was redundant.

This was the second time the word had fallen from grace: "dirigible" was formerly used mostly as an adjective derived from the Latin *dirigibilis,* and by the early nineteenth century had come to refer to the alleged control of the mind over its own functioning. By the late nineteenth century, whether the mind was believed to be a stream, a hypnotizable dupe, or tied to a *dirigiste* unconscious, few people thought the old meaning plausible. Naming the space of printed speech a speech balloon was therefore doubly appropriate, since the implicit ambiguity as to whether this balloon is dirigible or not corresponded both to the history of intense interest in the dirigibility or otherwise of the mind, and the modernity of what was then the latest form of transport.

William Blake's verbal art did not use speech balloons or anything equivalent—he wanted his text to be written across the cosmos of his images to emphasize both that language inhered in this visualized world, and that the actual word-crossed image's representations could be trusted just because they manifested the visibility of understanding rather than retinal memory. Pictorial conventions of the comic, one of the most commercially active forms of art, would set speech apart from the visible world, although the sounds of the deconstruction of material culture by explosions and other forms of damage have been represented by letters dancing in the picture plane.

"For H.D. the written image is already a palimpsest, written-over and redacted through centuries. Far from the young Pound's optimistically generative turbines, the 'image' in H.D. cannot forget the errors and miswritings of the past" (Willis 69).

From the north and into Middle English came *bal,* a globe or globular body to give the English the ball; from the south came the French *bal,* dancing, and from Italian, *ballo,* to give the ball as dance party; from Italian also came *ballone,* a "great ball or footeball" mentioned by Florio, giving us balloons; and from the Latin *balare* came ballad and ballet, the latter of which gradually gave way to ballad in order to distinguish the dance of the intellect in verse from the dance of the social body. Globes, balls, dancing, balloons, poems: the dictionary cautions us not to confuse *bal* (ME) with *bal* (FR) or, presumably, balloons with poems.

> As balloons are to the poet, so to the ground
> Its varied assortment of trees. The more assorted they are, the
> Vaster his experience. Sometimes
> You catch sight of them on a level with the top story of a house,
> Strung up there for publicity purposes. Or like those bubbles
> Children make with a kind of ring, not a pipe, and probably
>   using some detergent
> Rather than plain everyday soap and water. Where was I? The
>   balloons
> Drift thoughtfully over the land, not exactly commenting on it;
> These are the range of the poet's experience. He can hide in trees
> Like a hamadryad, but wisely prefers not to, letting the balloons
> Idle him out of existence, as a car idles. (Ashbery 1997, 200)

Poems as child's play, self-advertisement, nondirigible wandering thought (one perception leads directly to a further perception but not at the poet's will), reports on the self buffeted about by other systems as it proceeds on the journey of life, glimpsing "unknown horizons" and, like another Los, always "inventing systems." All these are familiar enough in contemporary poetry. This is not the end of Ashbery's meditation on the seeming helplessness of the poet, however, because he subsequently allows that the poet does sometimes take responsibility, is "best" when "placed squarely in front of his dilemma, on all fours before the lamentable spectacle of the unknown." Poet on all fours, animal, fully embodied, and at last acknowledging the boundaries of knowledge, the omnipresence of the unknown in everyday life.

The metaphor finds its way into Charles Altieri's discussion of Ashbery's poem "Self-Portrait in a Convex Mirror," where its power of entrapment supersedes any airborne freedoms it might offer:

> The terms themselves suggest an implicit motive for the entire meditation, the obsessive desire to find some kind of peace and release from the burdens of thinking. When all the reflections keep

> returning to the same note, and this note does not seem required by the content of each section, we are invited to see the thinking as motivated not only by the painting but also by some unstatable need in the subject. This need seems at once relieved and intensified by the encounter with the painting, as if the speaker's own mental hand were divided between the desire to identify and a desire to break out of the balloon of his own endlessly circling monologue. The purest abstractions remain complex emotional acts dramatically grounded in a rich sense of thinking as an act balanced between idealizing power and the pathos of distortion. . . . The fifth section, then, in effect breaks the balloon once more and urgently faces up to a sharpened sense of contingencies—both of the painting's place amid historical events and of the speaker as agent within his historical setting. (158)

Or is this a speech balloon? Whichever it is it needs to watch out for these sharp points.

"How do we understand this boundary," is a question that Lyn Hejinian also asks:

> Along comes something—*launched in context.*
> How do we understand this boundary?
> Let's begin by posing it as a dilemma. The term comes from the Greek, *dilemmatos,* and means "involving two assumptions," and so we begin by proposing that the boundary is not an edge but a conjunction—that the dilemma bears the *meaning* of conjunction: encounter, possible confusion, alteration exerted through reciprocal influence, etc.—the kind of situation that is typical, I might add, along borders between nations, between speakers of different languages, between neighboring ecosystems, etc. . . . *Dilemma* in this sense, constitutes that part of a poetics which we could call its *prepoetics*—a prepoetics functioning not as a condition either logically or chronologically prior to the formulation of a poetics but as a condition necessary and simultaneous to it—a current running through it. (Hejinian 339)

She is wary of any dirigibility of poetic imagination, "a reason that plows its way to authority," and cites Hannah Arendt's discussion of the boundlessness of action in *The Human Condition* in support of the belief that "authority over being is thus dispersed . . . in the boundlessness" (Arendt 352) (although the use of such citation might appear to spring from the furrow of authorship's power), and so concludes that poets should "enter and inhabit" the boundaries, not try to rise above them in their vehicles of poetic imagination or "totalize" them with systems of explanation. Prepoetics is the condition of the poetry for which Hejinian speaks, although to use this word "condition" so ballasted with philosophical freight might be misleading, since what she is outlining might be better named, in Giorgio Agamben's words, a "being-thus," or more conventionally, a context. But what is this condition?

Arendt's discussion of action's unbounded range of effects is careful to emphasize that although these futural ripples cannot be known at the launch of an action, and can never be encompassed by one perspective, they are nevertheless actual and specific, and potentially intelligible, however unpredictable. Unboundedness is therefore only one face of the unknown, although as she points out, such unpredictability does all too often present a terrifying face to the "frailty of human institutions and laws" (191). Dirigibility can only emerge from the labor of recognitions and histories that painstakingly sustain the tattered public realm.

The recent convergence of thoughtful essays on Prynne's later poetry by John Wilkinson, Robin Purves, and Drew Milne is cause for celebration. They have made explicit the difficulties of reading and interpreting the later poetry of J. H. Prynne in a manner that is at once highly perceptive, well argued, attentive to aesthetics, philosophy, and psychoanalysis, and, above all, willing to admit with admirable honesty to their own provisional understandings and residual doubt. All three openly speculate as to whether the poetry's tone of confident asseveration, which enfolds readers by the force of its syntactical emulations of urgent moral appeal and its apparent promises of achievable insight, should be trusted, by drawing attention to an alleged interpretative deficit in the accounts of Prynne's work over the past fifteen years and offering model remedies. Wilkinson does this by reading *Not-You* (1993) closely, and Milne by reading *For the Monogram* (1997). Purves goes farthest in expressing doubts: "Critical consensus about the ethical centre of Prynne's poetics *flourishes* without seeming to have understood anything he has written in the last fifteen years, being a consensus with baffles attached, evincing a fixation with a dogma which no single constituent seems willing, or able, to profess" (53). Leaving aside the polemical exaggeration of total incomprehension, there is considerable agreement that there is justice to this criticism. But what is this dogma and its secret bond to which Purves alludes?

My copy of Webster offers as a main definition of poem, "a composition in verse," which still seems evasive even when this definition is compounded with the entry for "verse": "metrical language." Although the second definition for poem appears at first sight just as circular, its concentration on the unity of the text and the link to the readership perhaps unwittingly does reveal the tacitly assumed ontology of poetry with considerable accuracy—"a piece of poetry designed as a unit and communicating to the reader the sense of a complete experience." A poem is a "piece" that is, it is all of a piece, a "unit," which communicates with another unit, the "reader," and what is communicated is "complete." The poem's essential characteristics are imagined in terms of a relation between a single agent, the poet, composing the text with the intention of producing something that forms a coherent whole, and a single reader, whose eyes track across the writing as his or her mind processes the information. For some purposes this simplified abstraction can be adequate, but it occludes many strategies that modernist and avant-garde writers deliberately chose to practice and leads to the neglect of some features of earlier poetry too.

Close reading of poetry is perilously out of date. Available languages and concepts for discussing prosody, literary devices, emotion, cognition, ethics, genres, allusion, image, performance, and a myriad of other practices internal to the text's relation to readerships by which meaning may appear are cut back by narrowly conceived literary political debates and restricted canons of exempla. How has this come about given the opportunities presented by contemporary poets? Later modernist poets have attempted many new modes of utterance and invited different acts of reading that challenge and guide their readers, and in doing so they have opened many backward passages into earlier poetry's newly evident mitochondrial efforts, while literary criticism has proffered disappointingly few commensurate recognitions. The short answer would be that the rejection of the techniques of practical criticism as a naturalization of ideology by literary theorists, coupled with the shift to both ideological critique from the directions of feminism, postcolonialism, queer theory, and to the emulsification of literary texts into discursive economies managed by the New Historicism, has overdetermined the formalist stigma of such literary techniques. Meanwhile the readership of poetry became so adept at the formal steps of new critical and modernist hermeneutics that its skill led to a largely unnoticed impasse between such metropolitan command of the usual routes and the ollies and nollies of contemporary poets who wanted to show other possibilities to their readers. This is not to say that the problems raised by Wilkinson, Purves, and Milne can be resolved by running up some new interpretative tools and decks according to a few designs by contemporary poets. A more promising response would be to unfold the social histories sedimented in the tail *slizzers,* the *gnar* potential, raging *seshes,* or for those of you not familiar with the chilled skateboard zones, the repertoire of semantic music emanating from the instruments, forms, friendships, beliefs, authorities, anarchisms, and even deaths of reception.

Structure? Visual admiration of the building is only a small part. Its rooms, halls, stairs, mezzanines, orifices and passages, heights and basements, reflections and inlets to the sun all choreograph the movements of people who live or work there, protected, temperature controlled, and given easily circumnavigable horizons to fill with themselves. The building enters their memories as both continuity of experience and frame for innovation. It accommodates, stashes, feeds, and excretes, and usually fades into dailiness, however much awe inhabitation starts with. No, there is little to see compared to what is eidetic only in time. Buildings are no more poems than they are brick umbrellas or steel and glass boxes or concrete balloons, and this is also true of the visibility of the poem on the page.

"Prynne, it seems, can have it both ways, being a significant source of dissent whether his work signifies or not" (Purves's reproof to Wilkinson and others [53]). Whether the poetry "signifies or not"? The verb is deceptive here: it conflates singular historical actions of reception with logic's judgment. Can the question of interpretability be articulated as the polar alternatives of *tabula rasa* and abundant wisdom? Obscurity, difficulty, strangeness, and the upwelling of the unknown in a text are themselves part of the signification. Could we not argue that the effort, the false steps, the cogitation, the conversations, the letters, and the e-mails, even the frustration mentioned by Wilkinson, are part of whatever it is the poem is and means? It is much harder to represent the perils of incomprehension than it might seem—realism is an extremely effective solvent whose neurotoxicity can be underestimated.

Is solitary interpretation possible?

Texts vary in their capacity for temporally extended interpretation or what scientists might call the terminability of citation lifetimes: think of the *Talmud* alongside the U.S. Constitution or a recent best-selling novel. It is easy to underestimate how much we don't understand in seemingly accessible contemporary verse, let alone the exegetically encrusted poetries of the tradition. Prynne's recent eighty-six-page essay on a single Shakespeare sonnet might be intended as a demonstration of the persistence of the uninterpreted in even the most overrun of texts.

In 2001, Prynne self-published a pamphlet of about ninety pages that is a phrase-by-phrase analysis of Shakespeare's Sonnet 94, "They that have power to hurt and will do none," a bravura *S/Z* (more an *S/T* perhaps—sweet, sense, soul, speech/they, them, themselves, threat, terminally) that takes each significant unit in turn and offers several interlocking modes of analysis. Most salient are the discussions of other written usages from the immediate period of composition as guides to the sonnet's lexical field, which frequently lead to the observation of contradictory potential meanings ("adversary semantic pressures" [*Powre To Hurt* 39]), as well as the micaceous complexity of possible meaning ("congested possibilities" [39]). A second mode of analysis is afforded by the presumed universality of emotion, which can be calculated according to our own norms and observations. The poem's presentation of a behind-the-scenes activity by the implied speaker trying to make a "decision about which of his many conflicting emotions to acknowledge as uppermost" has to be inferred by the modern reader: "the reader has a secondary access to the question only by reconstruction of this route." What, we might ask, does such reconstruction amount to—is this an affective hermeneutics at work? In Prynne's words, "the reader is not much encouraged towards guesswork along these lines, nor provided with information" (22). The final sentence of the essay rings out with a resonant anguish: "By what ultimate measure of emotion, then, in a high-risk uncharted hazard, could it be that losing everything might still be less hurtful than merely not winning, or prudently not playing against such risks?" (86) Reconstruction is a backward-looking temporal relation, which may implicitly assume that the present has a privileged access route toward this past because the present in which the reconstruction occurs carries this past as a latent information within itself. We should at least recognize the possibility that in some ways our moment may not be an outcome of, or a direct causal link to, that past, and that features of that past may have been irreparably lost. To assume that a reader can reconstruct effaced lines of passion, even as a possibility, is to vote for the optimistic option that at least in the area with which the analysis is concerned, continuity works, and to trade on a confidence that our own time's presumptions of what it is to read can be carried across to a distant past.

Poems that wear their literalism on their sleeves and are bedecked with realist flair may nevertheless be much more secretive and uninterpretable than is usually allowed. Hear Lavinia Greenlaw talking about the new communication technologies in the one poem ("A World Where News Travelled Slowly") by which she is represented in Armitage and Crawford's standard anthology of UK verse, a poem that also won the Forward Prize (Greenlaw 39). This passage from the third stanza follows what are meant to be amusing images of earlier modes of communication, the mail coach and the semaphore:

> Now words are faster, smaller, harder
> . . . *we're almost talking in one another's arms*
> Coded and squeezed, what chance has my voice
> to reach your voice unaltered and then to leave no trace?
> Nets tighten across the sky and the sea bed.
> [ellipses in original]

The stanza ends with a metaphoric play on the fireworks that celebrated the first successful connection between London and New York and the enthusiasm with which its creators and users were fired. The condition of the language of intimacy has changed, insists the poem, and so forcefully that asseveration almost overrides everything else. But where does this assertoric force stem from, what legitimates it, on what authority does it speak, and how much credence is expected? Look and listen more closely. Are *words* really faster, or is it their transmission, and doesn't the distinction matter? Text messaging may encourage verbal squeeze, but elsewhere verbal haploidism is more the norm. Harder? Small words are cognitively easy catches. The echo of Yeats's description of the young, "those dying generations," who can only sing about their romance of desire and reproduction, leaves a trace intertext lying about unexplored. What is an unaltered voice? And it is not just the slack logical assembly here, it is the inattention to interim semantics and sound (the subdued pun on *coded/co-dead* and the pause after *leave* both suggest a quite different attitude to the intimacy) and the lack of questioning of the voice's own confidence that it can speak in and to a public without the very distortion it mentions that all contribute to a chaotic noise of meaning when in close proximity to the text. The closer in we get the less interpretable this becomes—are the words of the poem, the tiny kernels of hug, also supposed to be on speed, and how does chance shift them along, and why does the voice they represent want to leave no trace? Polymorphous enigmas and fuzzy clichés combine to create an ordinarily secretive discourse.

From the omniscient altitude of an airship, the world below has one horizon, a circle that fuses only with itself, as if it were a metaphor of a hermeneutics for which all other horizons had disappeared in a vision of total comprehension.

Although the average contemporary poem has only a title and lineation to mark the boundaries, its voice markers usually indicate that the entire poem is a speech balloon ("my voice") into which an author is imagined blowing her or his spirit in words ("to reach your voice"). Balloons drift with the air currents determining weather unless chained to the ground (and as Lisa Robertson writes of climate's place in our lives in *The Weather:* "It's an outcropping of cumulus; we are a sum of inescapable conditions" [33]) and the speech balloons of personality poems also require the strong cables of individuality's affirmation to prevent their becoming wet or lost in cloudy uptake.

"A text is just the surface, in some ways the skin and there is flesh underneath it and underneath that the bones. One single word, let's say 'Hamlet,' or even in one single letter of that, 'H,' can contain everything a man has ever felt, experienced or suffered" (Wilson 103). Can one letter contain the history of friends, kin, community, nation? The first line of *For the Monogram* has ten words and forty-two letters, enough for the answer to the universe. Hyperbole of course.

Milne's scrupulous essay sets out the framework for a precise reading of Prynne measured against pertinent concepts from transcendental philosophy, phenomenology, and aesthetics to check potential alignments and crosstalk. Hence, for example, a Kantian formulation that

> language is understood [in Prynne] as a condition of possibility rather than as a site of communicative action. The decisive issue is whether the recognition of expressive contradictions can mediate its inclusion within determinate structures of communication and not remain trapped within the fundamental presuppositions of language which encode experience.

Such care with the conceptual exactions allows us to read reflexively and ask whether these theories might themselves be part of the difficulty Milne investigates. Code is widely used as a metaphor of language's interdependence on signs and cognition for its practice, with significant consequences for our theories of language. Some philosophers and linguists, notably Wittgensteinians like G. P. Baker and P. M. S. Hacker, and the historian of linguistics, Roy Harris, have therefore questioned code's appropriateness as metaphor to represent the generativity and interpretive work of language. Of greater difficulty is the knowability of language, which necessarily exceeds all structuring models and theories, so that to talk of "fundamental presuppositions" can be misleading. We speakers may make such presuppositions in a particular cultural moment, but there is no inevitable fit between them and language's worlds, and they could not generate language from the ground up as an ultimate linguistic axiomatics. Perhaps the Kantian concept of a transcendental condition is too aprioristic to grasp the parametric material conditions of reading? Milne himself admits that *For the Monogram,* because it resists reformulation as "philosophical counter-proposals" or, indeed, distillation into any conceptual theme, might be better thought of as "a phenomenological exploration of the conditions of the possibility of experience which is qualitatively different from Kant's, and which invites reading and thinking beyond the explicit horizons of the text's language array" (82) (making the implicit suggestion that these are poems whose words are set out more like the elements of a mathematical matrix than a typical block of sentences and phrases). By the end of his discussion, these conditions of possibility have been deflated to the scale of poetry itself: "Prynne's poetry explores the limits of poetry in ways that could be described as a critique of poetry's conditions of possibility, but this poetry resists criticism without affirming or denying the limits of the speculative readings it provokes" (86). There is a sense of defeat here, criticism on the ropes. Compare Steven Mailloux on reading nineteenth-century American literature: "the current talk about historical acts of reading provides a welcome opportunity for more explicit consideration of how reading is historically contingent, politically situated, institutionally embedded, and materially conditioned" (Mailloux 5). Or Willis Buckingham on his methodology for study of the early reception of Emily Dickinson in the eighteen-nineties: "in drawing on all known writing about the poet from the decade, it seeks what is common among poetry audiences as their fulfillment conditions for the reading of verse" (Buckingham 165). These historians of reading point us to a possible way through the dilemma that halts a criticism so scrupulous with its critical and phenomenological terms; they point us to the intersubjectivity and consequent extended temporality of reading as a plural act.

When Jacques Derrida writes of the rhetoric that has sustained the concept of structure that "the history of metaphysics, like the history of the West, is the history of these metaphors and metonymies" (Derrida, "Structure," 279) is he making anything more than a specialist's claim to have met a force and tone important enough to become the leading predicate of history, in a sentence whose functor could be replaced with money, technology, drains, or disease? Reverse the flow of this assertion and it deflates: trace out the implications and inferences of dominant metaphors and you will find their filaments reach into almost every domain of cultural life. Saggy contours of ordinariness are now evident. This is similar to the claim by George Lakoff and Mark Johnson for the centrality of certain atomic metaphors formed out of our sensorimotor experiences of being in the world, which combine to create the dominant metaphors of our culture. Comparing life to a journey works according to Lakoff by carrying over the inferences embedded in our experience of transport to the much more difficult to articulate concept, because largely intangible, of living a life.

An early poem from Prynne's *The White Stones,* "Charm Against Too Many Apples," presents a speaker whose matter of fact reflections on an at first seemingly literal journey, knowingly alludes to prestigious variants of this Western metaphor of life as a pilgrimage to the Eternal City:

> Still there is much to be done, on the
> way into the city, and the sky as yet
> only partly written over; we take all
> our time and the road is lined with apple trees.
> That's where we go, then, and if this sounds
> too obviously prolonged, remember that
> the ice was our prime matter. Flame is only
> just invisible in sunlight
>   and the smoke goes
> wavering into the atmosphere with all the
> uncertainty of numbers. And so we can't
> continue with things like this, we can't simply
> go on. In this way through the forest, we
> lose too much and too quickly: we have
> *too much to lose.* How can anyone hope,
> to accomplish what he wants so much not
> finally to part with. We even pick up
> the fallen fruit on the road. (68)

All the metaphoric resonance of apples, fruit, falling, numbers, "too much," and other terms are worked across the voice of an ethical urgency that folds back onto itself. The poem does not directly coincide with the concerns and hopes of its speaker, whose concerns are themselves products of the very problem that he tries to elucidate. Prynne wants the readiness of these metaphors to elicit questioning.

Lakoff and Turner's argument that such metaphors work by carrying the inferential patterns of one domain of thought over to another underestimates the significance of these domains themselves, which must already contain the inferential structures, and therefore rely on other cognitive and affective processes than metaphor. For Derrida's key metaphors and metonymies to wield such influence (his global statement only makes sense if these are a small number of "A-C-G-T" metaphors and metonyms; otherwise it would be tantamount to saying that history is equivalent to a subset of all utterances), there must have been similar domains of understanding for comparison and extension to do their work of persuasion. This is questionable. The "is" of Derrida's argument, its simulation of the transferential moment of metaphorical enlightenment, which treats language as a metaphor for history and thereby presupposes what is being argued, creates a circularity waiting for rhetorical inflation. Metaphor and metonymy are an important part of our history, but these language forces are not metonymically the source code, or core pattern, repeated through a homogenous ontology.

Lakoff and Johnson argue that metaphor is intrinsic to all reasoning, and in particular, that "there is no ethical system that is not metaphorical. We understand our experience via these conceptual metaphors, we reason according to their metaphorical logic, and we make judgments on the basis of metaphors" (Lakoff 325). This confidence in the ubiquity of metaphor is based on the belief that the complex activities of rationality, imagination, and visualization all depend upon analogies with bodily experiences.

> We acquire a large system of primary metaphors automatically and unconsciously by functioning in the most ordinary of ways in the everyday world from our earliest years. We have no choice in this. Because of the way neural connections are formed during the period of conflation [when young children cannot fully distinguish between their thoughts and their sensory experiences], we all naturally think using hundreds of primary metaphors. (47)

These primary metaphors are built up into complex ones through "conceptual blending," whereby connections are made between different fields and these produce inferences that may be "either conventional or wholly original." The authors' repeated message is simple: even the most abstract concepts derive from metaphors felt as deep habit. If theorists do not reflect on the initiating metaphors, they will derive inferences that appear logical to them even though they are generated by the matrix chosen from the unconscious metaphors. Here is a nascent poetics that treats originality of metaphor as a work of perceptive articulation of existing connections developing mostly below the surface of common recognition, connections that occasion this poetic representation of the historical experience and accompanying understanding seeded in the conditions that permit the metaphor, rather than showing off the freedom of creative will—a poetics in which accuracy, observation, care, prolonged thought, and acuity are indistinguishable from the more usually salient inventiveness, wit, and imagination. Unfortunately, these linguists don't notice the deliberate mental labor accrued over history by the vast network of metaphors, nor do they reflect on the body's fashioning by sociohistorical conditions. Without such correction their linguistics folds back into a new positivism.

Beginning to read the first stanza of *For the Monogram* (1997):

At a point tunes beating and striking the plate for
    sylvatic break and drop there not so sunken away
as in stay-put agreement; set off put off these crowds
    no free sky conversely. Will you jag up the tippet
over a new bow thrown down if for implored at five
    apace, floating across bars in black? In green
flash scraping ionic burn? Why ever not they split
    a tooth and spoil quickly by ricochet and fine
tremor's lull, singing and dying along the shore
    of the loud-roaring season: he'll position his
best eye at the planet boy too little, in three days
    notice of man too fat. Floating star, even up the
score of a radial plot and maze over or spoken by
    the sad sea ways. Afloat oblique and limping
at this the monocline in agreement for interrupted
    wings, nodding thistle to melancholy orchid.
(418)

Beginning to read *For the Monogram* uneasily, discomforted, in doubt of understanding and the text's designs, a sense of waking from slowly receding anesthetic or a stroke, when words have lost their meaning, self-awareness and other subjects are suddenly beside the self or gone without in-betweens. Do I *have* to keep reading this? A weariness "beating and striking" my will, a "wave shaping" my revealed stupidity "from its own wreck in shadow play" of incomprehension, "the sad sea ways" of knowledge for which I am no Newton, I cannot sing like Wallace Stevens's shoreline diva "beyond the genius of the sea," indeed a "counter search" and a "gain in deception" is all that seems to happen and I am unable to "select an object with no predecessors" (418–20) from these short poems since I hear Olson, Stevens, Arnold, Valèry, and Lucretius constantly at my back. How to read a fractal syntagma. If the sublime forces the imagination back on itself as it fails to comprehend the vast magnificence of the "hot glory" of this creation, this feels to my educated doubt a reminder of intelligence's mortality rather than its mercy. My immanence "passes through innervation" until I reach the "merciful injunction" to consider pity a vice rather than a virtue, its empathy "monoglot" with disavowed complicity in the object's predication. What does all this excess semantic complexity betoken: a secret communication, highly advanced expertise, hoaxing, an in-group elite's private exchanges, or a complex of ideas that I cannot grasp?

Beginning to read *For the Monogram* with excitement at this new "floating star," with feelings of expectation, and hope, anticipations of wisdom or at least hard-won insight from the "best eye" in British poetics. The thrill of such startling "long-glow deportment" of language at "dearest agile daybreak" of new meaning, the nurture of this "lactation" of possibility, and the sharp insights into the corruptions of our time, the "region combed out by fortune / ripping the nail bank it touched" (423). I too want "to shine in the code" like other skilled readers. The poem is surprisingly beautiful even when facing the worst of the times: "and adopt strike point rip barrens / swept barley, silver fennel, the sea streaked / red with flickering lights no issue" (431). Such a show of sustained skill is as much a delight as reading Henry James on wealth in *The Golden Bowl* or tracing the intricate visual analogies in Poussin. What does all this excess semantic complexity betoken: advanced communication, an offering of new expertise, a sophisticated entertainment, the first belongings of a new poetic community, or a field of ideas that one could appropriate for further research?

Could a prosody be constructed from a rhythm of interpretative demands experienced as operating on several axes of readerly obsolescence as it were (of difficulty, of register, of proximity to literary tradition), so that part of the poem's music was this complex cognitive and emotional movement over the time of a reading that would be irreversible, irreparable? It would not be reproducible. Once you know that lithium grease is an innovative lubrication for high-tech bearings do the exciting meanders recorded by Wilkinson in his reading of *Not-You* as he tries to elucidate the phrase without apparently realizing that lithium grease is an ordinary substance used by engineers, fade into the semantic murk, or does the slippery product speak more (poetry) than it knows? Am I meandering here?

Perhaps such a poem is a version of Brian Catling's impossible object the "stumbling block," that "atlas swallowing its tongue" and "ark of extinction" (Catling 13–15). Or a version of this pop-galactic McGuffin:

> The artifact . . . was black-body, an ambient anomaly . . . either almost completely massless, or—perhaps—some sort of projection; it seemed to make no impression on the skein, the fabric of space-time which any accumulation of matter effectively dents with its mass, like a boulder lying on a trampoline. The artifact / projection gave the impression that it was floating on the skein, making no impression on it whatsoever . . . almost as though it was a blister on the skein itself, as though the signals the ship was sending towards it could never connect with a *thing* there because all they did was slide flickering over that blister almost as though it wasn't there and pass on undisturbed into space beyond. . . . Well, if you take the definition of an excession as anything external to the Culture that we should be worried about, this is an excession all right. (Banks 89, 114)

Is Prynne's poem the hegemonic poetry culture's "excession"? Even more suggestive than the neologism's almost but not quite oxymoronic blend of destructive erasure with a coming forth that produces an inside far beyond what ought to be the limits of all interiority, are these awkward twin impressions that appear to cancel one another out, giving and taking away themselves. The gift of possibility in art—the gift as sign of impossibility—art as a hieroglyph of exchange that does not yet exist.

> The poet is affected by the "spirit" of language which is none other than the whole history of human imagination from which he draws his linguistic ideas. The appearance of the letter, its mere form, bespeaks a lost or unavailable content or referent. An event or experience is no longer associated with and hence intuited by such a sign; instead, a feeling of loss of meaning is generated. This loss not withstanding, the hieroglyph stands as a witness to a past without representing it to us and without signaling a meaning for us. (Rauch 134)

Rauch calls it a "psychic archive" because she argues that it needs to be part of a general background knowledge to find its potential, or one might say, it needs unimaginable readers. This subtly offers a different reading of Prynne's own persistent interest in such matters, in *Stars, Tigers, and the Shape of Words,* and in his afterword to *New Songs from a Jade Terrace:* "Their poems summoned that tradition, by summoning the whole through a knowing presentation of implicative fragments." This he calls a form of metonymy that

> depends on a pattern of figural components which are already associated together in the poetic discourse or context of formalisms from which combinations are produced, each local part of such a system pre-implying the larger whole . . . the stylistic history, or occasionally the cosmology or other typological ordering, comprises the precursory system which makes the use of coded metaphor a metonymic rather than metaphoric procedure; and it is the subtlety of intelligible allusion, varied and superimposed, which here shews [sic] the power of metonymy both to support metaphor and to exceed it. (Prynne, "China," 387, 368)

The hieroglyphs or monograms of Prynne's later poetry might be said to stand in such a relation to contemporary culture, as do such metonyms for a past set of traditions and their coeval signs ("precursory systems"?), and therefore loss might be one of the semantic effects of the fast metaphors.

The hieroglyphic "balloons" of comic-strip speech are metonymic of a complex history of both mind and flight, and their conflicts. They were named balloons at the only moment when cosmology and typological divisions of space could be figured by this then most modern vehicle. A decade or two earlier or later and who knows? Bulbs, balls, clouds, radios, or vehicles?

Beginning to read *For the Monogram* by starting with the title. Monogram: insubstantial, as of a god; a shadowy figure; a personal signature; a signature formed of letters that share lines that are salient spatial markers. It might be a pun on the letter I, a figure for the individuality of the author in a "mono writing," as much as a long shadow of absent ark or deity, or a singular measure of *gravitas.*

How does interpretation of a phrase like "stay-put agreement" begin (recall the opening lines of *For the Monogram:* "At a point tunes beating and striking the plate for / sylvatic break and drop there not so sunken away / as in stay-put agreement; set off put off these crowds / no free sky conversely")? Let's try the internet, which usefully makes available samples of usage within specialized lexical fields. Through Google I reach the website for the U.S. Individuals with Disabilities Education Act (IDEA) (http://clerccenter2.gallaudet.edu/KidsWorldDeafNet/e-docs/IDEA/section-2.html) and learn that they use this phrase to mean an agreement in which the parties agree to implement changes on which they all agree, whilst keeping unaltered those provisions related to issues over which there is still disagreement from the previous consensual decision. It might be a way of talking about how interpretive communities maintain their stability against attempts to change reading. Is much literary criticism a form of stay-put agreement? As important as the definitional restriction is to one's interpretation of the poem, more important still is the indication that the poem is working with a phrase whose significance derives from dissonance between one's naïve literalism (I had assumed that this was not specialized jargon and only searched for this phrase on a whim) and a more knowing user's habitus. Without the internet I would probably have remained in my meanders, because as is the case with many of Prynne's topical usages, "stay-put agreement" is not a phrase likely to be quickly traced in an ordinary dictionary. Searching for the phrase underlines for this reader the extent to which the culture in which Prynne's poetry floats is islanded into local specializations of the common language.

> This much only we can assert: the *image* is a product of the empirical faculty of the productive imagination; the *schema* of sensible concepts, such as of figures in space, is a product, and as it were, a monogram, of pure *a priori* imagination [*ein Produkt und gleichsam ein Monogramm der reinen Einbildungskraft a priori*], through which, and in accordance with which, images themselves first become possible. (Kant 183 [translation modified])

The significance of the monogram that Kant introduces with a poet's gesture, an "und gleichsam" or "as it were," is demonstrated in the very form of the gesture. The monogram is a sign of the way that, as Paul Guyer explains, "Kant clearly perceived that there was some inescapable connection between self-knowledge and knowledge of objects" because both were "intrinsically judgmental and necessarily involved logical structures as well as empirical inputs" (Guyer 155). Monogram is not only a metaphor for the working of the schema, but also its use in Kant's exposition metonymically demonstrates the coauthoring of expression by pure mind and by historical matters.

In his meditations on a future politics, Giorgio Agamben takes as one starting point Aquinas's oddly literal speculation on the future of the world of things once the day of judgment has passed. Agamben draws from Robert Walser the idea that this remainder of the Creation will

> be just as it is, irreparably, but precisely this will be its novelty. The irreparable is the monogram that Walser's writing engraves into things. Irreparable means that these things are consigned without remedy to their being-thus, that they are precisely and only their *thus* . . . but irreparable also means that for them there is literally no shelter possible, that in their being-thus they are absolutely exposed, absolutely abandoned. (38)

But this scholastic nicety is also metonymic of the balance between destruction and opportunity in our contemporary condition:

> Because if instead of continuing to search for a proper identity in the already improper and senseless form of individuality, humans were to succeed in belonging to this impropriety [that "even life in its nakedness is, in truth, improper and exterior to them, that for them there is no shelter on earth"] as such, in making of the proper being-thus not an identity and an individual property but a singularity without identity, a common and absolutely exposed singularity—if humans could, that is, not be-thus in this or that particular biography, but be only *the* thus, their singular exteriority and their face, then they would for the first time enter into a community without presuppositions and without subjects, into a communication without the incommunicable. (64)

Is this really "the political task of our generation" as Agamben says, or no more than John Rawls's "original position" that entails a hypothetical "veil of ignorance" (that for justice to be possible, of the parties involved "no one knows his place in society, his class position or social status" etc. [Rawls 137])? What would a monogram of this irreparable singularity of a humanity be like? Is this another version of the philosophical insight that to be modern is to believe that one's self-identity is chosen, and it is this that must be overcome?

Can one imagine an interpretive community in such terms? What responsibilities and care for friendship's thought and civic emotion would this require and what of its ethics?

Questions: they project a world before fact or truth, of hope and setting to, whiling and wait, assuming answerability is possible, just that, risking failure's erasure.

"To interpret is to impoverish, to deplete the world—in order to set up a shadow world of 'meanings'" (Sontag 7). Meanings as monograms (shadowy figures)? Does "for the monogram" translate as "for the interpretation?" But what does Sontag offer in place except an appeal to in-your-face experience, the "sensuous immediacy" of art? Is, as she argues, abstract painting really a flight from content? Doesn't such art have excessive content? Prynne's reading of an exceedingly nonfigurative painting, de Kooning's *Rosy Fingered Dawn at Louse Point,* flourishes a proposed content in the face of another critic's claim that the painting's radiance overwhelms any form that might outline such content:

> If I wanted to propose a kind of counter-mischief I should say that this was a painting formed out of a quadrilateral syllogism, and its logistic quality or obscured middle term is to do with that management or force which comes from alleging the power of ethos and its historical and even its epic dimensions, and of working its attachment to the other power of this lyrical presence here, of interior pathos and even of sublimity. (47)

"Lyrical presence" may sound like an attempt at a more licit nineties immediacy, cohabiting, as Prynne says, with expressiveness, yet his interpretation also replies to such fear of impoverishment through these figures of interaction (alleging, working), which reverse the monogram and unblock the illumination to dispel shadowy fears of pod art simulating the real with their mischievous insistence on a return to the painting's light.

In a hoarse voice through an oxygen mask he said to me: "They are listening to us now. We must find a way out." Patient reader, how paranoid is the text's belief that its attempt to speak in secrecy to those it trusts might be exploded by divulgence to those opposed to its plans? Compositional neoteny lingers in an encryption whose withheld evidence threatens even the closest kinships of reader.

What are the poetics of secrecy? Peter Riley recently castigated British poets whose alienation and accompanying ragey emotions impel them to "distort poetry into an ungainly and secretized discourse" through a writing "which is primarily opposition rather than inquiry" (19). This poetry "denies the reader's right of participation" (20) (to which I can imagine the answer that we have yet to establish such a democratic right and therefore a text that appears to be bound by such a right is lying to us), presumably because such secrecy, as many modern thinkers have reminded us, gives power to its controllers. I have considerable sympathy with this response to what Riley calls the "beast" in contemporary poetry, as this essay will demonstrate. But I also wonder if maybe this ungainliness isn't somehow the formalist admission of a secrecy that emulates other secrecies too? Michael Taussig would probably think so. He argues that "the methodology of human science unites with the ancient methodology of public secrecy as both blur into the charade of scientific detachment" (Taussig 75). It is the idea that "secrecy magnifies reality," however, taken from Georg Simmel, which enables Taussig to go further, and say that "attempts to unmask appearances may actually compound the mystery thereof" (56). Can it be that the more a poem like *For the Monogram* is unmasked or interpreted, the more interpretation becomes puzzling and overshadows insight?

Oppositional rage is certainly there in some of Prynne's prose. Prynne's essay in reply to Peter Handke is scoriaceous with the fallout from a volcanic anger at the West's "acts of barbarism which implicate every human domain" (26) in the Balkans. Greatest denunciation is shot at otherwise complacent liberals whose "protest [is] almost as distasteful as that against which it levels its superior moral allegation" (26). This might in other hands lead to the valuation only of highly visible, heroic gestures, kamikaze aesthetics, or the total personal sacrifice of all-out revolution, and never the small incremental and mostly invisible public acts of quiet generosity, resistance, and cultural reconstruction. Here the risk seems more that the state of language will be treated as the only measure of our ethical standing. Prynne argues that "human language is the tribal continuity of expressive human behaviour, and is marked in its very core by whatever depravity or nobility an exercise of linguistic analysis may discover within the human record" (24). Could this way of thinking reduce the entire situation of acts and events in which words are produced to a single projection onto a putative verbal plane orthogonal enough to miss nothing? Language is undoubtedly implicated, but the "partially observant bystander" he repeatedly castigates is lit by the radiant glow of television's mediation and is sitting down far away, not standing nearby, is not, in other words, able to observe observantly at all. Unless we acknowledge the intervening stages between bombs falling and everyday political comment, language could become the quark hypothesis of a fecundly generative hylomorphism.

For a poetics of secrecy? Poetry's once small art aesthetic has been so successful that all commerce and science are now practitioners, and poetry as once practiced becomes consoling nostalgia for the good life.

"Inventor, firstly, was always testing technology." What? Yes. This is what? Yes, it's a clue for the *Guardian* crossword set by Orlando on June 22, 2001, and the answer is Watt (acronym of last 4 words). Crosswords are popular enough to sell newspapers on their strength alone. Word puzzles pass time, enact the mystery of reference and signification, and offer consolatory answers to still fears of other less amenable secrecies and deeper unknowns; and they flatter intelligence as each clue is solved. An ability to solve crosswords was a high recommendation for the recruits to Bletchley Park code-breaking teams during WWII. A clue: Poetry registers yet newer nuances explicated.

And yet secrecy and alienated rage do sometimes go together. A certain perfectionism links them, a sense that every institution, public value, and consensual moral guidance falls so far short that an aesthetics of secrecy is the only fertile seed of a renewed public life because it enacts the necessary promissory rites of becoming known in shame and hope. And Riley is surely right that this mode can be dominated by rage against injustice written through the clenched teeth of elaborate verbal obliquity or, to switch metaphors, as a muffling anoxic foam protecting expression and reader from a destructive heat that might otherwise reduce language to crude polemic and its author to an easily dismissed polemicist. I don't find this in Prynne's poetry. Its interest in limited interpretability points to quite another mode of secrecy, a political form, the extensively repeated *habitus* of verbal secrecy of the governing institutions of modern Britain.

> The CX Milton gathered ["MI6's intelligence 'product' is known as 'CX' an anachronism from the earliest days of MI6 when the Chief, 'C' in popular fiction, was Mansfield Cummings" (Tomlinson 59)] from the meetings was encrypted using highly secure but commercially available PGP encryption software, then sent to London over the internet. . . . Reading an MI6 file can be a slow and laborious job. The papers are arranged in chronological order but that is the

> extent of their organization. They contain a vast jumble of information from many sources. Telegrams, letters, police SB reports, copies of military and DSS records of individuals mentioned in the file, titbits from GCHQ, contact reports, surveillance photographs. Many papers cross-reference to other files, so making sense of them means a trog down to the central registry to pull the file. One document in the file might be only peripherally relevant to the case, the next might be crucially important. It is easy to miss a vital titbit and so lose track of the big picture if not concentrating hard. (131, 180)

This vivid account of an extrapolation of contemporary reading competencies reminds us how these are shaped by power, gender, education, religion, and other institutions. To read is to inscribe and reproduce these socialities.

The viewer, the listener, the reader: useful abstractions when the simplifications they entail can be ignored. Messily historical, enfleshed, and distracted persons can be treated for the sake of textual analysis as just the one line of process wholly defined by this vector of attention: singular, present, and abstract sensory being are represented as if poised in perfect readiness in front of the art. This is a function with a restricted range, however, and its features may not remain stable when the scope is extended in time, community, and distance. For many texts whose readership is already established around shared ritual, the familiarity of extratextual encounters, expected behaviors, formulable prosodies, and a genre as fashion-conscious as any regular highstreet shopper, this abstraction works fine, but for Prynne's texts, which also repeatedly construct cross-register artifices that could not have a perfect reader, it does not. Poems like *For the Monogram* borrow from disparate languages that have split off into discrete, localized institutions of knowledge and economies, whose users might conceivably belong to several (the computer expert may be a botanist and musician), but because Prynne's poetry reaches out to so many registers, the fully consonant reader situated in all these linguistic communities is an impossibility; this person does not yet exist in our culture. Should we even try to imagine such readers and if so, how?

The firm, restrained, would-be informative sentences of *For the Monogram* show no tentative reaching for expression despite the constant strangeness of what is written, although this command of their resources is not why they could qualify as "unsayable" in Ann Banfield's sense. There is rarely an address or inscribed consciousness, and often little assertoric force. Affect is elusive, emulsified, streaky. Rhythmically, the poems are constructed around a six-beat foundation, and their vocalization (even sub) stretches the verbal muscles with elegant concatenations of syllable that suddenly jerk to a halt in anti-euphonious crash or stutter into a new rhythm (many words or phonemes are repeated, a troubling of expression that could be read as a sign of muting distress) in which beats pile up in spondees or other longer tight clusters of emphasis. Metapoetics hovers everywhere, notably in the third poem, which has the greatest homogeneity of register, because it uses a programming jargon that could also be a macro for the composition of the poem itself

> Select an object with no predecessors. Clip off its
>   roots, reset to zero and remove its arrows. At each
> repeat decrement the loop to an update count for all
>   successors of the removed object ranking the loop body
> at next successor to the array stack. Count back up
>   left and right scan, test for inert loops using
> 0 0 as sentinel pair. . . . (420)

"Select an object with no predecessors" might both describe the use of poetic devices like anaphora without precursor textual identifiers and also be readable ironically as the description of a poetics counter to Olson's injunction in his poem "These Days" that "whatever you have to say, leave / the roots on, let them / dangle," (Olson, *Collected Poems*, 106) when it continues "clip off its / roots." This poem's mention of an "array stack" offers a particularly inviting image of the poetic layout that recurs in the final poem where "the arrays lie packed in a dark light," although it's a sharply antipoetic concept that also endorses the prominence of the many scientific and medical terms (mostly from medical pathology). Certain words, images, topographies (notably the shoreline), and events repeat throughout the sequence in recursive patterns with intimations of a mind's circling dance and a world made significant. A dense etymological and idiolectical polysemy is used to the full, as are homonyms ("ponder arc setting" explicitly refers to an electrical arc for catalyzing gases but in the context of the fifth poem's many allusions to Jerusalem as the site of conflict between Palestinians and Israelis is also a pun on the Ark of the Covenant) and puns ("madder clouds" are both red and further signs of conflict; "flagrant unction" loops into "extreme unction" administered to those dying in such conflicts, as well as the emollient rhetoric used by some political leaders). Odd moments of comedy (in the poem on urban mall life: "Bored with fraud rowdy crowds flip / coin exchange macaronics like polar bear packs / propped on the escalator, freak anoraks heating up / with hormone replacement hints.") are not the regular hits of release from tension used widely in contemporary avant-garde poetry. Here such larking about is jarred by a subsequent allusion to the black charred shadows and genetic mutations of victims of the atomic bombs in Japan in WWII ("shadows in concrete / out to the *n*th generation"), and then the bitter repetition of "fun first fun rest" pushes at the limits of the poem's permitted expression of anger at injustice. Although the reading expected is the antithesis of the crossword solver's indifference to content, the phrasing repeatedly invites a similar first response in which an unarticulated "what is" might preface a phrase like "a clinical denouement sunk far past its frolic." No doubt about the task, but whose, to what end, with what promise?

The interpretation of a poem by Prynne is a set of readings that are also complex actions likely to include skimming, rereading closely, reading just a few lines, and remembering images and moods as well as lines or phrases, consequent discussions with others, ideas and expectations influenced by these readings as well as by misreadings, error, partial attention, projection, and the distortions of intense emotion. Each of these readings is located in time and space, in a material history that may or may not connect readily with other readings and related preoccupations with the poem, and these histories also coexist, running in parallel as it were, sometimes intersecting and sometimes developing their own semi-autonomous interpretative momentum. Metaphors of interconnection, such as web, weave, imbrication, network, and mesh, can help, but they all tend to underrepresent the extent, intensity, and complexity of the history of engagements with the poem, partly because the assemblage of microhistories also develops a certain autonomy of its own as particular interpretations and knowledges of the poem gain some visibility and other social interests push various aspects of the poem into prominence or oblivion. The time of readings may not be calendrically large, but the multiplicity of parallel histories of reading the text produces an aggregate depth of historical time that is. Phenomenologically speaking, the poem is not a unit or object capable of being fully apprehended by one perspective, it is all this historical activity, much of which will never be recorded in writing or any other durable form and could not be known in its entirety. There is nothing odd about this either, this is the condition of all texts in an age of rapid, cheap printing and other technologies of distribution, when there is a large Western audience of educated people potentially able to read it. All that is different about the poem from other forms of text is that it is much more likely to select features of its participation in this textual condition for a poetic emphasis that will complement the words and other poetic strategies that together compose its meanings. The "meaning" of this extended poem would be a fluorescence of the entirety of these myriad occasions of interpretative reception. To treat the poem on the page as capable of being encompassed by a singular reading by even the most highly trained and knowledgeable reader is similar to the treatment of a meaning of a word as exhaustible by a dictionary definition. Almost all contemporary poetry works to some degree, however limited, or unconsciously, with this condition of textuality, although just as emphasis on sound, prosody, etymology, or syntax may vary considerably, so does contemporary avant-garde poetry's selection of this deep time of reception for poetic salience.

Individual words and terse phrases are not the only carriers of a historical imagination and current sociality; clauses, sentences, and even paragraphs, or still higher levels of linguistic integration, can also do so. Breaking them down this way may work sometimes and in others produce symmetry groups rather than the thousand things of a universe.

Will there be a *Guide* to Prynne analogous to the guides to Pound, Olson, and other modernists? Many, perhaps most, of the surface obscurities of the first Pisan Canto, for example, can apparently be resolved within a few minutes by reading Carroll F. Terrell's *Companion*. Even the cage where he was incarcerated doesn't have to be imagined: the photograph in *Ezra and Dorothy Pound: Letters in Captivity 1945–1946* shows that it looked like a cross between a locked bicycle shed and an aviary. Canto 74's "ideogram of the guard roosts" turns out to be a remarkably apt description of the spindly legs of the boatlike lookout and its diagonal strokes of brace. What would it be like to read *For the Monogram* under similar conditions (or perhaps the question is whether such a guide would ever be possible?). Terrell is in no doubt about the gain his guide represents:

> Before a genuine dialogue is possible, the text of *The Cantos* must be made more easily comprehensible to a sizable audience of students and professors as well as critics. Although some progress has been made, it becomes clearer, as time goes on, that the problems are not so much in the abstruse levels of thinking as in the extraordinary and wide-ranging fields of reference. (Terrell ix)

So *The Cantos* have been thoroughly read and critique can begin (the two must therefore be separate, both analytically and temporally). What is this "genuine dialogue" (what other sorts of dialogue are there, and who is participating in this dialogue, and to what interim ends?) that cannot begin until the poem is "more easily comprehensible?"

A widespread model of interpretation is reading's hindsight, memory's abstraction of essentials from the ruck, a walker for self-consciousness. Reading may or may not be accompanied by degrees of verbal self-consciousness in its cognitive, emotional, and physical acts, which are not bounded by self, spreading into intersubjective projects and taking part in wider events.

George Butterick begins his preface to *A Guide to "The Maximus Poems" of Charles Olson* with a quotation from a weary Olson complaining about the burdens of poetry and adds that these also fall on the reader: "The major difficulty, and it can be discouraging, is the large amount of reference needed to populate a poem that seeks to occupy and extend a world. The *Guide to "The Maximus Poems"* provides the scholarship useful for reading these poems which are as complex and allusive as Pound's *Cantos*" (Butterick ix). Do informed interpretations become slowly "better," each scholar-critic able to use the discoveries of predecessors as tools for the making of their subsequent contribution to a series of recorded critical judgments forming interim stages on a passage toward an ever more established and enhanced interpretation that will supervene on those earlier ones? Such an assumption about the work of interpretation would make it negate the imperfect present in which actual criticism always unfortunately occurs. Interpretation would be always waiting for its own demise.

Is the difficulty of a contemporary poem by Prynne (or Bruce Andrews, Clark Coolidge, Lyn Hejinian, Maggie O'Sullivan, Tom Raworth, or John Wilkinson, all poets whose work demands sustained engagement with text that can seem initially almost unreadable and to anticipate eventual exegesis) a difficulty similar to that which afflicted Pound's earlier scholars? Are we living too soon to begin the dialogue that Terrell refers to? Is the difficulty a result of our limits as readers, limits that are temporal as well as the result of an informational deficit? Does induction promise a vacation from uncertainty?

A Kashye af a mayse—a Yiddish phrase that Jonathan Boyarin glosses as "[what's the point of asking] a logical question about a story?" (226) What sorts of questions can be asked of a poem also remain moot.

In *Stars, Tigers, and the Shape of Words,* Prynne talks of "reading with a heightened sense of the accumulated layers and aspects of association which form the significant resonance of previous usage: the whole prior history of the language-community can be tuned to allow and invite the vibrations of sense and suggestion and historical retrospect" (18). But who is doing the "tuning" here? The first part of this sentence starts with reading, so it might seem logical that it is the reader who works to tune the instrument, making its remoter harmonies accessible enough to elicit those more distant and less commonly audible historical cries and hopes. Or is it the composition that facilitates this, already carefully set to make such evocations possible? Does the reader alone have sufficient opportunity to take words as onion-layered time capsules, to loosen the forces of syntax that insist on completed and disambiguated propositions, and to be the entrepreneur of what the nameless narrator of Robert Browning's *Sordello* calls the "dim / Abysymal past?" (126) Or do readers need at least the cooperation of the poets who "know the dragnet's trick" because whether fate has decided to let the past live on as "silence or song," poets control "a realm wherein she [fate] has no right" and with their art: "Lo, the past is hurled / In twain" (127). Although Browning acknowledges that his readers must bring their attention to the text, hence the powerful emphasis on the single syllable (placed in the midst of a line), the "lo," the injunction to "look," whose poetic lexis brings to bear the long vowel associated with the emphatical language of a feeling that is still reaching for words, his poem's own power is doubly underlined by the force of verb and adverbial phrase. And the past is divided in two.

The second lecture of *Stars, Tigers, and the Shape of Words* ends with a brilliant summary of the consequent intricacy of this bilateral past. Prynne is primarily interested to show how the challenge to structuralist linguistics represented by the poetic strategies of literary language, its "secondary transgressions," might be incorporated into a broader schema that would not require complete abandonment of Saussure, and in doing so he adumbrates a historicity of reading that might be a less material form of the medieval *catena* (Carruthers 215):

> How far these secondary transgressions can then be allowed to be themselves sense-bearing is a function of the intepretative consensus, or of the author/reader contract, or of the successive sense-productiveness of generic text-types and sub-types; all of this makes up a network of practice which is socially and historically available around a central core of pragmatic accord, a working repertory. It is a counterpart and complement to essentialist analysis of structure, not so much because it operates more in one dimension than another (e.g., historical time rather than conceptual space), but because it is an aggregating and proliferative instigation, recursively back-folding and cross-linking, and this kind of incorporative opportunism is idiomatic for a whole pattern of cultural practice in which language is a centrally-mediating agency. (Prynne, *Stars,* 34)

There is still an ambiguity about the sense in which this network is *available,* and to whom. What restrictions and what openings might control this availability: education, specific knowledge of the local aesthetic, introspection, the raising of the *habitus* or background expectancies to at least partial consciousness, historical (possibly requiring extensive work of recovery if considerable time has passed since composition), leisure, intellectual or other special capacities (a musical imagination perhaps), or even inside information about author and circumstances of the text's launch? To talk of "accord," "consensus," a "whole pattern," or collective "agency" could be to presuppose what does not yet exist, a condition that has to be worked for, just as democracy or the willingness to run a little magazine always requires present effort and both prospective and retrospective orientations. One might counter by saying that the poem's composer can only work with what has already precipitated itself into the wells of language possibility, but this would then concede that we are talking now more of inception than reception and cut the present in twain, effacing the projective in favor of the already "corporate & prolonged action / of worked self-transcendence" ("Questions for the Time Being" [Prynne, *Poems,* 112]), available in language.

If, however, we give more weight to the "aggregating and proliferative instigation" as pointing along a temporal axis of rereadings that will certainly become part of the new reader's "working repertory," in both the scholarly sense of a secondary literature and as everything from remembered gossip, perceived subsequent influences on other poems, to the end results of long chains of cognitive and emotional intersubjective activities that momently converge on this new reader, then this reader splits into a conceptual space and a history. The reader as abstraction does not then impose an invariance of cognitive reaction onto an unbounded series of specific historical readerly engagements with the poem.

My reasoning may be adrift in one dimension at least. Am I treating Prynne's few prose texts as parts of an integral project in which every line is consistent and continuous? In a recent essay on the continuing dominance of organicism in literary criticism, Mary Poovey notes that this tendency "simultaneously makes contemporary criticism resemble a romantic lyric and converts its analytic objects into lyric-like organic wholes" even where tropes of "structure" replace overt organicism. She argues that "the developmental narrative which links parts of the textualized and spatialized analytic object to the whole that theoretically contains them is affiliated with the metaphor of organic unity because the trope of development implies an organism that grows into maturity" (Poovey 434). Endemic literary criticisms produce a ballooning Pound and Olson (and shortly may even produce a Prynne ready for take-off) whose vast shapes supposedly still retain the contours of the man and poet as they hover (or drift) across the landscape of contemporary critical industry.

For obscurity? Henges, staddlestones, neolithic "circuses." How the words break up into pleading syllables repeating themselves for emphasis: "sylvatic" into sylvan vatic and sylvan tic and even sly vatic. A break from the metropolitan vatic of high seriousness?

Both Milne and Wilkinson speak of the need to confer some authority on Prynne's poems, since the "speculative inquiry," as Milne calls it, of interpretation is "a costly and expensive investment" and "the poetry needs to be read against the faithful trust of expositors." For Milne, the poetry's field of production is the imaginative activity of response to the poetry that is engendered, so that speculative inquiry "makes concessions to the authority of the work as an object which works against the interests it is made to serve" (84). Wilkinson is more explicit about the authority he discerns in Prynne's poetry, even if he is puzzled, and asks in the face of the resistance to interpretation of the opening lines of *Not-You*, "why the authority which marks these lines, the impression that they say something which ought to be said? Their authority is a puzzling attribute, by contrast with the work of poets with whom Prynne has been compared—the eschewal of authority has been a cardinal principle of postmodernist practice" (191). A key principle for some of the more caricatured versions perhaps. Wilkinson offers some tentative explanations to his question, saying that it is all in the syntax, the connectives, the absence of heart-wrenching appeals, explanation, or justification, and of arm around the shoulder empathy (formality=authority?).

Aristeas (1968) includes "A Note on Metal" in which Prynne speculates on the archeological moment when "the magical implications of transfer" (129) of objects lost out to the force of mercantile distance, a situationist reading of prehistory that genuflects to the authority of scientists (citing *Proceedings of the Prehistoric Society* and *The Quaternary of the United States* for example in footnotes). "The Glacial Question

Unsolved" is given support from *Quarterly Journal of the Geological Society* amongst several other similar references. *Wound Response* cites an apparently scientific text with quotation marks ("'By this I mean a distribution / of neurons . . . some topologically preserved transform'" [223] in "Of Movement Towards a Natural Place"), but neither this nor other similar citations are footnoted, nor are many other allusions to current scientific work even minuted, and this appears to be because the poem is asking what has happened to the values evident in earlier discourses of an agrarian cosmology's sacral ethics now that medical functionalisms ("The warmth of cognition not / yet neuroleptic but starry and granular") assume the power to cure wounds to body and reason. *The Plant Time Manifold Transcripts,* from the same period, cleverly parodies scientific rhetorics of diminished agency and ballooning, but allegedly dirigible, abstractions ("Willbeen function has always been most powerfully implicated in bilinear time systems with differential enzyme signal rates [. . .] Monophasic dilation in stem-system time has now confirmed this model for plant process" [240]). By the time of *News of Warring Clans* the anthropological register (and by implication all these professional discourses of knowledge) seem little more than a "mendacious gab" in the words of the poem, an authority best met with laughter and rage.

The poems of *The White Stones* try various means of resolving a recurrent difficulty with the address of the poem, its claim to authority for its judgments. Throughout the volume the poems pass judgments with the backing of a first person whose sincerity is frequently guaranteed by a tone of sad resignation that rises to poignancy and falls to gloom, and whose reliability is supported by the intellectual acuity, quickness, and scope of the expression. But this only exacerbates the problem. "Foot and Mouth" cleverly allows the poet to portray his own naivety as he waits for his "skilfully seasoned 10 ½ oz. treat" of canned soup, and the cleverness coexists with the gullibility sufficiently to raise the question again that hovered above the opening assertion that "Every little shift towards comfort is a manoeuvre / of capital loaned off into the jungle of interest" (107). When the poem "Questions for the Time Being" (a title whose pun might wait patiently through many readings before triggering itself: these are indeed questions for Heidegger's *Dasein* or the Being whose existence is temporal) announces with a numeral three that

"What goes on in a / language is the corporate & prolonged action / of worked self-transcendence," the statement carries itself syntactically and rhythmically as if taking part in a debate between professional philosophers or linguists, but it has only the poem at its back, unless a reader adduces some putative authorial authority (the author who is himself a brilliant intellectual etc). Irony, incompletion, metaphorical involution, etymological twists of literalism, and many allusive references to poetry and philosophy are not enough to either secure or sufficiently test this authority, so that, almost against its will, the poetry is repeatedly compelled to gestures of defiance that paradoxically only intensify the dilemma. This greatest twentieth century British book about the plight of the intellectual leaves us in its final poem, "The Corn Burned by Syrius," with near despair as virtue still appears almost within reach, but the civic meets a red light, the passions fade, the sense of nothing is palpable, and the poet's own best self-description is as a nomad, with the diminishing authority this probably entails.

At some point in Prynne's poetic career, trust in science's authority is lost as countervalues from "the accumulated layers and aspects of association which form the significatory resonance of previous usage: the whole prior history of the language-community" (18) become more and more evident to him. Now the "mean square error" may be a measure whose meanness for those on whom it worked can be glimpsed. A "fulminant offertory" (*For the Monogram*) may be an angry anthem, a terrorist explosion (the gift of a bang) but it also allows that the sudden disease of giving (bribes, credence, faith) might have some wider ethicosacral intent. Mutterings of historical experience that scientific language mostly silences are picked up by this aural and etymological amplification and add to the thick semantics.

"'Our confidence is end-up like a roller towel' is a characteristically Prynnian witticism which tends to make exposition sound laboured—but in a roller towel the end goes up to be recirculated, and fresh confidence, fresh promise are guaranteed," writes Wilkinson (201). And to end up like one too, with all its associations of civic management of the hygiene risks from public filth. But why not just say that our confidence is endless and make the poem more accessible to the reader? Is it the need to stay in authorial character, or the demands of wit, that insist on this intricate monogramming of ideas? Is the metaphor that unfurls the contemporary politics of confidence somehow more necessary than such explanations allow? One answer might be that the roller towel is not just a wilfully chosen poetic metaphor: just as the appropriation of the balloon metaphor for comics in the eighteen-nineties was determined by a deep historical matrix of interests and topical concerns, the use of roller towels in public conveniences might also be a symptomatic manifestation of belief, action, and sociality out of which an abstraction like confidence emerges (we are a roller-towel society), rather than a metaphor with the roots clipped off.

For the Monogram raises questions for its readership about the problem of acknowledging, critiquing, and expressing outrage at contemporary political violence. The seventh stanza (or poem in the sequence—either description could be apt) picks up Steve Reich's own "array" composition, "Come out to show them," a loop tape recording of a black civil rights campaigner saying that he had to make the "bruise blood come out to show them" (the people trying to help him challenge the use of violence by the police):

> Brisket world animation come out to flay runtime take
> further as for them for him in novel good form
> other notice all allowed tufts of any hot white dis-
> persion; promote your charm in silver salt brisance.
> Stars fading to clement destroyed fixture to show them
> up milky too mindful cry to clamping hue, arraign
> set niche by a ripped fulsome sensor. Clip act out
> out to show weft of profile in whitened detaching,
> brain peeler now set on coals out to show at a fork. For
> the quick alight cut thirty-eight touching on each
> position and peel back this vivid failed bruise, baleful
> to scale and burning. You got scarlet out to show it
> in the toy-pack acerbic notation, in less significant to
> hands off warning come out for out now long and easy
> bleed pastime, henceforth to show round a bone stricture
> flaunted out and peeled easily off from these shores.
> (424)

The poem's vector is already evident in the first line's exaggerated description of such action as a "flaying." The second-person pronoun that produces the scarlet at the beginning of the final sentence of the poem could be variously the poet (the more American idiom of saying "you" instead of "one"), the reader, the young man whose voice is the music, and the artist who treated this report on his own suffering and the brutality of the white police in the world that treats black men as easy meat ("brisket world"), as an aesthetic object: "you got scarlet out to show it / in the toy-pack acerbic notation" and "easy / bleed pastime." Does the painful recollection "flaunted out" by art effect any change of heart, or is it "peeled easily off from these shores" ('sures? 'sureties?). Perhaps there's a fading echo of Olson's opening of *Maximus*, "I, Maximus, off shore" etc., which indicates from the start of the sequence the problematic of the poem, the poet as prophet's relation to the city, its politics and history, inward and necessarily complicit or outside in what Gillian Rose called "the holy city" of his own judgment? Poem ten also has many images of terrible violence to the body, and some of these recall Joseph Beuys's self-mythology of his rescue by nomads in the Caucasus when he crashed as a Luftwaffe pilot and almost died, and the felt and fat that kept him alive. The end of this poem invites reflection on the career Beuys created out of this suffering and the war that occasioned it ("rush impure for famous eclectic margins"). Much of the poem makes of me a speculative agent (to echo Milne).

"Accessible" poetry can hide the obscurity of history and intersubjectivity in poetic form and create a false confidence that distracts attention from the harder questions. With "difficult" poetry mere success in decoding can signal feet up from labor. The poem with echoes of Beuys doesn't allow me that leisure, but instead of perpetual labors of my own and a goal of understanding, I could think of this as a poem that is at this present largely elsewhere and elsewhen, so only partially available as impetus to thought and feeling. At some later date I may read along with others more and find time has altered it, that more conversations, exchanges, history, and writing have enabled it to say more (or less). I try to imagine Wilkinson, Purves, Milne, and others talking and writing this poem again, and after all, although I first read Yeats's poem "Sailing to Byzantium" thirty odd years ago it remains a guide to thoughts on art and vocation and is not by any means a finished reading. I have confidence *For the Monogram* will push on a good way yet.

"You like to feel what the Americans call closure?," you recall an actor saying in a British TV mystery. How does closure feel?

Left with awe at the sustained sprezzatura of long sentences perfectly controlling verbs, clauses, and the rapid cutting from register to register, metametonymics. The intelligence and beckoning ethical implications of the prose now at work behind the barely scenes. Admiration sampling unaskable questions: take me through this slowly? Bosch-like images of war in no. 14 "By sorrow or swallow"; the ethnographics of the mall in no. 16 "Prior guesswork"; or the glimpses of the Middle East in no. 10 "For cycle down lower done to tire" where the pun on Tyre/tyre indicates the overpainting at work. I try to find informative parallels. Joysprick? Not full-mouthed revels keeping their puns open. Clark Coolidgean circumventions of all but the striking together of sharply noticed words? This is a poetry with more design on a readership: "the now livid / face of a captured city centre immersed in colorants" is the face of a demand Coolidge would never make. And now I notice again with the pleasure of speculation, which Wilkinson, Purves, and Milne also report, that the final line is dirigible: "shadow under wing chalking the egg yolk cartoon." But where is this buoyancy taking me, where are we, is this under control?

Finish with that first successful dirigible, a giant pair of closed lips waiting to speak, still circling the great symbol of the new France, its industry and confidence. The pilot doesn't know what the future will have to say, although he is hoping that this trip will prove that directed flight is possible. All it takes is control, luck, and the wind behind him. Time will be the only measure of this latest version of the *bal.*

Chapter 8
Eat Write

"For many years I had a postmodern illness."

I would like to begin without scare quotes but I can't. Even anaesthetizing the assertive force of the statement may not be enough to save its logic from consuming itself. A postmodern self ought not to be capable of the unitary identity needed to be the subject of an illness. The very concept of illness, whose nominalizing "ness" turns process into metaphysical substance, belongs to a genre of realism that postmodernism has supposedly overturned. After all, an illness usually has a narrative, a disease or two as protagonists, and with any luck, a heroic medical antagonist ready with the cure.

This is far from all that is wrong. From the tone of some theorists of postmodernity you might think that "postmodern illness" was close to tautology, because they write as if postmodernism itself were a pathology. Fredric Jameson, who was one of the early proponents of the idea that ours is a postmodern cultural condition, diagnosed a loss of the historical sense so acute as to be schizophrenic and a "waning of affect" (which sounds like a description of autism). If you were postmodern you would already be ill.

Worse still are my own doubts about the validity of this era label. I am not convinced by *post*modernism's chronological superiority, nor even by subtle corrective attempts like those of Jean-François Lyotard, who argues that postmodernism has always been with us as potential for a redoubled modernism, because I doubt that such supermodernisms ever existed outside the discourses of postmodernism and its friends (but how they flourished there). Imperialism, capitalism, consumerism: they are still the terms of our historical situation, however much ideological excesses in their use may have made them nauseous to us. Much as I like the opening gesture, it won't do.

Why then do I still find this opening flourish so compelling? It helps me begin to reflect on an experience that still puzzles, threatens, and angers me and that I do not know how to write about because it has consistently undermined the capacity for articulate thought and so shaped my understanding of writing that I am not at all confident that I can separate whatever was my pathology from disarticulations of meaning in contemporary poetry and prose. Let me explain.

Looking back over the years, I can just discern a continuous development. It began as an ever widening anxiety in the solar plexus, which then spread out across my world, accompanied by the disorienting symptoms of a bad head cold: fluid pressing on the skull and a confusion of thought. At some point of maximum expansion, the symptoms that infected everything began to pull back slowly from the troubled scene and retreat into the inner world, then out of mind and into a smaller and smaller abdominal space. What I had explained to myself in a shifting montage of consoling ideas as a general condition of society, culture, and even writing, gradually became an individual problem of consumption. With what sometimes seemed a humiliating bathos, my digestive system progressively revealed a series of food intolerances.

To describe it like this from the outside misses almost all of what made it distinctive. It was nonreferential (its discomforts and disorientations were not symptoms of a sturdy, recognizable illness), virtual (it was the mind's eye the doctors and cranks often thought needed glasses), decentered (vague enervation, nomadic bloats and aches), a pastiche (of symptoms clumsily copied from other ailments), and lacking a sense of history (fade-outs of memory and disjunctions of bodily ego): all traits listed by Jameson as defining the postmodern. About the only postmodern manifestation my condition lacked was the schizophrenic, and the many experts I consulted may have suspected its imminence when they variously suggested tranquillizers, group therapy, transcendental meditation, reevaluation cocounseling, psychoanalysis, and antidepressants. The disease was always on the move, shifting back and forth from mood to thought to proprioception to bone to sight to a threatening world beyond.

Maybe the difficulty that the term "postmodernism" raises is due to its readiness to supplant those other capacious names for our condition: imperialism, capitalism, and particularly consumerism. After all, it might be more accurate to have begun by saying that "for many years I was more consumed than consuming." Apart from the strain of paradox, this interestingly evokes a now anachronistic name, "consumption," for the TB that once claimed the lives of many writers ("In TB the person is 'consumed,' burned up. In cancer, the patient is 'invaded' by alien cells" [Sontag 14]). Susan Sontag's contrast of an older with a more recent metaphorics of fatal illness points to the strange rehabilitation of the concept of consumption. We are all consumers now, and consumption is supposedly what we desire. The eating of food has become the main trope for everyday life, often extended far beyond shopping to any use of a public service, to learning (students as consumers), and even to reading (consuming the meanings—the references, the realism, the centers, the authenticity, and the history that constitute a text—and thereby taking them into ourselves). Consumption is one of the main ways we enact and circulate meanings in our culture. It is also a trope that conceals much of what goes on in our lives and makes it especially difficult to comprehend a chronic condition in which food eats the body or prompts the body to erode itself.

Simon Cohn's interviews with diabetic patients struggling to manage their diet and sugar intake elicit a division between sense of self and body that undermines treatment, because the body "can itself embody disorder, fragmentation or disequilibrium" (Cohn 210). If, as Nicole Brossard says, "We call body the form our bodies take once they have tried their hand at memory, imagination, and appetite" (90), we might be able to travel back through division and disorder to find figurations of memory, imagination, and desire.

How does one represent the disconnected states of mind induced by a mostly unnamable illness; how does one value its insight that the self is immersed in the world as Jonah was in the whale's stomach; and how does one incorporate incompatible theories and sciences of embodiment, dissociation, introjection, consumerism, textuality, and digestion into one's analysis? My current intuition is that postmodernism's attempt to conflate social ills with new forms of representation points to a possibility of reading consumerism, food intolerance, and performative writing as different manifestations of a common condition. An answering poetics would acknowledge the mutuality of hungers and the intermingling of individuals and environments and could take as a theme the radical implications of using food and eating as the experiential basis for our tropes of contemporary culture. A metapoetics that calls the reader to the surface of discourse in order to recognize the coproduction of ideology as meaning can still be idealist if it simply overwhelms words, phrases, and stanzas by incorporation, disembedding them from the actualities that once bit the apple of knowledge alongside them. Can we imagine a poetics that would allow the outside to share the work of consumption; time, memory, passion, collective rage at injustice, cellular imperatives, plants and animals all contribute their gifts of transformation.

Why do I still feel compelled to use this opening sentence? For one thing, its emotional ambivalence feels exactly right. Underneath the opening sentence's bold self-advertisement ("I was a victim of postmodernity") is a timid plea to be fed sympathy by the reader, and this tension between two quite different intensities of dialogic relation suggests a performativity that I believe necessary to begin to articulate this history. Performative writing is sometimes capable of the same rigorous originality and discovery as the experiments performed in a laboratory. Could the mode of avant-garde text that consumes reading—the text that is nonreferential, virtual, decentered, pastiched, and detemporalized —help my investigation of this history? The enlistment of postmodernism might after all have some use in concentrating attention on textual negativities, not least because it counters the danger in my presentation that blackouts and gaps in the avant-garde text will be explained as merely the product of an individual mind's faulty functioning, a flickering light bulb of perception. Could the modality of the disjunctive avant-garde text be read as an emulation of the new consumption without mocking writers' claims to originality? I don't know, but I shall try placing scholarly recipes and histories of consumption alongside the trestle tables of precooked memories, "raw feels," and leftovers as an invitation to cook something up. It may not be to your taste and appear too provisional, allegorical, or artificial—and risk sounding flippant, cynical, or like old food, just plain bad. These are the ingredients of a text I don't yet know how to make: I/a/modern/post/ill/for/many/had/years/for/ness.

The Mind-Belly Problem

The usual stages of a life span occur backward, exhausted old age in one's twenties, late middle age in one's thirties, a transition to full strength over the next decade, becoming more alert and sharp-witted at fifty than at thirty. I don't know how much of this is my own invention. It may be a mixture of wishful exaggeration and the usual accumulation of more mental know-how over half a lifetime. Nor am I confident that I understand what was so wrong with the past that one could have a job, a family, and friendships and yet feel one was bleeding energy out of one's middle to nowhere. And I wrote out of one's middleton first. This language is too reserved. There's anger at the loss of years of attention, and the life guttering out instead of flaring up into illuminating intensity. Envy at those whose life is calorific with heat and light over long years as muscular intent only slowly concedes to entropy. Longing for a body able to stay late when needed, to press on for days, to think on the move, and to bear up under labor. Struggle not to resent such stamina, and the common willingness of friends to test this gift to the limit and turn down the flame with tobacco and bottle. My secret

The Mind-Belly Problem

When Adorno explains in blunt, polemical terms that "idealism," the ideology of European culture, which he believes has led eventually to Nazism, draws on instinctual sources despite its grand claims to the highest rationality, he traces these sources to the animal necessity of the predator: "predators get hungry, but pouncing on their prey is difficult and often dangerous" so they need the assistance of a rage against the other that will terrorize it. "The 'rational animal' with an appetite for his opponent" projects evil onto the other and thereby justifies its extinction. "Idealism—most explicitly Fichte—gives unconscious sway to the ideology that the not-I, *l'autrui,* and finally all that reminds us of nature is inferior, so the unity of the self-preserving thought may devour it without misgivings. This justifies the principle of the thought as much as it increases the appetite. The system is the belly turned mind, and rage is the mark of each and every idealism." (Theodor Adorno, *Negative Dialectics,* trans. E. B. Ashton [New York: Continuum, 1973], 23) [*leaving the servicing references obtrusively in the text, like the intestinal ducts left visible on the surface of a "postmodern"*

wish is to be able to time travel, to observe what was not recorded by long-term memory (and there was much), to offer advice in the twenty-five-year-old ear, to say don't live with fatigue, it is not you, food is poisoning you, question what you consume. To think we used to believe it was cool to call money bread. And I regret regret—even regret my thinking that the story "Flowers for Algernon" (by Daniel Keyes) could be my own autobiography: a man of low intelligence is given an operation to rev up his brain and the result is so successful he becomes a near genius capable of exceeding the efforts of the doctors who have helped him, until the effect begins to wane and he is just able to write a complex theoretical paper explaining the effect in mathematical language before his mind begins to regress without remedy, although he can faintly remember what it was like to be bright ("Thats why Im gonna keep trying to get smart so I can have that feeling agen"). His diary tells the story, making his writing a changing measure of intelligence's soar and fall. Eating was one of the last signs of my mother-in-law's personality after Alzheimer's emptied her mind of all its storytelling (the early days of her marriage during World War II went last), and she had no verbal language left.

building to display "truth to materials," will soon wear thin, so I shall revert to standard practice now] It is hard to believe that Adorno took these proofs seriously. As an explanation of the drive to overcome nonidentity it seems at first absurd, and even looks unconvincing alongside much better arguments elsewhere in his work, but as so often it needs to be read as an observation "inseparable from an increasingly self-totalizing society" (Jarvis 172). We could paraphrase Adorno's argument even more simply and say that consumerism is an ideology of eat or be eaten, although this would risk implying that there is some alternative possibility in which no consumption would need to occur.

Adorno doesn't envisage such a possibility since our very existence depends to some degree on the negation of difference. Our minds do need our bellies. The painter Agnes Martin describes aesthetic experience in a similar manner, except that joy replaces rage in her account, and her use of the digestive trope emphasizes the necessity and pleasure of some types of predation: "We are in the midst of reality responding with joy. . . . Let us now consider response to the concrete. Sometimes some things look very beautiful and we are moved to happiness and joy. Sometimes

Waffle and Syrup

Trouble begins at the surface of the body. Itchy red patches of dermal scarring, where testicles and underpants rub against thigh, appear after a weekend on the dunes near Ocean City. It was already 1964, Kennedy was now assassinated and the nation that disappeared for several days until everything had been seen and said and shot was back, this was when we were in high school, still smoking Marlboros in the john (shared out from a carton hidden in a locker), sizing cocks in the changing rooms after muddy football, and the Beatles went long hair. Sun, sun everywhere, and not a hope of shade. We were shown how to spot Reds. Must be the sand rubbing soft skin. It is satisfying each day to be able to peel off a new swatch of myself. Hungry after the exercise due to what I learned ten years later to call low blood sugar, I eat what will long be my favorite food (until wheat is eliminated from my diet), real maple syrup on fresh waffles, and feel that this is the living sap of the trees in my school textbook of Americana. It doesn't hurt a bit, and it can't be poison ivy. Adolescent discontent with appearances. Tremors are next, taut limbs vibrating. Lethargy begins at the middle of my way of life, at the navel, a drain down

some things taste very good and we enjoy them and are satisfied. . . . We enjoy watching the plants grow and the fruit develop. Imagine a pear tree covered with golden fruit. Suddenly we pick the fruit and eat it and it is entirely destroyed" (94). The conclusion she wants to draw from this way of representing our experience of the everyday sensory world is that it necessarily includes "violence, destructiveness, and possessiveness." To perceive the world is to eat it, and to eat is to respond to the world. Memory simulates digestion: "experiences recalled are generally more satisfying and enlightening than the original response. It is in fact the only way to know one's whole response" (94). Self-consciousness is nourished by consumption. Such an aesthetic could perhaps be used as an alibi for predatory violence and exploitation, but Martin espouses it to point out the unavoidability of the mind-belly problem: to be in, or thrown into, the world is to need to negate some of its difference in order to survive. The politics of this demand still keeps debates alive between liberals and others. Its aesthetics are less evident.

Waffle and Syrup

Valèry's Socrates has an elitist perspective subtly different to Plato's

which strength spirals away. Cells flatten to dead, horny squames rubbed off on the environment. Pink with calamine lotion, white with Cortisone cream, this redness persists like the Oedipal memory of dad saying, "Take your hand out of your pocket and stop playing with yourself." Inertial body, swooning head at daybreak, an itchy groin, what do you expect when rock music has become the teenager's guide to infinity? Drugged asleep for ten minutes by afternoon heat and calculus lesson, by discontinuous integrals, glandular messages. The short steep walk up the scarp to see the Malvern Hills out beyond the flat plain of fields and houses is more exhausting than it used to be when my legs were shorter. These falls into unconsciousness will increase until every afternoon irresistible sleep seizes hold for a few minutes and leaves a hangover behind. Thoughts of resistance only occasionally surface.

What Is It Like To Be Yourself?

I don't remember much, I tell my friend, and as we talk I am daydreaming Oxford University again. From the doctor's office I can see the crenellated walls of a college while I complain that I am tired and unable to concentrate. He talks about bites of the cherry, a metainvention: "*Socrates.* O physician that you are, I was silently admiring the acts of all these feeding bodies. Each of them, all unknowing, fairly gives its due to each chance of life, to each germ of death within itself. They know not what they are doing, but they do it like gods. *Eryximachus.* I have long observed it: all that enters into man very soon comports itself as the Fates decree. It is as though the isthmus of the gullet were the threshold of capricious necessities and organized mystery" (Valèry 28). This "unknowing" is anachronistic. Here is a philosopher-poet who knows the society excoriated by Adorno, knows the ruthlessness of its appetites as well as its unwillingness to admit its dependence on material necessity and the consequences. Like the narrator-poet in E. E. Cummings's poem, "My Love," the modern thinker discerns a pervasive amnesia in the passion to consume. Ostensibly, Cummings's poem is a typically self-conscious and quirky reprise of the trope of woman as exotic landscape, in which he uses the kind of neologism he often coined, "eatage":

> thy legs are the trees of
> dreaming
> whose fruit is the very
> eatage of forgetfulness

phor that confuses me—cherry as in cakes, virginity, spitting the pips out, or the flowering cherry trees given by the penitent Japanese to the Nation's Capital, that adults insist on driving past each year? My sight is as unreliable as my insight. It dims in low artificial light and brings on vertigo, vision tunneling, overreaching shadows, fright. Try Mars bars for the dread. Man fins (finds?) self in the empty ocean between thoughts. The doctor tries group therapy, an experiment for the psychiatry journals, where there is no spoken intervention at all, except that the shifting bodies of psychiatrist observers, his confident shoulders, her long legs open to the edge of a distractingly sexy skirt, their knowing foreheads, are intervention enough. One's face really does fall, the display of person collapses, and one feels the blood leave the cheeks while running to buy a cup of sugary tea to fill up with. And again. Still can't remember and think at the same time. Red is the worst, red consumes vision, and as a member of a socialist fraction I'm not unaware of the ironies. Consciousness may fall through red holes into the body without skin and the mind without reason. Time swallows all that's gone. The doctor tries hospitalization. Writing—nil by mouth. After Erotic fascination with her legs makes him want to devour them: she is ripe, juicy food for the male lover to consume in a negation of her independent subjectivity. So far this is no more than the "edible woman" of Margaret Atwood's satire. What takes this beyond mere masculine stereotype is the recognition that this fantasy induces forgetfulness and loss of self, so that to eat the other is to find one's own consciousness eaten too. Cummings gives us little more than this echo of Tennyson's lotus eaters, but we might add that self-forgetfulness is strongly associated in most cultures with particular acts of eating and drinking (poppy, alchohol, marijuana, cactus, and so forth).

The most brilliant of all the poets of the ontology of self, Emily Dickinson, also has a poem in which such tropes are briefly flown. In "It would have starved a Gnat" (Dickinson, #612, 301), watching a fly attempt to escape her room prompts a series of increasingly ironic reflections on commonplace comparisons between the imagined appetites and abilities of a gnat and those of human beings. She lives in a world even more straitened than that of the fly, and she lives, at least metaphorically, on less. But the poem

three days of starvation in the Radcliffe hospital I feel better than I have since I was ten years old. Omelet fantasies in which the butteriness, the creaminess of the egg, the possibility of cheese, tomato, mushroom fillings, create unlimited plot possibilities. The last test I have is for a pancreatic tumor, and what they do is give you an injection of a drug, and if you have one of these tumors, which can cause severe hypoglycemia, you have a measurable reaction, and this young doctor about my age, who'd been running the other tests, inserted a tube, hooked up a monitor, and then became awkward and refused to carry out the last step, nor would she explain why. A registrar pushed the plunger. When nothing had happened after a half hour, my doctor returned and admitted that people occasionally died during this test. She told me that she had been one of the people sitting in on my interview several days before admission, and later saw me in the Oxford Playhouse, and knowing that I might have a dangerous fit right there had found me a more interesting subject to watch than the play. No one listens to illness. Idiopathic hypoglycemia means there is no cause except my self-pathology. For the next year I am supposed to eat a high protein, low carbohydrate diet, and will

pushes far beyond this beginning to trace further implications of the comparison: the gnat is always in fear of a predatory claw that will kill it as prey; the gnat sucks blood from animals and people; the gnat can fly, one of the greatest symbols of freedom of action, and yet it cannot find its way through the apparently nonexistent barrier between captivity and this world of freedom. The poet's comparison of herself to the fly begins with the confession that she too is driven by material, bodily hungers: "With food's necessity / Upon me—like a claw." This necessity eats at her like a leech and yet also has the power of that mythical creature of the underworld, the dragon, and therefore apparently cannot be defeated. She can't simply give way to the power of this urge either, less because (the logic of the poem goes) she has ethical objections to the vampirism of the gnat (she is writing at the time that other authors, notably Bram Stoker and Henry James, are exploring ideas of intersubjectivity as a blood-sucking absorption of the other's energies—Amerigo's witty repartee to his wife Maggie in *The Golden Bowl* points to a deeper truth about the intimate relations in this novel: "Well, I'm eating your father alive" [H. James 4]), and more because she cannot fly (or as the im-

have to ask for extra helpings of meat at lunch in the college cafeteria, and refuse sugary puddings and cakes. Stop eating sugar. Stop drinking coffee. Then stop drinking tea to get rid of the stomach bubbling it produces, then eliminate dairy products and their narcotic effects, then yeast and bread. On the wall of the university where I am studying, every day I pass a line of poetry written in paint: "Moloch whose fate is a cloud of sexless hydrogen." Did you ever have those doctoral fantasies that your work will undergo a text change and explain how society, nature, and even poetry works? As I finish my PhD, and find temporary lecturing work, I begin to wonder what my final food will be. Memories cloud over, lines of inference break up, depression crashes reason.

No Sucking or Spitting

Forget yesterday. Cut the connections. Writing at the second-hand kitchen table in a tiny flat in Dalston, troubled by the hand-body problem (this is before computers). Graffito at Hampstead High Street railway station: "Let them eat Valium, we'll snort Sulph(A)te." The A is for anarchy—every letter has its own politics. Pages of the novel accumulate, narrative moves forward, but each day's work is a unit in an atemporal series written

plicit pun would have it, imagine what it would be like to be a fly). No fly, and certainly no angel, lacking the freedoms even of men of her time, she must stay earthbound. Her final stanza produces a twist in which she confesses that she even lacks the gnat's "art," the art of suicide, but unlike the fly, she has the consolation of originality, of being able to begin life again and again, through the recreation of herself in her own art. Her metaphors hint that by living small she is best able to create. This smallness requires acknowledgement of the force of bodily and spiritual hunger as the outside that makes the window, or self-creation, possible. [*In Dickinson's poetry the silence of the years of delayed and distorted transmission becomes intrinsic to reading. Her torque on words and meanings never energized the verbal culture from which she began. Hence a great fluidity of interpretation that contemporary poets find full of possibility.*] The vampire gnat also creates ontological ambiguity. Pasi Falk argues that the cultural categorization of creatures is bound up with not only "whether a 'thing' is edible, but also with whether it will consume us, or contend with us for our basic resources" (76). Extremes of the inedible are commonly associated with the "uncon

as if there were no work already done and none to follow. At midday, the poet (who later became a novelist famous for his portraits of shaman poets and his ability to show London's spectrum of arts "extinguished in execution") is at his trestle table in the market, wearing a jaunty cap, watching over his second-hand books wrapped in both dust-jackets and cellophane. Who thinks the recent murder of a tramp in the Islington public toilets may have been ritual. Censorship makes even small cuts count. When you want to read a book you don't read your own writing or remember it. The doctor says everyone has off days. Another lunchtime, the English department gathers to meet an American whose world according to fiction is already successful enough to be sent on a British tour, and all these foreigners do is eat the excellent free lunch and talk shop to each other, leaving the novelist to wrestle with silence. Lacunae create mystery and meaningfulness. As he lies in bed he feels parts of his body slowly dissolve into a protoplasmic matrix from which new structures will emerge to create more space and light inside. Rebuilding will soon be finished but right now he flows. Snot runs out of his nose, his eyes water, he pees shuddering torrents of clear urine all the time, and pain trollable" and the "unknown" and "violators of the subject-object distinction."

What Is It Like To Be Yourself?

What it is like to eat the whole world? The vampire bats that devour any wildlife they meet, as well as livestock and even farmers and tourists in Martin Cruz-Smith's novel *Nightwing,* know: "From every other warm blooded animal they could feel the pulsing of the Food, or taste it in the air so rich with sweat and exhalations. As a result, to the bats there were no natural enemies, not even man. There could be no enemies, when all was the Food" (Cruz-Smith 66). Several times the novel allows the narrative to enter their bat-consciousness and show us what it is like to be a vampire bat. [*Cruz-Smith writes popular novels with a subversive purpose, to show Native Americans, Russians, and in this novel, although only glancingly, Mexicans, from the inside—I suppose one could argue that the bats represent an American fantasy of their southern neighbors. Do I say this defensively in case I'm thought to be unable to discern literary quality?*] Behind the gothic narrative is a challenge to philosophy, specifically to the debate started by the philosopher Thomas Nagel. He argues that although we are likely

sloshes against the dam of his forehead. He doesn't mind—only the snot and tears are exceptional. His body's hydraulics have always been excessive. He calls this formation of new internal distances the flu, and it looks like being a succesful illness, because the prospects of managing an effective conversion using the limited materials available are very good. Reading, television, visitors, and dreams provide constant stories between sleeps, and he spends most of his remaining mental energy recalling them to their originating categories. That was on television, this was what a friend told him, this is a poem. He asks the pains in the neck what is happening, and they say, "impossible to explain." Wishing he was better, he finds himself at the end of the day sitting at dinner with three friends arguing about the impossibility of doing anything in this political climate of a government breaking the miners' strike. One friend says that people are greedy for money and don't want change. Another talks of the patriarchal fraud. The third friend believes that politics doesn't matter, all that counts are a few strong friendships sustained by regular dinners, drinks, and phone conversations. The only sign of his illness is recurrent tiredness, but he knows he must be better. Does his come to assume that "bats have experience," and that therefore "there is something that it is like to be a bat," we surely have to accept that because bat experience is primarily sonar, nothing in our human experience enables us to imagine just what it is like to be a bat: "the fact that we cannot expect ever to accommodate in our language a detailed description of Martian or bat phenomenology should not lead us to dismiss as meaningless the claim that bats and Martians have experiences fully comparable in richness of detail to our own" (Nagel 168–70). You can't say what it is like to be a bat, even a bat with such evident single-minded interest in eating all blood-dwelling creatures as a vampire bat. The distance between bat joy and human excitement would be an instance of a much bigger limit to human knowledge of being: "there are facts which *could* not ever be represented or comprehended by human beings, even if the species lasted for ever—simply because our structure does not permit us to operate with concepts of the requisite type" (171). At best, "we can be compelled to recognize the existence of such facts without being able to state or comprehend them." Cruz-Smith's bat-consciousness may now begin to sound unconvincing because too much like a bat-man's,

really taste bitter or is this a rejection slip? Occasional failure is normal. Are his food allergies contagious? She eats an entire packet of biscuits sitting up in bed in the night, having eaten only small, weighed amounts of bread and cheese during the day. Mental white noise or, the favorite descriptor, fog (is this a consoling attempt to make it seem the ordinary weather of a depression or anticyclone) intervenes to obscure what would otherwise emerge into the lighted streets of thought. Fog disables thought is an example of this metaphoric thought's confusion. A retrospective image: daily life is a flight over intermittently clouded terrain through which patches of actuality are only occasionally visible. Extrapolate an entire landscape, trying to hold on to the corrective knowledge that there might be unglimpsed anomalies, mountain ranges, cities, hours, nouns. Miners' wives are collecting money to provide food and support for those most in need and I wish I had more time to collect myself and listen to him. It's only recently that I took on this research report, I have to go to the supermarket, my students are hungry for their results, and I'm consumed by guilt whenever I look at all the unanswered letters and think of what I haven't had a mind to read.

since he relies on the humanly recognizable senses of taste, touch, and smell, and attributes an unconvincing bravado to his creatures, but his weird philosophical allegory seems to say that at least one desert of the unknown is not after all so distant from the terra firma of human beings. Vampire bats and the culture of consumption may have much in common. This could be an example of the "schematic" guess that Nagel concedes is as far into the battiness of the unknown as our human capacities can reach. The bats could also be a paranoid representation of the way the world outside ourselves regards the human self.

No Sucking or Spitting

Adam Phillips likes to tease his readers with paradoxes and arguments not pursued in his elegant yet modest justifications of psychonanalysis. To say that art appeals to a taste for consumption because "judgment, or aesthetic valuation, is fundamentally a question of whether something is edible," is typically provocative with undeveloped promise (Phillips 23). Lest we think this is wholly implausible, he cites from Freud's essay "Negation," where introjection is compared to eating and rejection to spitting out or refusing to eat. "The judgment is, 'I should like to eat this,' or 'I should like to spit it

Soft Conceal Corrector

Truly my mind could not then carry the weight and duration of this writing. Any text longer than a page requires rests, and if memory has to carry over most of what happened on the first page, it's usually too hard to continue. Wonky drawers in the walnut chest keep jamming. Guess what is inside the top one to get your attention out. Is there any poetry in it? His body flows steadily down to his waist where it piles in folds on the chair. Let me tell you about the beauty I saw on the wall where sunlight's emphasis pushed the window frame off-center from the print beside it. She says that all paintings are representational, just look at the abstract patterns of color and line in the objects around you when seen up close or in small fragments. Later one of the men jokes that she is known for her forefront. Many books are simply too long to read in their entirety, hence a private system of short cuts, redactions, summaries, and conclusions is needed to gut the text quickly, ignoring outlying curves and minor differences of hue and scale to produce conversant knowledge sufficient for workaday needs. The painting carries a reflected globe of white lines on greenish blue wallpaper the artist remembered from some-out'; and, put more generally: 'I should like to take this into myself and to keep that out.' That is to say, 'It shall be inside me' or 'it shall be outside me' . . . the original pleasure-ego wants to introject into itself everything that is good and to eject from itself everything that is bad. What is bad, what is alien to the ego, and what is external are, to begin with, identical." Phillips then moves on to speculate about the implications of these metaphors of lunching on experience for the understanding of memory and forgetting. Do we need spittoons or stomachs, he wonders. "Spat out it will be, as it were, metabolized by the world in a future you hope to have exempted yourself from; taken in, it will be metabolized by your body, and fuel your future." What if the experience can be neither digested nor expelled? And what sort of art might be resistant to both introjection and rejection, like the claw of a world dragon upon the audience? [*The caution of questions, the unquestionable authority of the clinician who cites Freud, the tease of a poetics of saliva.*] Is the poetic form of the canto developed by Ezra Pound an example? Is its capacity to absorb any information, language, or allusion and neutralize objections to inaccuracy as well as the claims of prior contexts, an in-

where. The roses were already part of the wallpaper design, so all he had to do was copy them into a squeezed vase. I was reading the book on the table in the picture but one of the stems kept falling across my face and gradually I realized that I could no longer read the painted lines. They were only rough brushstrokes meant to indicate the shiny absorptive black of the print. Intermittence becomes a mode of reading in itself, an emulation of the condition of all things, disjunct, bounded, separated by picnoleptic time as Paul Virilio calls it, much more satisfying than linear braced text. Small gatherings of light on East Anglian brick, a yellow flowering weed, the enduring brown of a telephone pole. Is this beauty? Okay skin. Once the peaches and glass were arranged on the glossy tray, the artist painted the glossy peaches and the shiny glass, and seeing this made me wander into the kitchen to find a rice cake and a mug of coffee substitute. Fortunately the painted carpets are almost mouths, some with faces. Sometimes feeling unworthy of the exchange and, at others, just about capable of settling the whole picture. Let's do that reaction again. Why not save moments of unbearable response against a future recovery with interest? Hunched forward, the globe's reflection is now stance of an art that can neither be digested nor repudiated?

Soft Conceal Corrector

One way to pursue this mythical art that neither consumes experience nor returns it unopened for a refund would be to imagine what the inverse of consumerism would look like. I say consumerism and not consumption because it is time to distinguish them. Consumerism is dependent upon a prior stage of production, and our commonplace ideas about consumption tend tacitly to assume a similar prior condition in which there is a given world waiting to be consumed, eaten. What would happen if instead of starting with production and then of necessity consuming it, a culture started with consumption, or what Roy Wagner describes as "the affirmation and enactment of anti-production" (Wagner 339), which might then incur some form of production in its wake. He believes that the Usen Barok of New Ireland practice "anti-production" in their complex mortuary feasts. These are wealthy and politically successful Papua New Guineans who combine what looks to Westerners to be a basic agricultural economy and simple social structure with modernisms that include a liking for Hollywood movie heroes

the artist's chair and the leaves of the dahlia. What you see is made possible by its internal light. Then cannot say what I was. And in the end it was all live. The artist knew the difference between peaches and painted peaches was enough for one work of art. Writing always seems wiser than conversation.

Axonal Pathways

Writing poetry on the edges of my life, outland where I can try anything, no rules, no requirements, an opportunity to see and hear what rises out of the mists of thought, what sounds can be heard, and what stories might begin. Later this seems an unnecessarily hermetic practice, at times cathartic, at others deliberately experimental, regrettably almost never observational. Am unable to write the poem of environment that registers an event in time, space, thought, and feeling in its discrete moment. Divinatory elicitation of words jumbled in the day residues of consciousness, letting arguments appear out of associative exploration, hearing voices call from the vast blocky formulae in the massed anonymities of news texts, guide texts, memo texts, science texts, and classed texts. Finding whose thoughts and feelings litter the cities of the aftermath, glimpsing narrative in the efflorescence. Unfinished work mailed as Roy Rogers, whom they admire as being "tricky." They sustain cultural reproduction by what Wagner calls "gastroenterprise, a format for the digestion and incorporation of the new as well as the old, of capital as well as of labor" (343), largely through ritual feasts that have the force of what we might call performatives (like a senate vote or a marriage ceremony). For them the fundamental concepts at work in these social events are *kolume* (containment) and *gala* (elicitation) rather than representation or substance. An important feast is a transformation of the social world, "achieved through a negation of the cultural meanings or categorizations that ground social life" (340). Such occasions can be described as performances as long as we don't imagine that there is a script: "For what happened is contained (*kolume*) in the images that circumscribe (but do not *describe* it) and is elicited (*gala*) in the presentation of those images. History is then a matter of how the images happen to *you* (as it perhaps always is anyway), a subjectivity that does not need verbalization" (344). By contrast, we write histories in which words construct rhetoric of material and spiritual transformation, and "what is left to the imagination is how these tropes and their implied transformations

to the future, the date on the address smudged or shelved in the museum once the act of discovery is over. Reworking the clay to achieve a satisfying sound container only to realize the material will never set. Sometimes an amphora arrives from the firing unready for transport to its new users. This way, says the interpreter, is a route through the debris. "Portrait of an Unknown Man" found lines for my hitherto unsayable history. Began during a holiday visit to the island of Poros in 1985, using a university notebook prepared with pasted scraps (or where there were no convenient photocopies, handwritten extracts) from books, letters, poems, and diaries, even bad translations of Greek brochures. Other sources were the few books with me, a mix of Kant, Plato, trashy fiction, and poetry. Interlineated passages copied out into long columns of scumbled registers. A photo-fit narrative made from many bits of anecdote and memory of various men and women, insinuated with gender theory and infused with first attempts to decode passages of childhood and seeming exile in Washington D.C. when my father worked for NSA, the decoders of the communications of otherness, in the late fifties and again in the mid-sixties. A collected biography of could possibly take place without words" (345). Wagner then draws on his New Ireland anthropology to speculate about Western concepts of history, society, and transformation. Although ours is a consumer culture, so-called, it is really a culture of production that we then consume without any art to the process. The world is there first, and then we consume it. If we were to think of ourselves as first of all skilled consumers rather than skilled producers (of commodities, art, "empires, roles, principles, institutions, ideals, peoples [345]") who consequently need to consume what we produce (buy, use, read, belong to, subscribe to, identify with), we might find ourselves capable of a different, and more empowering relation to history. What would a modern writing that began with consumption look like? [*When the poet was asked after his reading about a particularly abstract, non-referential poem by the students in the audience, he gave a line-by-line exegesis. This image was something he saw on a visit, he had been reading that book, a friend used these words, a different society would think this. No reader, no future scholar, could ever hope to decipher some of these references that had been so completely metabolized by the text's implicitness.*] Would it leave words out, would it display its

those who came of age around 1970 and again at the end of socialism in the eighties. "He and he," as the poem names this "unknown man" because of his generic masculinity, eventually dismisses his former allies, saying, "start . . . with sensible people / no pacifist dorks or junkie punks / leave round the clock activism / to trot cults." Who wrote that "the earliest sexual memory / glued his terror in place / in a letter full of errors." This glib Freudian genuflection by the social democratic narrator now seems gratuitous, but the terror-error rhyme spot-on. When the anonymous man sneers at the narrator's "new isonomia," the narrator thinks his friend is being politically unrealistic and seeing only "microconsciousnesses," and yet the narrator's SDP irony about the government—"the elegance of our establishment / forms are a daily source of pleasure"—is an inadequate response to his friend's criticism. How hard it became to feel one had an articulable history at that time in the nineteen-eighties in Britain when usable public words for community had been pulped. Outlandish poetry loves the sounds made by words from lives distant to each other. As laughing critics say, in the reading every line has time and sense, if you can find out what they are.

powers of transformation openly, would it devour meaning? Thinking like capitalists, we wonder what would be left of our productions. Thinking like the Barok we would find a new power of production as transformation, a writing that neither merely contains nor simply elicits meaning, but one that contains the elicitation of meaning and elicits the containment of meaning. And its transformations could well seem disjunctions inviting readers to wake up to their potentially politically significant powers to reconstruct meaning.

Axonal Pathways

Why are unexamined assumptions about food and consumption so hard to analyze? Elizabeth Mayes argues that we take for granted a narrative of intellectual development that at the very least should be reexamined. Early peoples supposedly thought of their feelings and actions as the result of possession by some external spirit or deity and did not fully demarcate their own bodies from the environment. Modern intellectuals as diverse as Adorno and Horkheimer, Arendt, Dodds, Freud, Girard, Ricoeur, and Taylor all assume that moderns are "partially or wholly insulated against intrusion of otherness" (102).

Pathological Sequelae

Write ahead of time. Chronic physical weakness at thirty-seven, thirty-eight, thirty-nine, forty, forty-one, forty-two. After our first child is born I have postnatal perception: I can't look at a smoker without seeing a ghostly nipple in place of the fag. Britain in the eighties looks shabby, temporary, episodic. Performing an endless grief, you search out occasions for mourning, wanting to cry in empathy at others' loss and wanting everyone to recognize how difficult it has been for you. You seem alright. Now I will always be on the train from the university job back to Cambridge where I live. My three-year-old son watches from his push chair and thinks I live behind these sliding doors all week. And I even copy out a long passage from Raymond Williams's first novel where the protagonist, Peter, talks about the commitment to research: it is capable of redeeming the way "he had lived badly, in all his immediate relationships," a failure that although it feels personal is the result of the "settlement," working class accommodation to its exploitation, and "the man who had been made, by this social process, still contained the child, who had not really grown at all" (138). In my own tongue I have wanted to eat you, a lick be-

One explanation of this, she says, is that we now have a "prohibited fantasy of a body moved without conscious effort, a body whose various parts effortlessly are harmonized by, and may even merge with, manifold external forces" (102). Instead we expect to have control over our bodies and their relation to what is other and want to be consumers of a given, produced world: "Rather than a state of being effortlessly moved and fed, in ceaseless communication with the surrounding environment, mingling with otherness across fuzzy or nonexistent boundaries, the 'after' stage figures a compulsive need to differentiate, through one of two acts: ingestion or repelling, manipulations that presume an objectified world" (103). Freud's theory of introjection, like those of the other thinkers she mentions: "is a necessary theoretical artifact of the construction of the subject as discrete and isolate. Lacking such a premise, identities might alternately be conceived as overlapping, mingling, shared, dispersed, varifocal, or fluctuating; in other words, the intermingling of individuals, through the sharing of psychic contents, gestures, habits, feeling states, and the like, would either occasion no comment or be otherwise accounted for. . . . Ironically, although internaliza-

coming a bite just hard enough to be more than mock, and a long inhalation of your flesh in glory. Then I was what I cannot say. Disability encourages an almost infinite self-exculpation for selfish acts, insufficient attention, or stupidity due to exhaustion and fear. How to persuade one's courage away from managing the artifice of personality into a wider field of action. A terrifying leaky world is not so much out there as I thought. You can now read *Nature* and *Mind*, and other intellectually demanding texts. Reason is Contact Improvisation, a dance of thought and emotion, controlling muscles, falling with gravity, letting the floor press up, and the other dancers enfold space with their delight and repulsion. You dream: Siamese twins who have been made subintelligent by the fierceness of their disagreement struggle over whether the arms should write or cook—they are hungry enough but experiences will be lost if not written down. Interesting times, dangerous grains. Recently I visited a large art installation of brilliantly colored plastic tunnels, each done in single colors in a labyrinth that crisscrossed a play park in Hereford. When I ducked into the red room I was amazed by its unique effect, quite distinct from the other colors. Red's retinal overtion would seem to promise escape from subjugation to unpredictable possession by alien spirit forces and, analogously, protection from societal control of the individual, it in fact creates a new form of possession, for the internalized energies organized into imitative forms can gain autonomy inside the subjective system and potentially take it over from within" (Mayes 109). The food, the world, eats us.

Pathological Sequelae

If, as Nicole Brossard says, "We call body the form our bodies take once they have tried their hand at memory, imagination, and appetite" (90), we might be able to travel back through division and disorder to find figurations of memory, imagination, and desire. An answering poetics would acknowledge the mutuality of hungers and the intermingling of individuals and environments and could take as a theme the radical implications of using food and its consumption as the experiential basis for our tropes of contemporary culture. A study of the effects of the introduction of bakery-produced bread on the eating habits of a small town in Sardinia showed that although it may have saved labor, it caused a loss of social connection because eating the new bread meant par-

load eliminates detail and produces a light mist that appears to hang outside in the air, not in the eye. Being clear-headed is an odd sensation, like being in a room after the furniture has been removed, or going outside after a full-volume movie. Don't give us this day our daily bread. I begin to think of doing a book on mind and body one day, and even that I might morph the disjunctive style of the eighties for it. She says, "It's all head." Jellywobbles in the stomach are a food reaction, not a sign of danger. The diaries from that time are so boring, one long complaint, and don't tell me what I want to know. I sometimes wasn't sure I'd live long enough to meet him at the other end of the immense prolepsis he had set forth, but now I will have to eat my words.

ticipating in a world economy beyond the influence of these people. Previously, "meals involved consumption of a near-one's labor: one's father, brother, or son in the wheat; one's mother, sister, or daughter in the loaf" (Counihan 291. See also Mintz). A poetics of consumption, or antiproduction, would allow the outside to share the work of consumption; time, memory, passion, collective rage at injustice, cellular imperatives, plants, and animals all contribute their gifts of transformation. *They* can say what then I was. A new poetry that enacts its rituals of containment and elicitation in such ways that what remains is neither an essence of everything said, nor a lasting representation of the world and the author. It cooks in the actual.

Notes

CHAPTER 2

1. Garfinkel is talking about the typical "member of a society" rather than poets.

2. Cited in Eshleman, 41.

3. Steve Benson, introductory note to "The Birds," *Language Alive* 2 (1996): no page nos.

4. See for example Parker and Sedgwick, 1–18.

5. This is the title that David Antin gives to one of his performance pieces in *talking at the boundaries.*

6. "The *Responses* project originated as an exploration of the ways people apprehend literature; of the processes of continuation that an engagement with texts provides; of the relationships (negative and positive) between writer and reader. This is not an anthology of contemporary poetry, it is an investigation into the union or interaction of creation and response, though some of the contributors are among the best and most interesting writers of today." Statement at the beginning of *Complete Responses,* edited by Pereira and Rollinson. The Maggie O'Sullivan issue was #6 and published in 1991.

7. I have discussed her concept in some detail in "On Ice: Julia Kristeva, Susan Howe and Avant-garde poetics," in *Contemporary Poetry Meets Modern Theory,* edited by Antony Easthope and John O. Thompson. Hemel Hempstead, UK: Harvester Wheatsheaf, 1991: 81–95. Kristeva's theory can be found in *La révolution du langage poètique* (Paris: Seuil, 1974). A part of the book can be found in English in *Revolution in Poetic Language,* translated by Margaret Walker (New York: Columbia University Press, 1984), although it is advisable to check the translations against the original wherever possible.

8. Page 100 in French edition, hereafter indicated with square brackets.

9. William Fitzgerald argues that a musical concert is beset by a tension between

cognitive and bodily responses in a manner that sounds similar to the complexities of the poetry reading. The concert may aim at a "spiritualized musing," but

> paradoxically, it may be that the institution of the concert makes possible the very experience that it would repress. Once the audience neither dances nor talks during the music, but sits, watches and listens, it delegates its corporeality to the stage, combining the playing/feeling bodies of the performers and the sounding/responsive bodies of the instruments into a new corporeality. The de-corporealization of the concert listener is an unstable condition which may lead either to a spiritualized musing or to incorporation in the autoerotic body of musical 'feeling'.

William Fitzgerald, "'Music is Feeling, then, not Sound': Wallace Stevens and the Body of Music," *SubStance* 21, no.1 (1992): 47.

10. A brilliant discussion of this can be found in Thomas Nagel's *The View from Nowhere.*

CHAPTER 3

1. This account is based on biographies by Schumacher, Miles, and Kramer and on Davidson's study of *The San Francisco Renaissance.*

2. For bibliographies and introductions to the field, see Ong, Finnegan, and Edwards and Sienkewicz.

3. Many poets would dispute the use of this term but there is no more commonly acknowledged term to designate the linguistically innovative modern poetries and their challenges to existing norms and beliefs. Terms like "new," "postmodern," and "experimental" are all too vague or caught up in other controversies.

4. These terms are used loosely to distinguish say the poets of the *American Poetry Review* and Faber and Faber, from feminist and antiwar poets, from poets whose work verges on cabaret and comedy. In practice, many poets cross these boundaries but the categories do usefully distinguish different audiences and forms of reception.

5. Walter Ong, "Text as Interpretation: Mark and After," in Foley.

6. High cultural writing is rarely given the same kind of treatment that popular literature receives in work like Janice Radway's *Reading the Romance.* Shakespeare is a partial exception to this generalization. See for example Terence Hawkes, *Meaning by Shakespeare.*

7. This was part of the statement on the masthead of *Alcheringa.* Rothenberg cites it in "From a Dialogue on Oral Poetry with William Spanos" (31).

8. Talking of her parents she says "they loved to read aloud and so do I" (Fallon 41).

9. See Louis James, *Fiction for the Working Man 1830–1850.*

10. This and the remainder of the biographical information is taken from Mariani's biography of William Carlos Williams. These details are taken from p. 137.

11. Andrew Duncan, "The Material Practice of Bad Writing," p.105. This articulate dismissal of both sound and concrete poetry should not be dismissed as mere prejudice; it raises useful questions about the value of both forms of writing that I believe can and should be addressed. Most of those who dislike such work simply don't bother to address it at all.

12. William Carlos Williams to Ronald Lane Latimer, 25 Feb 1935.

13. Aristotle, *Rhetoric,* translated by W. Rhys Roberts 1403b 37–38 (Howell 152).

14. I discuss the concept of intersubjectivity at length in my essay "The Burden of Intersubjectivity: Dialogue as a Communicative Ideal in Postmodern Theory and Fiction."

15. See for instance Talbot J. Taylor and Deborah Cameron, *Analyzing Conversation: Rules and Units in the Structure of Talk.*

16. See in particular Talbot J. Taylor, *Mutual Misunderstanding: Skepticism and the Theorizing of Language and Interpretation;* Roy Harris, *The Language Myth;* John McCumber, *Poetic Interaction: Language, Freedom, Reason.* Taylor and Harris are both critics of current trends in linguistics. McCumber is reading aesthetics in the context of Habermas's insights into the significance of interaction for the constitution of society.

17. This is from one of David Antin's early talks, "what am i doing here" collected in *talking at the boundaries,* p. 23.

18. See Thomas L. Hankins and Robert J. Silverman on the history of the *Vox Mechanica.*

19. Jonathan Morse presents compelling examples of the temporality of texts, which support this hypothesis. See Jonathan Morse, *Word by Word: The Language of Memory.*

CHAPTER 4

1. I would like to thank Bob Perelman for the opportunity to deliver an earlier version of this paper at King's College, London, as well as the constructive audience who attended and generously demonstrated, as throughout the series, that talks can live up to his ideals of exchange.

2. Bob Perelman, "*Speech Effects:* The Talk as a Genre" (C. Bernstein 201).

3. Eavan Boland, "Distances" (Hulse 55). *The New Poetry* is an anthology that offers a representative selection of the poetry that is currently dominant in Britain.

4. All in Hulse, Morley, and Kennedy, eds., *The New Poetry:* John Burnside "Septuagesima" (105); Michele Roberts "Lacrimae Rerum" (153); Peter Didsbury "A Winter's Fancy" (109); Lavinia Greenlaw "From Scattered Blue" (309).

5. Raymond Carver, "Quiet Nights" (Shapcott and Sweeney 94).

6. For a full discussion of this poem, see Middleton and Woods, chapter 7.

7. Tom Leonard, "100 Differences Between Poetry and Prose." (Caddel 129).

8. Douglas Oliver, "Walnut and Lily" (Caddel 174). Also in *Penguin Modern Poets,* vol. 10 (Harmondsworth, UK: Penguin, 1996).

CHAPTER 6

1. The original prompt to write this essay was an invitation to "remember the nineties" at a conference at Birkbeck College, "Remembering the 1990s," 8 September 2000.

2. See my essay "The Burden of Intersubjectivity."

3. A few examples: J. M. Coetzee, *Foe;* Laurie R. R. King, *The Beekeeper's Apprentice;* Jacqueline Rose, *Albertine.*

4. Compare this with J. H. Prynne's poem "Acquisition of Love," which takes on the history of 'mower' poems as well as Heidegger's critique of tools and technology (Prynne, *Poems,* 111).

5. News item, *Poetry News* (winter 2000/1): 1.

Works Cited

Adorno, Theodor. *Negative Dialectics*. Translated by E. B. Ashton. New York: Continuum, 1973.

Antin, David. *talking at the boundaries*. New York: New Directions, 1976.

Appardurai, Arjun. *The Social Life of Things: Commodities in Cultural Perspective*. Cambridge: Cambridge University Press, 1996.

Appelbaum, David. *Voice*. Albany: State University of New York Press, 1990.

Arendt, Hannah. *The Human Condition*. Chicago: University of Chicago Press, 1958.

Armitage, Simon, and Robert Crawford, eds. *The Penguin Book of Poetry from Britain and Ireland Since 1945*. London: Viking, 1998.

Ashbery, John. *April Galleons*. Manchester: Carcanet, 1988.

———. *Houseboat Days*. Harmondsworth, UK: Penguin, 1977.

———. *The Mooring of Starting Out: The First Five Books of Poetry*. New York: Ecco Press, [1966] 1997.

Augustine. *Confessions*. Edited by Henry Chadwick. Oxford: Oxford University Press, 1991.

Baker, G. P., and P. M. S. Hacker. *Language, Sense Nonsense: A critical investigation into modern theories of language*. Oxford: Basil Blackwell, 1984.

Banfield, Ann. *Unspeakable Sentences: Narration and representation in the language of fiction*. London: Routledge & Kegan Paul, 1982.

Banks, Iain M. *Excession*. London: Orbit, 1996.

Barthes, Roland. "The Grain of the Voice." In *Image/Music/Text*. London: Fontana, 1977.

Bartlett, Lee, ed. *Talking Poetry: Conversations in the Workshop with Contemporary Poets*. Albuquerque: University of New Mexico Press, 1987.

Beach, Christopher. *Poetic Community: Contemporary American Poetry between Community and Institution*. Evanston, IL: Northwestern University Press, 1999.

Bell, Alexander Melville. *The Principles of Elocution*. New York: Edgar S. Werner, 1887.

Bell, Catherine. *Ritual Theory, Ritual Practice*. New York: Oxford University Press, 1992.

Benson, Steve. Introductory note to "The Birds." *Language Alive* 2 (1996): no page nos.

Bergvall, Caroline. *Éclat.* Lowestoft, UK: Sound & Language, 1996.

Bernstein, Charles, ed. *Close Listening: Poetry and the Performed Word.* New York: Oxford University Press, 1998.

Bernstein, J. M. *Adorno: Disenchantment and Ethics.* Cambridge: Cambridge University Press, 2001.

Birdwhistell, Ray L. *Kinesics and Context.* Harmondsworth, UK: Penguin, 1973.

Boswell, James. *Boswell's London Journal.* Edited by Frederick A. Pottle. London: Heinemann, 1950.

Boyarin, Jonathan. "Voices Around the Text: The Ethnography of Reading at Mesivta Tifereth Jerusalem." In *The Ethnography of Reading,* edited by Jonathan Boyarin. Berkeley: California University Press, 1993.

Brandt, Joan. *Geopoetics: The Politics of Mimesis in Poststructural French Poetry and Theory.* Stanford, CA: Stanford University Press, 1997.

Brito, Manuel, ed. *A Suite of Poetic Voices.* Santa Brigida, Spain: Kadle Books, 1992.

Brogan, T. V. F., and Alex Preminger, eds. *The New Princeton Encyclopedia of Poetry and Poetics.* Princeton, NJ: Princeton University Press, 1993.

Bromige, David. "Allen Fisher." In *80 Langton Street Residence Program 1982.* San Francisco, CA: 80 Langton Street Publications, 1983.

Brossard, Nicole. *The Aerial Letter.* Toronto: Women's Press, 1988.

Browning, Robert. "Sordello." In *The Complete Works of Robert Browning* Vol. 2. Edited by Roma A. King Jr. Athens: Ohio University Press, 1970.

Buckingham, Willis. "Poetry Readers and Reading in the 1890s: Emily Dickinson's First Reception." In Machor, *Readers in History.*

Burke, Seán. *The Death and Return of the Author: Criticism and Subjectivity in Barthes, Foucault and Derrida.* 2nd ed. Edinburgh: Edinburgh University Press, 1998.

Burnside, John. *The Asylum Dance.* London: Jonathan Cape, 2000.

Butler, Judith. *Bodies That Matter: On the Discursive Limits of "Sex."* New York: Routledge, 1993.

Butterick, George F. *A Guide to "The Maximus Poems" of Charles Olson.* Berkeley: California University Press, 1978.

Caddel, Richard, and Peter Quatermain, eds. *Other: British and Irish Poetry since 1970.* Hanover, NH: University Press of New England, 1999.

Cage, John. "45' for a Speaker." In *Silence.* London: Marion Boyars, 1968.

Carrier, David. *The Aesthetics of Comics.* Pittsburgh: Pennsylvania State University Press, 2000.

Carruthers, Mary J. *The Book of Memory: A Study of Memory in Medieval Culture.* Cambridge: Cambridge University Press, 1990.

Catling, Brian. "The Stumbling Block Its Index." In Sinclair.

Char, René. "l'âge cassant." In *René Char: Dans l'atelier du poète.* Edited by Marie-Claude Char. Paris: Gallimard, 1996.

Chartier, Roger. "Leisure and Sociability: Reading Aloud in Early Modern Europe." In *Urban Life in the Renaissance,* edited by S. Zimmerman and S. Weissman. Newark: University of Delaware Press, 1989.

Chaucer, Geoffrey. *Canterbury Tales.* Edited by A. C. Cawley. London: Dent, 1958.

Clark, Tom. *Charles Olson: The Allegory of a Poet's Life.* New York: Norton, 1991.

Clunies-Ross, Pamela. "Promoting Poetry Events." In *Poetry Live: British and Irish Poetry,* edited by John Medlin. London: Poetry Society, 1987.

Coetzee, J. M. *Foe.* Harmondsworth, UK: Penguin, 2001.

Cohn, Simon. "Being Told What to Eat: Conversations in a Diabetes Day Center." In *Food, Health and Identity,* edited by Pat Caplan. London: Routledge, 1997.

Coleman, Joyce. "The Solace of Hearing: Medieval Views on the Reading Aloud of Literature." *Nordic Yearbook of Folklore* 46 (1990): 123–34.

Counihan, Carole, and Penny Van Esterik, eds. *Food and Culture: A Reader.* London: Routledge, 1997.

Creeley, Robert. *The Collected Essays of Robert Creeley.* Berkeley: University of California Press, 1989.

Crozier, Andrew. *All Where Each Is.* London: Agneau 2, 1985.

Dasenbrock, Reed Way. "Do we write the text we read?" In *Literary Theory after Davidson,* edited by Reed Way Dasenbrock. University Park: Pennsylvania State University Press, 1993.

Davidson, Donald. *Inquiries into Truth and Interpretation.* Oxford: Oxford University Press, 1984.

Davidson, Michael. *The San Francisco Renaissance: Poetics and Community at Mid-Century.* Cambridge: Cambridge University Press, 1989.

———. "'Skewed by Design': From Act to Speech Act in Language-Writing." *fragmente* 2 (1990): 44–49.

de Certeau, Michel. *The Practice of Everyday Life.* Translated by Steven Rendall. Berkeley: University of California Press, 1984.

Deguy, Michel. Interview with Serge Gavronsky. In *Towards a New Poetics: Contemporary Writing in France.* Edited by Serge Gavronsky. Berkeley: University of California Press, 1994.

Derrida, Jacques. *Of Grammatology.* Translated by Gayatri Chakravorty Spivak. Baltimore, MD: Johns Hopkins University Press, 1976.

———. "Structure, Sign and Play in the Discourse of the Human Sciences" In *Writing and Difference.* Translated by Alan Bass. London: Routledge & Kegan Paul, 1981.

de Saussure, Ferdinand. *Course in General Linguistics.* Translated by Roy Harris. London: Duckworth, 1983.

Dickinson, Emily. *The Complete Poems of Emily Dickinson.* Edited by Thomas H. Johnson. London: Faber and Faber, 1975.

Duncan, Andrew. "The Material Practice of Bad Writing." *Angel Exhaust* 9 (1993): 104–12.

Economou, George. "Some Notes towards Finding a View of the New Oral Poetry." *Boundary 2: The Oral Impulse in Contemporary American Poetry* 3 (1985): 653–63.

Edwards, Viv, and Thomas J. Sienkewicz. *Oral Cultures Past and Present: Rappin' and Homer.* Oxford: Basil Blackwell, 1990.

Eshleman, Clayton. *Antiphonal Swing: Selected Prose 1962/1987.* Edited by Caryl Eshleman. New York: McPherson, 1989.

Evans, J. Claude. *Strategies of Deconstruction: Derrida and the Myth of the Voice.* Minneapolis: University of Minnesota Press, 1991.

Falk, Pasi. *The Consuming Body.* London: Sage, 1994.

Fallon, Janet Ruth. "Speaking with Susan Howe," in a special issue, edited by Tom Beckett, of *The Difficulties: Susan Howe Issue* 3, no. 2 (1989): 28–42.

Fenton, James. *The Memory of War and Children in Exile: Poems 1968–1983.* Harmondsworth, UK: Penguin, 1983.

Finnegan, Ruth. *Oral Poetry: Its Nature, Significance and Social Context.* Bloomington: Indiana University Press, 1992.

Fisher, Allen. *Brixton Fractals.* London: Aloes Books, 1985.

Fisher, Allen, Bill Griffiths, and Brian Catling. *Future Exiles.* London: Harper Collins, 1992.

Fisher, Catherine. Review of *Gunpowder. Poetry Wales* 31, no. 3 (1996): 64–65.

Fitzgerald, William. "'Music Is Feeling, Then, Not Sound': Wallace Stevens and the Body of Music." *SubStance* 21, no. 1 (1992): 44–60.

Fogerty, Elsie. *Rhythm.* London: George Allen & Unwin, 1937.

———. *The Speaking of English Verse.* London: J. M. Dent, 1923.

Foley, John Miles. *Oral Tradition in Literature: Interpretation in Context.* Columbia: University of Missouri Press, 1986.

Gadamer, Hans-Georg. *Truth and Method.* No translator given. London: Sheed & Ward, 1979.

Garfinkel, Harold. *Studies in Ethnomethodology.* Cambridge, UK: Polity Press, 1984.

Gaylord, Alan T. "Reading Chaucer: What's Allowed in 'Aloud'?" *Chaucer Yearbook* 1 (1992): 87–109.

Geary, Patrick. *Phantoms of Remembrance: Memory and Oblivion at the End of the First Millennium.* Princeton, NJ: Princeton University Press, 1994.

Ginsberg, Allen. *Collected Poems.* Harmondsworth, UK: Viking, 1985.

Ginzburg, Carlo. *The Cheese and the Worms: The Cosmos of a Sixteenth-Century Miller.* Translated by John and Anne Tedeschi. London: Routledge & Kegan Paul, 1980.

Glassco, John. "A Real Good Noise: The Poet as Performer." In *The Insecurity of Art: Essays on Poetics,* edited by Ken Novies and Peter VanToorn, 57–59. Montreal: Véhicule Press, 1982.

Glazier, Loss Pequeno. *Digital Poetics: The Making of E-Poetries.* Tuscaloosa: University of Alabama Press, 2002.

Golding, Alan. *From Outlaw to Classic: Canons in American Poetry.* Madison: University of Wisconsin Press, 1995.

Greenlaw, Lavinia. "A World Where News Travelled Slowly." In *A World Where News Travelled Slowly.* London: Faber and Faber, 1997.

Greenwald, Ted. "Spoken," *L=A=N=G=U=A=G=E* 7 (March 1979): no page nos.

Guyer, Paul. "The Transcendental Deduction of the Categories." In *The Cambridge Companion to Kant,* edited by Paul Guyer. Cambridge: Cambridge University Press, 1992.

Habermas, Jürgen. *The Theory of Communicative Action.* Vol. 2, *Lifeworld and System: A Critique of Functionalist Reason,* translated by Thomas McCarthy. Oxford, UK: Polity Press, 1987.

Hall, Donald. "The Poetry Reading: Public Performance / Private Art." *American Scholar* 54 (1985): 63–77.

Hankins, Thomas L., and Robert J. Silverman. "*Vox Mechanica:* The History of Speaking Machines." In *Instruments and the Imagination.* Princeton: Princeton University Press, 1994.

Harris, Roy. *The Language Myth.* London: Duckworth, 1981.

———. *Reading Saussure.* London: Duckworth, 1987.

Harrison, Tony. *The Gaze of the Gorgon.* Newcastle upon Tyne, UK: Bloodaxe Books, 1992.

Havelock, Eric. *Preface to Plato.* Cambridge, MA: Harvard University Press, 1963.

———. "The Pre-literacy of the Greeks." *New Literary History* 8, no. 3 (1977): 369–92.

Hawkes, Terence. *Meaning by Shakespeare.* London: Routledge, 1992.

Heaney, Seamus. *Beowulf.* London: Faber and Faber, 1999.

Helms, Mary. *Ulysses' Sail: An Ethnographic Odyssey of Power, Knowledge, and Geographical Distance.* Princeton, NJ: Princeton University Press, 1988.

Hinton, Leanne, Johanna Nichols, and John Ohala, eds. *Sound Symbolism.* Cambridge: Cambridge University Press, 1994.

Hoover, Paul. *Classroom Guide to Accompany Postmodern American Poetry: A Norton Anthology.* New York: W. W. Norton, 1994.

Howe, Susan. *Singularities.* Hanover, NH: Wesleyan University Press & University Press of New England, 1990.

Howell, Wilbur Samuel. *Eighteenth-Century British Logic and Rhetoric.* Princeton, NJ: Princeton University Press, 1971.

Hughes, Ted. *Tales from Ovid.* London: Faber and Faber, 1997.

Hulse, Michael, David Kennedy, and David Morley, eds. *The New Poetry.* Newcastle upon Tyne, UK: Bloodaxe Books, 1993.

Husserl, Edmund. *Cartesian Meditations: An Introduction to Phenomenology.* Translated by Dorion Cairns. Dordrecht, Netherlands: Kluwer, 1991.

Irving, John. *The World According to Garp.* London: Black Swan, 1986.

James, Henry. *The Golden Bowl.* London: Methuen, 1905.

———. "The Question of Our Speech." In *The Question of Our Speech. The Lesson of Balzac: Two Lectures.* Boston and New York: Houghton Mifflin, 1905.

James, Louis. *Fiction for the Working Man 1830–1850.* London: Oxford University Press, 1963.

Jameson, Fredric. *Postmodernism, or, The Cultural Logic of Late Capitalism.* London: Verso, 1991.

Jarvis, Simon. *Adorno: A Critical Introduction.* Cambridge, UK: Polity Press, 1998.

———. "Prosody as Cognition." *Critical Quarterly* 40, no. 4 (1999): 3–15.

———. "Prosody as Tradition." *Dalhousie Review* 79, no. 2 (1999): 151–72.

Johnson, Nicholas. *Foil: Defining Poetry 1985–2000.* Buckfastleigh, Devon: Etruscan Books, 2000.

Kane, Daniel. *All Poets Welcome: The Lower East Side Poetry Scene in the 1960s.* Berkeley: University of California Press, 2003.

Kant, Immanuel. *The Critique of Pure Reason.* Translated by Norman Kemp Smith. London: Macmillan, 1933.

Katz, Jack. *How Emotions Work.* Chicago: University of Chicago Press, 1999.

Keyes, Daniel. "Flowers for Algernon." In *Science Fiction Hall of Fame,* Vol. 2. Edited by Robert Silverberg. London: Victor Gollancz, 1971.

King, Laurie R. R. *The Beekeeper's Apprentice.* London: Collins, 1996.

Knights, Ben. *From Reader to Reader: Theory, Text and Practice in the Study Group.* Hemel Hempstead, UK: Harvester Wheatsheaf, 1992.

Koch, Kenneth. *Selected Poems.* Manchester, UK: Carcanet Press, 1991.

Kramer, Jane. *Allen Ginsberg in America.* New York: Random House, 1969.

Kristeva, Julia. *Revolution in Poetic Language.* Translated by Margaret Walker. New York: Columbia University Press, 1984.

Kugler, Paul. *The Alchemy of Discourse: An Archetypal Approach to Language.* Lewisburg, PA: Bucknell University Press with Associated University Presses, 1982.

Kyger, Joanne. "October 11." In *Going On: Selected Poems 1958–1980.* New York: E. P. Dutton, 1983.

Kyle, Jim. "Looking for meaning in sign language sentences." In *Language in Sign: An international perspective on sign language,* edited by Jim Kyle and B. Woll. London: CroomHelm, 1983.

LaBelle, Brandon, and Christof Migone, eds. *Writing Aloud: The Sonics of Language.* Los Angeles: Errant Bodies Press, 2001.

Lakoff, George, and Mark Johnson. *Philosophy in the Flesh: The Embodied Mind and Its Challenge to Western Thought.* New York: Basic Books, 1999.

Langer, Suzanne. *Philosophy in a New Key: A study in the symbolism of reason, rite, and art.* Oxford: Oxford University Press, 1951.

Latour, Bruno. *We Have Never Been Modern.* Translated by Catherine Porter. Hemel Hempstead, UK: Harvester Wheatsheaf, 1993.

Lazer, Hank. *Opposing Poetries.* Vol. 1, *Issues and Institutions.* Evanston, IL: Northwestern University Press, 1996.

Lee, Dennis. "Writing in Colonial Space." In *The Post-Colonial Studies Reader,* edited by Bill Ashcroft, Gareth Griffiths, and Helen Tiffin. London: Routledge, 1995.

Levertov, Denise. "An Approach to Public Poetry Listenings." In *Light Up the Cave.* New York: New Directions, 1981.

———. *Footprints.* New York: New Directions, 1972.

Levin, David Michael. *The Listening Self: Personal Growth, Social Change and the Closure of Metaphysics.* London: Routledge, 1989.

Lynd, Robert S., and Helen Merrell Lynd. *Middletown: A Study in American Culture.* New York: Harcourt, Brace and Co, 1929.

———. *Middletown in Transition: A Study in Cultural Conflicts.* New York: Harcourt Brace Jovanovich, [1937] 1965.

Lyotard, Jean-François. *The Postmodern Condition: A Report on Knowledge.* Translated by Geoff Bennington and Brian Massumi. Manchester, UK: Manchester University Press, 1984.

Macdonald, Helen. *Shaler's Fish.* Buckfastleigh, UK: Etruscan Books, 2001.

Machan, Katharyn Howd. "Breath into Fire: Feminism and Poetry Readings." *Mid-American Review* 12, no. 2 (1992): 120–26.

Machor, James L., ed. *Readers in History: Nineteenth-Century American Literature and the Contexts of Response.* Baltimore, MD: Johns Hopkins University Press, 1993.

MacIntyre, Alasdair. *After Virtue: A Study in Moral Theory.* London: Duckworth, 1985.

———. *Whose Justice? Which Rationality?* London: Duckworth, 1988.

Mac Low, Jackson. *Stanzas for Iris Lezak.* Barton, VT: Something Else Press, 1971.

Mailloux, Steven. "Misreading as a Historical Act: Cultural Rhetoric, Bible Politics, and Fuller's 1845 Review of Douglass's *Narrative.*" In Machor, *Readers in History.*

Mariani, Paul. *William Carlos Williams: A New World Naked.* New York: McGraw-Hill, 1981.

Marilyn, Strathern. "Partners and Consumers: Making Relations Visible." *New Literary History* 22 (1991): 581–601.

Martin, Agnes. *Writings / Schriften.* Edited by Dieter Schwarz. Ostfildern-Ruit, Germany: Canz, 1991.

Masefield, John. *So Long to Learn: Chapters of an Autobiography.* London: Heinemann, 1952.

———. *With the Living Voice: An Address.* London: Scottish Association for the Speaking of Verse and William Heinemann, 1924.

Mayes, Elizabeth. "The Fantasy of Internalization in the Theoretical Imaginary." *Representations* 62 (Spring 1998):100–101.

McCaffery, Steve. "Sound Poetry." *L=A=N=G=U=A=G=E* 7 (March 1979): no page nos.

McClatchy, J. D., ed. *The Vintage Book of Contemporary American Poetry.* New York: Random House, 1990.

McCumber, John. *Poetic Interaction: Language, Freedom, Reason.* Chicago: University of Chicago Press, 1989.

McGann, Jerome. *Radiant Textuality: Literature after the World Wide Web.* London: Palgrave, 2001.

Merleau-Ponty, Maurice. *The Visible and the Invisible.* Evanston, IL: Northwestern University Press, 1968.

Middleton, Peter. "The Burden of Intersubjectivity: Dialogue as a Communicative Ideal in Postmodern Theory and Fiction." *New Formations: The Future of Dialogue* 12 (Autumn 2000): 31–56.

———. "On Ice: Julia Kristeva, Susan Howe and Avant-garde Poetics." In *Contemporary Poetry Meets Modern Theory,* edited by Antony Easthope and John O. Thompson. Hemel Hempstead, UK: Harvester Wheatsheaf, 1991.

———. "Portrait of an Unknown Man." *Temblor* 7 (1988): 131–40.

———. Review of *Nearly Too Much: The Poetry of J. H. Prynne* by N. H. Reeve and Richard Kerridge. *Cambridge Quarterly* 26, no. 4 (1997): 344–53.

Middleton, Peter, and Tim Woods, *Textual Memory: History, Time and Space in Postwar Literature.* Manchester, UK: Manchester University Press, 2000.

Miles, Barry. *Ginsberg: A Biography.* London: Penguin, 1990.

Miller, J. Hillis. *The Ethics of Reading: Kant, de Man, Eliot, Trollope, James, and Benjamin.* New York: Columbia University Press, 1987.

Milne, Drew. *The Gates of Gaza.* Cambridge, UK: Equipage, 2000.

———. "Speculative Assertions: Reading J. H. Prynne's Poems." *Parataxis* 10 (2001): 67–86.

Mintz, Sidney W. "Time, Sugar and Sweetness." *Food and Culture: A Reader.* Edited by Carole Counihan and Percy Van Esterik. London: Routledge, 1997: 357–69

Morse, Jonathan. *Word by Word: The Language of Memory.* Ithaca, NY: Cornell University Press, 1990.

Motherwell, Robert, ed. *The Dada Painters and Poets: An Anthology* 2nd ed. Cambridge, MA: Harvard University Press, 1981.

Mullen, Harryette. "An Interview with Harryette Mullen" conducted by Elisabeth A. Frost. *Contemporary Literature* 41, no. 3 (2000): 397–421.

Murphy, Michael. "On Not Reading Chaucer Aloud." *Medievalia* 9 (1987): 205–23.

Murray, Janet H. *Hamlet on the Holodeck: The Future of Narrative in Cyberspace.* Cambridge, MA: MIT Press, 1997.

Nagel, Thomas. *The View from Nowhere.* Oxford: Oxford University Press, 1986.

———. "What is it like to be a bat?" *Mortal Questions.* Cambridge: Cambridge University Press, 1979.

Noakes, Susan. "Gracious Words: Luke's Jesus and the Reading of Sacred Poetry at the Beginning of the Christian Era." In *The Ethnography of Reading,* edited by Jonathan Boyarin, 38–57. Berkeley: University of California Press, 1993.

Norman, Margot. "Poet of His Generation." *The London Times,* December 1, 1993.

O'Donoghue, Bernard. *Gunpowder.* London: Chatto & Windus, 1995.

O'Hara, Frank. *The Collected Poems of Frank O'Hara.* Edited by Donald Allen. Berkeley: University of California Press, [1971] 1995.

Oliver, Douglas. *Arrondissements.* Edited by Alice Notley. Great Wilbraham, Cambs., UK: Salt, 2003.

———. "Poetry's Subject." *PN Review* 21, no. 7 (Sept.-Oct., 1995): 52.

Oliver, Mary. *A Poetry Handbook.* New York: Harcourt Brace, 1994.

Olson, Charles. *The Collected Poems of Charles Olson.* Edited by George Butterick. Berkeley: University of California Press, 1987.

———. *Human Universe and Other Essays.* Edited by Donald Allen. New York: Grove Press, 1967.

———. *The Maximus Poems.* Edited by George Butterick. Berkeley: University of California Press, 1983.

———. *Selected Writings of Charles Olson.* Edited by Robert Creeley. New York: New Directions, 1966.

Ong, Walter. *Orality and Literacy: The Technologizing of the Word.* London: Routledge, 1982.

O'Sullivan, Maggie, ed. *Out of Everywhere: Linguistically Innovative Poetry by Women in North America & the U.K.* London: Reality Street Editions, 1996.

Palmer, Michael. "An Interview with Michael Palmer." By Thomas Gardner. In *Regions of Unlikeness: Explaining Contemporary Poetry,* edited by Thomas Gardner. Lincoln: University of Nebraska Press, 1999.

Parker, Andrew, and Eve Kosofsky Sedgwick, eds. "Introduction: Performance and Performativity." *Performativity and Performance.* New York: Routledge, 1995.

Pereira, Steven, and Anthony Rollinson, eds. *Complete Responses.* Swansea, UK: Responses, 1992.

Perelman, Bob. *The Future of Memory.* New York: Roof, 1998.

———. *The Marginalization of Poetry: Language Writing and Literary History.* Princeton, NJ: Princeton University Press, 1996.

Perloff, Marjorie. "Crisis in the Humanities." See http://wings.buffalo.edu/epc/authors/perloff/articles/crisis.html.

———. *Poetic License: Essays on Modernist and Postmodernist Lyric.* Evanston, IL: Northwestern University Press, 1990.

Phillips, Adam. *On Flirtation.* London: Faber & Faber, 1994.

Poetry 130 (April–September 1977).

Poovey, Mary. "The Model System of Contemporary Literary Criticism." *Critical Inquiry* 27, no. 3 (Spring 2001): 408–38.

Prynne, J. H. *Aristeas.* London: Ferry Press, 1968.

———. "China Figures." In *New Songs from a Jade Terrace,* edited by Anne Birrell. Harmondsworth, UK: Penguin, 1986.

———. "A Discourse on Willem de Kooning's *Rosy-Fingered Dawn at LousePoint.*" In *act: Beautiful Translations,* edited by Juliet Steyn. London: Pluto, 1999.

———. *Poems.* Newcastle upon Tyne, UK: Bloodaxe Books, 1999.

———. "A Quick Riposte to Handke's Dictum about War and Language." *Quid* 6 (November 2000): 23–26.

———. *Stars, Tigers and the Shape of Words.* The William Matthews Lecture, delivered 1992 at Birkbeck College, London. Published by Birkbeck College, 1993.

———. *They That Haue Powre To Hurt; A Specimen of a Commentary on Shake-speares Sonnets, 94.* Cambridge: No publisher given, 2001.

Purves, Robin. "Apprehension, or, J. H. Prynne, His Critics, and the Rhetoric of Art," *The Gig* 2 (March 1999): 45–60.

Quasha, George. "Dialogos: Between the Written and the Oral in Contemporary Poetry." *New Literary History* 8 (1977): 485–506.

Radway, Janice. *Reading the Romance: Women, Patriarchy and Popular Literature.* Chapel Hill: University of North Carolina Press, 1984.

Rasula, Jed. *The American Poetry Wax Museum: Reality Effects, 1940–1990.* Urbana, IL: National Council of Teachers of English, 1996.

Rauch, Angelika. *The Hieroglyph of Tradition: Freud, Benjamin, Gadamer, Novalis, Kant.* London: Associated Universities Press, 2000.

Rawls, John. *A Theory of Justice.* London: Oxford University Press, 1972.

Raworth, Tom. *Eternal Sections.* Los Angeles: Sun & Moon, 1993.

Reid, Constance. *Hilbert.* New York: Copernicus, 1996.

Richardson, Joan. *Wallace Stevens: The Later Years 1923–1955.* New York: William Morrow, 1988.

Ricoeur, Paul. *Freud and Philosophy: An Essay on Interpretation.* Translated by Denis Savage. New Haven, CT: Yale University Press, 1970.

———. *Time and Narrative.* Vol. 3. Translated by Kathleen Blarney and David Pellauer. Chicago: Chicago University Press, 1988.

Riley, Peter. "Two Letters to British Poets (2nd Letter)." *Quid* 6 (November 2000): 18–21.

Robb, Mary Margaret. *Oral Interpretation of Literature in American Colleges and Universities.* New York: H. W. Wilson, 1941.

Roberts, Susan, ed. *More Poetry Please! 100 Popular Poems from the BBC Radio 4 Programme.* London: BBC Publishing, 1992.

Robertson, Lisa. *The Weather.* London: Reality Street Editions, 2001.

———. *Xeclogue.* Vancouver: Tsunami, 1993.

Rodefer, Stephen. "Pretext." *Four Lectures.* Berkeley, CA: The Figures, 1982.

Rodenberg, Patsy. *The Need for Words: Voice and the Text.* London: Methuen Drama, Reed Publishing, 1993.

Rose, Gillian. *The Broken Middle: Out of Our Ancient Society.* Oxford: Blackwell, 1992.

Rose, Jacqueline. *Albertine.* London: Vintage, 2002.

Rothenberg, Jerome. *Prefaces and Other Writings.* New York: New Directions, 1981.

Sacks, Oliver. *Seeing Voices: A journey into the world of the deaf.* London: Pan, 1991.

Sandburg, Carl. "Smoke and Steel." In *Modern American Poetry,* edited by Louis Untermeyer. New York: Harcourt Brace and Company, 1921.

Sansome, Clive, ed. *Speech in Our Time.* London: Hinrichsen, 1948.

Schneeman, Carolee. *More Than Meat Joy: Complete Performance Works & Selected Writings.* Edited by Bruce McPherson. New York: Documentext, 1979.

Schumacher, Michael. *Dharma Lion: A Critical Biography of Allen Ginsberg.* New York: St. Martin's, 1992.

Shapcott, Jo, and Matthew Sweeney, eds. *Emergency Kit: Poems for Strange Times.* London: Faber and Faber, 1996.

Sheridan, Thomas. *A discourse being introductory to his course of lectures on Elocution and the English Language.* Los Angeles: William Andrews Clark Memorial Library, Augustan Reprint Society, [1759] 1969.

Silliman, Ron, et al. "Aesthetic Tendency and the Politics of Poetry." *Social Text* 19/20 (1988): 261–275.

Simon, Clarence T. "Appreciation in Reading." *Quarterly Journal of Speech* 16 (1930).

Sinclair, Iain. *Conductors of Chaos.* London: Macmillan, 1996.

Sivier, Evelyn M. "English Poets, Teachers, and Festivals in 'A Golden Age of Poetry Speaking,' 1920–1950." In *Performance of Literature in Historical Perspectives,* edited by David W. Thompson. Lanham, MD: University Press of America, 1983.

Slevin, James. *The Internet and Society.* Cambridge, UK: Polity Press, 2000.

Smith, Martin Cruz. *Night Wing.* London: Macmillan, 1987.

Sontag, Susan. "Against Interpretation." *Against Interpretation.* London: Vintage, 1994.

Stern, Frederick C. "The Formal Poetry Reading." *The Drama Review* 35, no. 3 (Fall 1991): 67–84.

Stewart, Susan. *Poetry and the Fate of the Senses.* Chicago: University of Chicago Press, 2002.

Strathern, Marilyn. *After Nature: English Kinship in the Twentieth Century.* Cambridge: Cambridge University Press, 1992.

———. "Partners and Consumers: Making Relations Visible." *New Literary History* 22 (1991): 581–601.

Stubelius, Svante. *Balloon, Flying-Machine, Helicopter: Further Studies in the History of Terms for Aircraft in English.* Göteborg, Sweden: Gothenburg Studies in English, 1960.

Svenbro, Jesper. *Phrasikleia: An Anthropology of Reading in Ancient Greece.* Translated by Janet Lloyd. Ithaca, NY: Cornell University Press, 1993.

Sweeney, Matthew, and John Hartley Williams. *Teach Yourself Writing Poetry and Getting Published.* London: Hodder Headline, 1997.

Taussig, Michael. *Defacement: Public Secrecy and the Labor of the Negative.* Stanford, CA: Stanford University Press, 1999.

Taylor, Mary. "A Finger Pointing." *Tears in the Fence* 30 (Autumn 2001): 99.

Taylor, Talbot J. *Mutual Misunderstanding: Skepticism and the Theorizing of Language and Interpretation.* London: Routledge, 1992.

Taylor, Talbot J., and Deborah Cameron. *Analyzing Conversation: Rules and Units in the Structure of Talk.* Oxford: Pergamon Press, 1987.

Terrell, Carroll F. *A Companion to the Cantos of Ezra Pound.* Berkeley, CA, and Orono, ME: University of California Press and National Poetry Foundation, 1980.

Tomlinson, Richard. *The Big Breach: From Top Secret to Maximum Security.* Edinburgh: Cutting Edge, 2001.

Tsur, Reuven. *What Makes Sound Patterns Expressive: The Poetic Mode of Speech Perception.* Durham, NC, and London: Duke University Press, 1992.

Turner, Victor. *The Anthropology of Performance.* Baltimore: Performing Arts Journal Publications, 1988.

Valèry, Paul. "Dance and the Soul." *Dialogues.* Translated by William McCausland Stewart. Princeton, NJ: Princeton University Press, 1956.

Vincent, Stephen. "Poetry Readings / Reading Poetry: San Francisco Bay Area 1958–1980." In Vincent and Zweig, *The Poetry Reading.*

Vincent, Stephen, and Ellen Zweig, eds. *The Poetry Reading: A Contemporary Compendium on Language & Performance.* San Francisco: Momo's Press, 1981.

Virilio, Paul. *The Aesthetics of Disappearance.* Translated by Philip Beitchman. New York: Semiotext(e), 1991.

Wagner, Linda. "A Colloquy with Robert Creeley." *Robert Creeley, Contexts of Poetry: Interviews 1961–1971.* Edited by Donald Allen. Bolinas, CA: Four Seasons Foundation, 1973.

Wagner, Roy. "New Ireland is shaped like a rifle and we are the trigger: The power of digestion in cultural reproduction." In *Clio in Oceania: Toward A Historical Anthropology,* edited by Aletta Biersak. Washington D.C.: Smithsonian Institution Press, 1991.

Ward, Geoffrey. *Statutes of Liberty: The New York School of Poets.* Basingstoke, UK: Palgrave, 2001.

Wardle, Sarah. "Homing Instinct." *Times Literary Supplement* (February 9, 2001): 15.

Watten, Barrett. *Conduit.* San Francisco: Gaz, 1988.

———. *Progress.* New York: Roof, 1985.

Waugh, Linda. "Against Arbitrariness: Imitation and Motivation Revived, with Consequences for Textual Meaning." *Diacritics* 23, no. 2: 71–87.

Weiner, Annette B. *Inalienable Possessions: The Paradox of Keeping-While-Giving.* Berkeley: University of California Press, 1992.

Weiss, Jeffrey. *The Popular Culture of Modern Art: Picasso, Duchamp, and Avant-gardism.* New Haven, CT, and London: Yale University Press, 1994.

Wellmer, Albrecht. "Truth, Semblance, Reconciliation: Adorno's Aesthetic Redemption of Modernity." *The Persistence of Modernity.* Cambridge, UK: Polity Press, 1991.

Wesling, Donald. *The Scissors of Meter: Grammetrics and Reading.* Ann Arbor: University of Michigan Press, 1996.

Whalen, Philip. *On Bear's Head.* New York: Harcourt, Brace & World and Coyote, 1969.

———. *Scenes of Life at the Capital.* Bolinas, CA: Grey Fox Press, 1971.

Wilkinson, John. "Counterfactual Prynne: An Approach to *Not-You.*" *Parataxis* 9 (1996): 190–202.

———. *Effigies Against the Light.* Applecross, Western Australia and Great Wilbraham, Cambridge: Salt, 2001.

Williams, Archibald. *Conquering the Air: The romance of the development and use of aircraft.* London: T. C. & E. C. Jack, 1926.

Willis, Elizabeth. "'All This Very Queer Knowledge,' or, From Ornament to Ontology: The Gender and Dualism of the Modernist 'New.'" *Sagetrieb* 16, no. 3 (1997): 63–73.

Wilson, Robert. "Hear, See, Act: Robert Wilson interviewed by *Der Spiegel*." In *The Intercultural Performance Reader,* edited by Patrice Pavis. London: Routledge, 1996.

Winters, Nancy. *Man Flies: The Story of Alberto Santos-Dumont, Master of the Balloon.* London: Bloomsbury, 1997.

Winters, Yvor. "The Audible Reading of Poetry." *Hudson Review* 4, no. 3 (1951): 433–47.

Wojahn, David. "A Kind of Vaudeville: Appraising The Age of the Poetry Reading." *New England Review and Bread Loaf Quarterly* 8, no. 2 (1985): 265–82.

Zukofsky, Louis. *A.* Berkeley: University of California Press, 1978.

———. *A Test of Poetry.* New York: C. Z. Publications, 1980.

Index